Korean-Americans:
Past, Present, and Future

Korean-Americans:
Past, Present, and Future

Edited by

Ilpyong J. Kim
University of Connecticut

www.hollym.com

HOLLYM International Corp.
Elizabeth, NJ

Korean-Americans: Past, Present, and Future

First published in 2004
by Hollym International Corp.
18 Donald Place
Elizabeth, NJ 07208
Phone (908) 353-1655 Fax (908) 353-0255
www.hollym.com

Cover design by Jin Woo Bum

ISBN: 1-56591-121-0
Library of Congress Control Number: 2004106752

Printed in the United States of America

TABLE OF CONTENTS

PART II. THE PRESENT

Preface

In preparation for the next 100 years

One hundred years after 102 Koreans made their first step onto the land of freedom and opportunity with great defiance and courage, one century has just concluded, ushering in a new century that holds promise and potential for even more prosperity for all of us.

Leaving their homeland in great pain after centuries of foreign invasions, our ancestors were brought to the sugar cane farm in Hawaii and became the foundation for our prosperous emigration history. Recalling the last 100 years of our immigration history, it is one in which our ancestors confronted hardship and survival with their hopes and determined spirits. They helped their mother country of Korea by donating more than half of their earnings to the independence resistance. Seeing the need to prepare future generations for the challenges ahead, they focused on the education of their children, making us who we are today.

The immigration was discontinued for 30 years but became active again in 1965 by students and many immigrating families. It is estimated that more than two million Korean-Americans are now living in the United States.

To commemorate our centennial year of immigration history since 1903, we celebrated in 14 different regions across the United States, including at the Rose Parade in Los Angeles on Jan 1, 2004. Especially noteworthy was the closing ceremony in New York in which we showcased the growth and prosperity we attained through 100 years of our immigration history. Notwithstanding their own financial difficulties, many of our fellow Korean-Americans, including 1.5 and 2nd generations were actively involved and helped make the centennial celebration gatherings a memorable event. More than just commemorating the past 100 years of our immigration history, the centennial celebration helped us to plan for the next 100 years, holding onto the legacy and lessons of our ancestors whose lives continue to guide us and inspire us as we prepare for this new century.

For the next 100 years, it is our responsibility to impart the spirit of our ancestors to the next generation and to guide and assist them in building stronger and prosperous Korean-American communities. To achieve such goals, it is important to gain political power and self-determination by acquiring citizenship in order to vote, and empowering ourselves economically and culturally for enrichment of the life that our children will live in. With the publication of the Korean volume released in 2003, my hope is that this English work will serve, in some small way, the future of our next generation, while guiding the mainstream to understand a little more about our culture and history.

I would like to take this opportunity to extend my appreciation to Dr. Ilpyong Kim, the editor, and to the officers of the Korean-American Foundation for their financial assistance.

Thomas (Byung T.) Cho
General Chairman
Korean American Foundation

Korean American Foundation

<u>Regional Headquarters</u>
General Chairman - Thomas Byung T. Cho

Honorary Chairman - Yoon Soo Park, Ph.D.
Honorary Chairman - Byung Wook Yoon
Vice General Chairman - Pyung Yong Min
Vice General Chairman - Sang Won Park Ph. D.
Vice General Chairman - Yung Mook Lee
Secretary General - Bo Young Chung

<u>Regional Chairmen</u>
Hawaii
Regional Chairman - Duk Hee Murabayashi
Los Angeles
Regional Chairman - Ki Shik Ahn
San Francisco
Regional Chairman - Kun Tai Kim
Chicago
Regional Chairman - Hyuck Chun
New York
Regional Chairman - Paul P. K. Kim
Washington D.C.
Regional Chairman - Sekwon Chong
New England (Boston)
Regional Chairman - Kyung Min Park, M.D.
Philadelphia
Regional Chairman - Myung-Sook Yi (Lee)
Louisville
Regional Chairman - Charles Park
Sedona
Regional Chairman - Seung-Bae Chun
Miami
Regional Chairman - Woo Ho Lee
Fresno
Regional Chairman - Marn Jai Cha

Acknowledgements

The Centennial Committee of Korean Immigration to the United States-Greater New York appointed me to chair the Editorial Committee of the Centennial History of Korean Immigration in the Greater New York Area. The main task of this committee was to publish two history books, one in Korean and the other in English. The second book, which you now hold in your hands, is entitled *Korean-Americans: Past, Present, and Future*, and each chapter has been penned by an expert in his or her field of scholarship. The editor would like to acknowledge the efforts these contributors have made to meet the book's demanding publication deadline.

The editor would also like to express his appreciation to those senior scholars who have undertaken specific research assignments in their personal areas of expertise. Professor Yong-Ho Choe of the University of Hawaii contributed the original essay on the Korean Church in Hawaii, while Professor Han-Kyo Kim of the University of Cincinnati contributed a paper on the Korean independence movement, which was presented at the panel I organized and chaired for the 2002 conference in Washington, convened jointly by the Centennial Committee of Korean Immigration to the United States (CCKI) and the International Council on Korean Studies (ICKS). I was the founder and president of ICKS from 1996 to 2000, during which we began publishing the *International Journal of Korean Studies* to address the issues of Korean unification and the roles of Korean-Americans in U.S. policy-making concerning the Korean Peninsula.

Part II of this book has been contributed by the younger generation of Korean-Americans, who wrote their doctoral dissertations on current issues of Koreans in America or who conducted research on specific problems of Korean-Americans in the U. S. community. I would like to acknowledge their contributions to this volume, written while actively engaged in teaching and research at various colleges and universities.

Part II covers almost every pertinent issue of Korean-Americans, ranging from adaptation, assimilation, and identity problems to the status of Korean children adopted by American families, cultural adaptation, and value changes, to the conduct of Korean businesses and the role of Korean churches in American society.

Part III addresses the future role of Korean-Americans in the American community. Part III has essentially been written by Korean-American students currently enrolled at colleges and universities in the northeast United States, the essays for this section being drawn from an essay contest sponsored by the Korean Community Foundation for Korean-American college students. Special thanks are due to Brian Lee and Howard Han of Yale University, who contributed essays to help first generation Korean-Americans understand the aspirations and thinking of second generation Korean-Americans, which are quite separate and distinct.

Mr. Thomas B. T. Cho, Chairman of CCKI, and Vice Chair Jin Hyung Seo facilitated the publication of this book.

Ilpyong Kim
Editor

Introduction

There have been quite a few books written by experts on Koreans in America from cultural, historical, and sociological perspectives. Moreover, several hundred Ph.D. and D.D. dissertations have been written by Korean scholars and theological students in various universities and seminaries in America. Why then is one more book on Korean-Americans needed? This book is unique because it captures the main thrust of the historical, cultural, and value changes among Korean-Americans, as well as addressing the vision of Korean-Americans for the 21st century.

Part I covers the centennial history of Korean immigration from 1903 to 2003 by surveying the origin of Korean immigration to the development of Korean organizations such as church groups and the national independence movement which spurred the growth and development of the Korean community in America. My own chapter surveys the centennial history of Korean immigration from 1903 to 2003, with special focus on the growth of the Korean community, the development of Korean political organizations for national independence during the Japanese colonial rule in Korea from 1910 to 1945, and the role of Korean churches organized and developed by Korean immigrants. More than half of the population of Korean-Americans participates in Korean ethnic churches, which now number more than 3,500 in the United States.

Also in Part I, Dr. Yong-Ho Choe discusses the development and organization of the first Korean church in Hawaii by the first generation of Korean immigrants, which became the model by which second and third wave Korean immigrants to the United States organized and operated *their* Korean churches. Dr. Han-Kyo Kim addresses issues of the Korean national independence movement among the first generation of Korean immigrants in America. The three approaches to Korean national independence developed by political leaders such as An Ch'ang-Ho, Park Yong-Man, and Yi Sung-Man (Syngman Rhee) shed much light on the factional struggles among Korean immigrants in support of the Korean independence movement.

Part II consists of a collection of essays by the second generation of Korean-Americans, born and raised by the first generation and well educated by American colleges and universities. The topics they cover are diverse but their analyses are rigorous and incisive. Angie Chung traces the historical formation of Korean-American organizations in Los Angeles in the context of ethnic power structures, exploring various dimensions of inter-organizational conflict and cooperation that affected community politics in the post-1992 Los Angeles Riots.

Eunju Lee bases her essay, "Gender and Immigrant Small Business Ownership," on her in-depth interviews with the Kim family and others in New York City. Her argument is that the current thinking on immigrant small business ownership is largely based upon the experiences of men who are officially recognized as owners and that gender profoundly shapes the decisions and outcomes related to immigrants and small business ownership. Miliann Kang contributed "Korean Immigrant Women's Work in the Nail Salon Industry," which focuses on gender, race and class in the service sector of New York City. This essay explores variations in the performance of body labor caused by the intersection of the gendered processes of beauty service work with the racialized and class-specific service expectations of diverse customers. These patterns demonstrate how Korean immigrant women learn to provide different kinds of service for customers of different races and classes, and in so doing they both challenge and reproduce existing forms of inequality within U. S. society.

Eleana Kim addresses the issues of Korean-Americans adopted by U. S. families. Korean adoptees in the United States number well over 100,000. Over half of these adoptees are now adults, and they have begun, in recent years, to publicize collectively their unique identity as Koreans and as Americans. Following a brief history of Korean adoption, Kim examines Korean adoptees' relationships to Korea and asks how the overseas adopted Korean community movement might help us to rethink what it means to be Korean in the diaspora. She concludes with some provisional thoughts about what the future role of Korean adoptees might be with respect to Korean unification. A closely related essay by Richard Lee and his colleagues examines the ethnic identity development and psychological adjustment of Korean adoptees who are now adults. Lee and his colleagues conceptualize and measure ethnic identity as a multidimensional construct that consists of affective pride, cognitive clarity, and behavioral engagement associated with ethnic *identification.*

Yoon Joh's essay, "Independent and Interdependent Self-Construals," investigates the self-construal of the 1.5 generation of Korean-American college students in relation to counseling and therapy. Self-construal is a critical concept for Korean-American college students who live in the United States and are raised by immigrant parents who impose traditional Korean culture upon them. Multicultural counseling literature currently overlooks challenges encountered by this generation positioned between two conflicting cultures. Therefore, the multicultural counseling of Korean-American youth is likely to need to address such challenges.

Okyun Kwon explores the ways in which Korean churches have played a role in the formation of the Korean community in the Washington, D.C. area. According to our study, Korean churches, especially Protestant churches, have not only been the center of the ethnic community from the beginning of Korean immigration but have also played a critical role in community formation. Their mono-ethnic tendency and limited interaction with other religious groups and the larger community, however, have deterred immigrant members' incorporation into U.S. society.

In Part III, second generation Korean-Americans currently enrolled in American colleges and universities look at their future role as Korean-Americans. This section combines specifically commissioned essays with prize-winning submissions to an essay contest sponsored by the Korean Community Foundation in New York for Korean-American college students. The future of Korean-Americans in the U. S. depends upon their active participation in American society, as they have already distinguished themselves

8

in professional fields such as science and technology, media and communication, medicine, and law. However, only a small number of Korean-Americans are active in practical politics. The empowerment of Korean-Americans will eventually increase their role in American politics, and they will become a more visible ethnic minority in American society.

I sincerely hope that this book will accurately reflect the current situation of Korean-Americans and that it will also encourage Korean-Americans to learn the lessons of Korean-American history and thereby avoid repeating the mistakes of their forefathers.

Ilpyong Kim,
Editor

PART I.

THE PAST

1. A Century of Korean Immigration to the United States: 1903-2003

Ilpyong J. Kim

Introduction

On January 13, 1903, the first shipload of Korean immigrants, aboard the *S.S. Gaelic,* arrived in Hawaii to work on the pineapple and sugar plantations. Thus, the long journey of Korean laborers to America began in 1903 and by 1905 more than 7,226 Koreans had come to Hawaii (637 women and 465 children) by sixty-five different ships. This group of Korean immigrants is known as the "first wave." The first part of this book will begin with a brief history of Korean immigrants from 1903 to 2003 in terms of their aspirations, achievements and contributions in the United States.

The First Wave of Koreans in America

Three waves of Korean immigrants have arrived on the American shores over the past century. The first wave of Korean immigration ended when the 1924 Immigration Act, which was known as the Oriental Exclusion Act, was adopted and excluded all Asians except Filipino laborers. The motives of the first wave of Koreans coming to America should be understood in their personal, economic, and political contexts. Some of the earlier studies of Korean immigrants in Hawaii, including the Oral History Project of the first generation immigrants, indicate that the Korean situation at the end of the 19th century was deteriorating economically due to draught or flood and famine which swept through Korea in 1901, as well as a political deterioration, due largely to the inept government of King Kojong who ruled Korea from 1864 to 1907.[1] Many Korean immigrants were attracted by the promise of money from working in the sugar plantations in Hawaii. Recruiters told Korean immigrants that the streets of America were paved with gold and there was abundant money to make if they came to America to work hard. Thus, Korean immigrants wanted to overcome their poverty by bitter labor in

America, returning home after saving enough money. However, the circumstances that led to the recruitment of more than seven thousand Korean laborers (7,226 to be exact) to work in the pineapple and sugar plantations in Hawaii should be explained in the context of Korean-American diplomatic relations.

In 1882, Korea established diplomatic relations with the United States by signing the Treaty of Amity and Commerce, opening itself to foreign relations after a century of isolation from the outside world. Western writers often referred to Korea as the Hermit Kingdom. When the first treaty on immigration between the United States and Korea was signed in 1882, a small number of students, merchants, and political dissidents began arriving in America. To open its doors to the West, the Kojong government dispatched its first diplomatic mission to the United States in 1883, led by Min Young-ik, a cabinet-level official in King Kojong's palace.

Upon completion of its mission, one of the delegation members, Yu Kil-chun, remained behind and enrolled at Dummer Academy in Massachusetts. He was the first Korean student to enroll in an American school and many more Korean students followed him to study in American colleges and universities. The United States also formally opened its diplomatic mission in Seoul. Horace N. Allen, a 26-year old medical doctor from Ohio, was sent to Korea by the Presbyterian Board of Foreign Missions in 1884. The development of his close relations with the Royal Family in King Kojong's court was due largely to Allen's medical treatment of the Royal Family, using Western medicine, and led to an opportunity for Allen to be appointed as the Minister of the U. S. legation in Seoul.

It was reported at that time that King Kojong formally requested that the U.S. government appoint Allen as the Minister of the U.S. legation in Korea. Allen's appointment to that U.S. diplomatic post, coupled with his close contact with the Hawaii Sugar Planters Association (HSPA), encouraged the HSPA to recruit Korean laborers to work in the pineapple and sugar plantations in

Hawaii. The background and negotiations by which Allen was able to help the HSPA to recruit Korean laborers is well documented in Wayne Patterson's pioneering book, *The Korean Frontier in America: Immigration to Hawaii, 1896-1910.*[2]

When Hawaii was annexed by the United States in 1898, the sugar industry, which required abundant and cheap labor, began to be affected by U.S. policies on foreign labor. The first influx of immigrant labor from China to work on the sugar plantations in Hawaii began in 1852 when 293 Chinese from the Canton area arrived. However, serious search for workers abroad did not begin until 1864 when an act to provide for the importation of laborers and for the encouragement of immigration was passed. Between 1876 and 1886, the influx of Chinese laborers reached 50,000. However, the Chinese Exclusion Act of 1882 was still in effect and the HSPA was no longer able to recruit Chinese laborers to work on the Hawaii sugar plantations.

When Japanese immigration began in 1885 it increased by leaps and bounds, becoming by the early 1890s the largest immigrant labor group in the Hawaiian islands. Like the Chinese before them, the Japanese originally intended to make money and then return home. However, many Japanese laborers stayed in Hawaii because of the lack of home ties, the better climate, and the difficulties of saving enough money to pay for the return passage. Japanese laborers moved out of the Hawaiian plantations before the Chinese did and thus engaged in many different occupations. The shortage of laborers forced the HSPA leaders to recruit Korean laborers, according to Patterson, and also to break the strike of the Japanese laborers who were demanding higher wages. The U.S. diplomat Horace N. Allen was thus able to play an important role in recruiting and bringing Korean laborers to work in the pineapple and sugar plantations in Hawaii.

Two distinctive characteristics of Korean immigrants emerged from the early years of 1903-1907. Koreans displayed a higher rate of religious participation, through building churches in which to worship, and self-employment than any other Asian immigrant group. Reverend George Herbert Jones, a Methodist missionary, played a prominent part in recruiting more than half of the first group of 102 members from the Naeri Methodist Church in the Inchon area. The first group came to Hawaii and established the first Korean Methodist Church in Honolulu. Korean churches functioned as a place where Korean laborers could get together to exchange information and also pray and worship to overcome the suffering and hardship of working at the sugar plantations. Thus, Korean churches were organized in seven different locations in the Hawaiian Islands and more than one half of Korean laborers attended church.[3] The growth and development of the Korean Methodist Church in Honolulu, as discussed by Yong-Ho Cho in Chapter 2, is a typical case study of the Korean churches in America. The number of Korean churches grew exponentially and today there are more than three thousand Korean churches in America. The rapid growth of Korean churches has been accompanied by many cultural, religious and doctrinal problems. However, during the national independence movement, Korean churches played a most significant role in the immigrant community because they were able to unite the Korean immigrants in their national identity and raise funds to support the national independence movement and the Korean provisional government in Shanghai, China. In the post-independence years the Korean churches lost their purpose and many forms of factionalism developed around minor issues of the Korean immigrant community.

David W. Deshler was hand picked by Horace N. Allen to serve as the official agent of the Hawaii Sugar Planters Association (HSPA) to recruit Korean laborers in 1902. He set up the East-West Development Company in Inchon, using funds provided by the HSPA. Koreans at the turn of the century were very isolated and stay-at-home people. They were not willing to go abroad and work in the pineapple or sugar plantations.

However, the deteriorating political situation caused by Japan's move to colonize Korea and unbearable economic conditions forced many Koreans to go to Hawaii to make their fortunes.

Some of them recalled in their oral histories that they had heard

Number of Korean Churches and Temples in the U.S. (Table 1)

Year	No. of Protestant Churches	No. of Buddhist Temples	Korean Immigrants
1903-1910	7	u	7,697
1911-1920	39	u	8,746
1921-1930	u	u	9,344
1931-1940	u	u	9,404
1941-1950	u	u	u
1951-1960	u	u	15,635
1961-1970	100	u	50,161
1971-1980	1,017	9	322,117
1981-1990	2,000	20	660,941
1991-2000	3,402	97	850,124

Source: (1) Number of Korean Protestant churches: Choy, Bong-Youn. *Koreans in America.* Chicago: Nelson-Hall (1979); Harris, Scott Collins, "Korean Church Growth in America, 1903-1990: History and Analysis." Ph.D. dissertation, South Western Baptist Theological Seminary (1990); *The Christian Press. 2000 Jun Miju Hanin Kyohoe Jusorok (2000 Korean Church Address Book).* (2) Number of Buddhist temples: Yu, Eui-Young. "The Growth of Korean Buddhism in the U.S.: with Special Reference to Southern California." *The Pacific World: Journal of the Institute of Buddhist Studies.* New Series. No. 4. (1988) pp.82-93; *Mi-ju Hyun-dae Bul-kyo (Modern Buddhism).* December 2000. u: Unidentified.

that the streets of Hawaii were paved with gold and one could become rich by sweeping the gold with a broom. So they contracted to work in the pineapple and sugar plantations for a monthly salary of fifteen dollars, working ten hours a day. It was bitter labor from dawn to dark, but they were able to save some money to pay back the passage and other expenses they owed to Deshler when they left Korea. When the labor contract expired, Korean laborers set up self-employed businesses such as laundry shops and restaurants. However, by the end of the labor contract in 1907 about 1,000 Koreans left Hawaii and moved to the mainland United States to engage in self-employment, and about

1,000 Koreans returned to Korea because they were unable to adjust to the foreign land and culture. Moreover, the majority of Korean laborers were illiterate because they did not have any formal education and were not able to speak English, which made them homesick and culturally alienated.

Another group of Korean immigrants came to Hawaii when 951 picture brides arrived in 1910 to marry Korean laborers, and by 1924 a total of 1,100 picture brides had come to the United States, according to the Annual Report of the U.S. Immigration and Naturalization Service. Of the "first wave," Korean immigrant men outnumbered Korean women ten to one. There were nearly 5,000 bachelors and Korean men insisted on marrying Korean women only. Therefore, they had to send pictures of themselves and have arranged marriages. Because Korean men often used old pictures of themselves that had been taken before they left Korea, an arriving picture bride would often find herself facing a groom who was ten or twenty years older than she.

Korean Students and the Independence Movement
Even before the first wave of Korean immigrants arrived in Hawaii in 1903, Korean students came to the United States to study at various institutions following the 1882 Treaty of Amity and Commerce. When the treaty was signed in May 1882, the Korean government dispatched the first diplomatic mission, headed by Min Yung-ik, to visit the United States in 1883. The delegation was received by President Chester Arthur on September 18, 1883 in New York, as he was visiting the city of New York and staying at the Fifth Avenue Hotel. One of the ten-member delegation, Yu Kil-chun, was given permission and financial support by the Korean government to remain in the United States to study at the Governor Dummer Academy in Massachusetts. Thus he became the first Korean government scholarship student. He enrolled at the Governor Dummer Academy in September, 1884 but was forced to return home in December 1885 due to the 1884 political coup that shook up King Kojong's palace in the young elites' attempt to reform the most corrupt conservative government. Another member of the Korean delegation, Pyon Su, was also given permission to study in the

United States and he was the first Korean to graduate from a U. S. college. He was enrolled at Maryland Agriculture College (now the University of Maryland) as a freshman in 1887 and graduated with a B.S. degree in June 1891. He returned to Korea briefly after his graduation but came back to the United States as a result of the lingering political crisis in Korea. He paid a brief visit to his alma mater in October 1891, but he was killed in a train accident while waiting at the platform. He was only 32 years old and was buried in Beltsville, MD.

In 1892, perhaps the first Korean graduate of an American medical college was Philip Jaisohn (So Chae-pil), who was one of the leaders of the 1884 political coup attempt (known as the Kap-sin chong-pyon) that aimed to reform the conservative Korean government. The coup attempt was crushed. After the collapse of the coup, many coup leaders escaped to Japan and some moved from Japan to the United States. So Chae-pil, one of the coup leaders, came to the United States in 1886 and graduated from Hillman Academy in three years. He was the first Korean student to become an American citizen in 1888. Four years later, in 1891, he became the first Korean to receive an American medical degree, graduating from Columbian Medical College (which later became the George Washington University). He was one of the leaders of the Korean students actively involved in the Korean independence movement during the Japanese occupation of Korea from 1910 to 1945. Subsequently, he served as an advisor to the U.S. military government in Korea after Japan was defeated in World War II. The U. S. military government ruled Korea from 1945 to 1948. Jaisohn was actively involved in South Korean politics, but when he failed to achieve his ambition to be the first president of the Republic of Korea in 1948, he came back to the United States and lived and worked in Pennsylvania.[4]

Warren Kim's pioneering book, *The 50 Year History of Koreans in America*, published in 1959, divides the history of Korean students in America into four periods. The first period spans from the 1882 treaty to 1903, when the first shipload of Korean laborers arrived in Hawaii. The above-mentioned students, Yu Kil-choon, Pyun Su, and So Chae-pil and Kim Kyu-sick belong in this category. Dosan An Ch'ang-Ho, Syngman Rhee, and Pak Yong-Man came to the United States in the early 1900s, and became the most prominent leaders of the Korean independence movement in the United States during the Japanese occupation period (1910-45).

The second period begins with the Japanese Protectorate Treaty of 1910 and runs to the end of Japanese colonial rule in 1945, during which a total of 891 Korean students and exiled patriots came to America to study at various colleges and universities. During this period, large numbers of Korean student leaders emerged to carry out the national independence movement in America.[5]

During the second period and beyond from 1910 to 1945, when the Japanese seized power and ruled Korea for three and a half decades, sixty to seventy students came to the United States to study at various academic institutions. It should be noted that the immigration of Korean laborers to Hawaiian pineapple and sugar plantations was halted after 1905 when Japan took control of Korea's foreign relations. However, the Japanese colonial administration in 1910 permitted about 1,100 picture brides to emigrate and marry Korean workers there.

Moreover, the Oriental Exclusion Act of 1924 was signed on July 1, 1924, banning all Asian immigration and ending the first wave of Korean immigration. To understand the discrimination and restriction of Asian immigration, we should know more about the Chinese Exclusion Act of 1882 and several other U.S. legislations forbidding the immigration of Chinese laborers into the United States. The original act of 1882 forbade Chinese immigration from 1882 to 1892. In 1892 another act was passed extending the ban until 1902, and again in 1902 another act was passed further forbidding Chinese immigration. Thus plantation laborers from Korea were recruited to work in the Hawaiian pineapple and sugar plantations in place of Chinese laborers. The Oriental Exclusion Act of 1924 banned all Asian immigration, but permitted students from Asia to study at various U.S. academic institutions.

The following chart shows the number of Korean students enrolled in various American colleges and academic institutions as well as the number of Koreans who settled in the United States from 1910-1919. The number of Korean immigrants in the United States was drastically reduced by the Japanese colonial administration in 1910.

(Table 2)

Year	1910	1911	1912	1913	1914	1915	1916	1917	1918	1919	Total
Immigrants	14	6	45	9	21	11	13	7	19	19	185
Students	--	2	3	2	7	--	4	3	--	5	26

The number of Korean students in the 1920s: (Table 3)

1920	1921	1922	1923	1924	1925	1926	1927	1928	1929	Total
17	18	31	38	31	26	45	55	39	32	332

These statistics are drawn from the publications of the Japanese Governor's office in Korea. The Korean-language newspaper, *Shinhan Minbo* (*New Korea*), published in San Francisco, reported that the number of Korean immigrants in the years between 1910 and 1919 was estimated at 8,326, including Koreans in Hawaii, while the number of Korean students who came to study in America was estimated at 150. The number of Korean students in the United States in 1920 more than doubled to 332 in the aftermath of the 1919 uprising of the Korean independence movement, which forced the Japanese colonial administration to adopt a more liberal cultural policy, thereby allowing more Korean students to study abroad. Of the 486 Korean students studying abroad, 78% of them came to the United States.

Following the 1919 independence uprising in Korea, a large number of Korean students came to the United States to study and many became the student leaders of the Korean independence movement in America. Cho Byung-ok became one of the more prominent leaders. He graduated from Columbia University with B.A. and M. A. degrees in economics in the 1920s and later served in the U.S. military government as the chief of police (1945-48). He then became the first cabinet member in charge of internal affairs, including the police force, in the Syngman Rhee government in 1948. He was one of many Korean student leaders who became politicians in post-WW II Korea. He came to the United States in 1914 and started his education in high school. He went on to college and graduate school in New York City.

Many Korean students emerged as political, educational and economic leaders in post liberation Korea. Cho Byong-ok was followed by Kim Do-yon, who came to the U.S. to study in 1922 and later became a cabinet member in the Syngman Rhee government. Kim Hual-ran (Helen Kim) came to America in 1922 and became the president of Ewha Women's University after receiving her Ph. D. in education from Columbia University. Yun Chi-young also came in 1923 and became a cabinet member during Syngman Rhee's presidency. Chung Il-hyung came in 1929, becoming a well-known politician and serving as foreign minister in the Chang Myun government in 1960-61. Paik Lak-chun (L. George Paik) came to the United States in 1918 and received his B.A. from Park College in 1922, his M.A. from Princeton in 1925 in history and his Ph.D. from Yale in 1927 in church history. His doctoral dissertation, *History of Protestant Mission in Korea, 1832-1910*, was a pioneering work on that topic. He was professor and later President of Yonsei University in Seoul. He served as Minister of Education and was elected to the upper house of the Korean legislature, serving as its Speaker during Chang Myun's democratic government in 1960-61.

Thus the students who came to the U.S. in the 1920s returned home after receiving their education and being actively involved in the Korean independence movement in America, and were appointed to leadership positions in government, education and economic institutions in post-liberation Korea. However, many Korean students who came to the U.S. during the Japanese colonial period (1910-1945) remained there, became American citizens, and worked in various positions in government, military, and other economic institutions during World War II. In 1924, when the Oriental Exclusion Act of 1924 was passed in the U.S., the Japanese colonial government in Korea halted the issuing of student passports to all Korean students who wanted to study in the U.S. The number of Korean students studying in the U. S. at that time did not exceed 900, but those students led the Korean community in the U. S. in the 1930s and 1940s. There were no more than 7,000 Koreans who were living in America, including students, in the 1920s and 1930s. The following chart shows the number of Korean students in the U. S. in the 1930s.

(Table 4)

1930	1931	1932	1933	1934	1935	1936	Total
31	28	12	5	6	6	10	98

The Korean independence movement in the United States began when the Japanese Protectorate Treaty was imposed on the government of King Kojong in 1905, depriving Korea of its diplomatic rights to conduct foreign relations. Thus the Korean national independence movement was organized in 1905 under the leadership of Korean intellectuals, students, and patriotic immigrants. The movement can be divided into two periods: the period of anti-Japanese activities in Hawaii and on mainland U.S. from 1905 to 1930, and the period of the united front against Japanese military expansion in China and Asia from 1931 to 1945. Korean immigrants as well as students thought of themselves as temporary residents in the U.S., prepared to return home when they made enough money or when the Korean political situation improved. Thus Koreans in America participated actively in the national independence movement.

As early as August 1903, Koreans in Hawaii formed the first political organization, Sinmin-hoe (New People's Association), under the leadership of An Jong-su and Yun Pyong-ku. The primary objective of this organization was to unite the Korean immigrants of Hawaii to oppose any foreign interference in domestic affairs of foreign powers and maintain the independence and sovereignty of Korea. In September 1903, the first social organization, known as Ch'inmok-hoe (Friendship Association), was formed by An Ch'ang-Ho in San Francisco. It had nine members and An was elected chairman of this organization. [6] Many more social and political organizations were established in Hawaii and on the mainland, but the organization formed by An played the leading role in the Korean independence movement in the United States.[7]

An Ch'ang-Ho organized the Corps for the Advancement of Individuals (Hungsa-dan) in San Francisco because he thought the education of Koreans would promote virtue, intellect, and health so as to raise the consciousness of all Korean-Americans, which was essential to achieve Korean independence. He also organized the Korean National Association in San Francisco in 1909 to bring about the unity of Koreans and the independence of Korea. After the Japanese occupation of Korea the State of California recognized the Korean National Association as an incorporated organization representing the interests of Koreans in America. The Korean National Association was authorized to issue permits in place of passports for those Koreans who wanted to enter the U.S.[8]

While An was dedicated to peaceful means for achieving the goal of national independence, Park Yong-Man, who came to the United States in 1904, was committed to the use of military means to overthrow the Japanese colonial government. Park finished his secondary education at Lincoln High School in Lincoln, Nebraska and was enrolled at Hastings College in 1906, graduating from it in 1909 with a political science major and a minor in military affairs. He majored in political science with military affairs as a minor to learn more about the political process by which he would be able to achieve the national independence of Korea by using military strategy to expel the Japanese colonial government.

Upon his graduation from Hastings College in 1909, Park established a school for military training for Korean youth at Hastings College. He was able to recruit twenty-seven students from the children of Korean immigrants and they began military training during the evenings, working on the farms during the day. He also served as the editor of the Korean people's newspaper, *Sinhan Minbo* (*New Korean News*), in 1910 and then moved on to become editor-in-chief of the weekly newspaper *Sin-hankook-bo* (*National Herald*) in 1912. When the Korean

National Association in Hawaii recruited two hundred Korean immigrants to the army corps, Park was invited to serve as the commander-in-chief of this Korean National Army Corps in 1914. The Korean National Army Corps trained more than 311 military leaders and a little over six hundred Korean immigrants participated in the training program. However, it is not clear if any of those trained in the military program were ever recruited to the independence movement under the Provisional Government of Korea in Shanghai, China.

Under the 1940 Alien Registration Act, Korean-Americans were forced to identify themselves as "enemy aliens" because Koreans were Japanese subjects during Japanese colonial rule. For self-protection, Koreans wore signs proclaiming, "I am not Jap" when anti-Japanese demonstrations spread along the West Coast after the Pearl Harbor attack by Japanese Kamikaze special forces. Koreans in America were eager to support America's war against Japan, and many Koreans volunteered to serve in the U.S. military as translators and intelligence officers. In 1943, Colonel Young Oak Kim, a highly decorated Korean-American, was the first Asian-American to command a combat battalion.

Moreover, Park served as the leader of the Korean National Association in Hawaii and invited Syngman Rhee, who had just returned from Korea where he was in charge of the YMCA training program after receiving his Ph.D. from Princeton University, to work with him for the publication of *Pacific News* and other newspapers. Thus the collaboration between Park Yong-Man and Syngman Rhee began in Hawaii for the sake of Korean national independence. However, disagreement developed between the two leaders over policy issues of Korean independence. While Park advocated military means to expel the Japanese colonial rule and achieve Korean national independence, Syngman Rhee wanted to achieve the goal of national independence by means of political and diplomatic actions. The three prominent leaders of the Korean national independence movement in the U.S. formulated three different approaches to that goal: An Ch'ang-Ho advocated the education and cultivation of Korean nationalism, Park Yong-Man dedicated himself to the military means, and Syngman Rhee was committed to political and diplomatic means.[9]

When Japanese colonial rule over Korea ended in 1945 following the military defeat of Japan by the Allied Powers, including the United States and the Soviet Union, a large number of Koreans who were dedicated to Korean national independence returned to Korea to help establish the Korean government. The factionalism that had developed among the leaders of the Korean national independence movement abroad in turn brought about the numerous political parties and groups in post-liberation Korea. The U.S. military government in South Korea recruited many Koreans in America to serve as interpreters and administrators. Many students who returned to Korea also participated in the establishment of the Republic of Korea's government and served in the National Assembly, the Cabinet and various administrative posts during the First Republic.

The Second Wave of Korean Immigrants: 1950-1964
During the second wave of Korean immigrants, from 1950-1964, three groups of Koreans emigrated to the U. S. One group was the Korean wives of American servicemen, known as the war brides, whose number increased from the days of U.S. military government (1945-48) to the Korean War (1950-53). Between 1951 and 1964 the number of Korean immigrants in the U.S. reached 14,027, according to the annual report of the U.S. Immigration and Naturalization Service, and by 1971 it increased to 14,297. The total number of war brides was 53,629 by the end of 1980. This group, like the first wave of Korean immigrants who came to work in the pineapple and sugar plantations in Hawaii, suffered from culture shock and a language barrier and was isolated from both Korean and American communities. Most of the war brides stayed on military bases or in military facilities and there have been reported many cases of physical abuse, suicide, and a high rate of divorce or separation.

The second group was the Korean orphans adopted by American families, whose number reached 6,203 in the period of 1955-66. Among adopted Koreans, 41 percent were full-blooded Koreans, 46 percent had White fathers, and the rest were Afro-Koreans. [10]   Most Korean children were adopted by White Protestant families living in rural and small communities and many adopted Korean children faced problems of national identity as they grew up.[11]

The third group of Koreans in America reached 27,000 people and consisted of students, visitors, businessmen, and many others engaged in trade. Many in this group were professional people such as medical doctors, lawyers, and college professors, who were well accepted by the middle- class community and who also made significant contributions to American society. Members of this group became integrated into American society and became the models of Korean-Americans. By 1965, Korean professionals had the highest per capita income and lowest unemployment rate of any immigrant group in America because of their higher education and professional training.

The Third Wave of Korean Immigration
The 1965 Immigration and Naturalization Act repealed the national origins quota system and gave priority to family reunification. The McCarran-Walter Immigration Act of 1952, passed over President Truman's veto, affirmed the national origins quota system of 1924 and limited total annual immigration to one-sixth of one percent of the population of the continental United States in 1920. The act exempted spouses and children of U.S. citizens and people born in the Western hemisphere from the quota. This act was so racially discriminatory that President Truman had even vetoed it. The quota system restricted the number of immigrants from Asia whereas unrestricted numbers of White Europeans could come to the U.S.

However, more than 28,000 Koreans were able to emigrate to the U.S. during the period from 1951 to 1964 because of the War Brides Act of 1945, which allowed foreign-born wives of U.S. citizens who had served in the U.S. armed forces to enter the

United States. The U.S. military rule of South Korea (1945-48), the Korean War (1950-53), and continued stationing of U.S. troops in Korea increased the number of Korean War brides in the 1950s and 1960s.

In 1965, the U.S. Congress recognized America's need for skilled professionals and lifted the national immigration quota system. Independent nations outside of the Western hemisphere were permitted to send up to 20,000 emigrants per year to join their families in the United States. The Hart-Celler Act of 1965, which President Johnson signed into law in October of that year, was actually intended to limit immigration. Congressman Emanuel Celler of New York stated: "Since the people of . . . Asia have very few relatives here, comparatively few could emigrate from those countries, because they have no family ties in the U.S." Congressman Celler had overlooked or was ignorant of the Asian-American population in the United States. In the year in which his bill was passed, only 2,165 Koreans were admitted to the U.S. However, between 1965 and 1980, 299,000 Koreans immigrated to the U.S. From 1970 to 1980, the Korean population increased by 412 percent and between 1980 and 1990 to 370,909. More than 30,000 Koreans have immigrated each year for the past decade and the population of Korean-Americans increased from 69,150 in 1970 to 1,076,872 in 2000, as shown in the U.S. Census.[12]

However, the number of Korean-Americans constitutes only 0.39 percent of the American population, and 10.8 percent of the non-Hispanic Asian and Pacific-Islander population. Census 2000 indicated that Korean-Americans live in large cities of major metropolitan areas, such as Los Angeles (24.0 percent), New York (15.8 percent), Washington (6.8 percent), San Francisco (4.3 percent), and Chicago (4.3 percent). Moreover the number of Korean immigrants has fluctuated in recent years. After two decades' surge, with more than 30,000 per year until 1990, when the Korean economy reached a substantial level, the number of Korean immigrants dramatically declined to as few as 12,000 per year until 1997. The number of Korean immigrants, however,

Number of Koreans Admitted to the U.S. as Permanent Residents, 1950-2001 (Table 5)

Year	New Arrivals	Status Adjusters	Total
1950-1954	538	N/A	538
1955-1959	4,990	N/A	4,990
1960-1965	11,686	1,583	13,269
1966	2,492	598	3,090
1967	3,956	1,424	5,380
1968	3,811	1,098	4,909
1969	6,045	1,820	7,865
1970	9,314	2,079	11,393
1971	14,297	4,049	18,346
1972	18,876	5,513	24,389
1973	22,930	4,961	27,891
1974	28,028	4,658	32,686
1975	28,362	2,364	30,726
1976	30,803	1,881	32,684
1977	28,437	2,480	30,917
1978	25,830	3,458	29,288
1979	26,646	2,602	29,248
1980	29,387	2,933	32,320
1981	28,819	3,844	32,663
1982	27,861	3,863	31,724
1983	29,019	4,320	33,339
1984	28,828	4,214	33,042
1985	30,532	4,721	35,253
1986	30,745	5,031	35,776
1987	32,135	3,714	35,849
1988	31,071	3,632	34,703
1989	28,248	5,974	34,222
1990	25,966	6,335	32,301
1991	12,754	13,764	26,518
1992	11,473	7,886	19,359
1993	8,133	9,893	18,026
1994	7,975	8,036	16,011
1995	8,535	7,512	16,047
1996	7,277	10,908	18,185
1997	8,205	6,034	14,239
1998	8,734	5,534	14,268
1999	5,360	7,480	12,840
2000	5,244	10,586	15,830
2001	(4,565)	(16,177)	20,742
Total	**677,907**	**192,959**	**870,866**

Source: Immigration and Naturalization Service

substantially increased again beginning in 1998, right after the Korean economy was under IMF bailout.

Although the number of Korean immigrants per year has steadily increased since 1997, it has not returned to the high numbers of

Although the number of Korean immigrants per year has steadily increased since 1997, it has not returned to the high numbers of the 1970s and 1980s, as shown in Table 5. Although occupation and family reunion cases are still the most popular entrance categories, approximately half of current Korean immigrants are visa change cases. These visa cases stay in the U.S. for a few months or years with temporary visitors' visas, usually as tourists, contract workers, or foreign students, and they become determined to live in the U.S. permanently when conditions are met. This means that many Korean immigrants experience immigration life on a temporary basis before they decide to become permanent residents. It is reported that there are still thousands of Koreans living illegally in the United States without any permanent resident status.

The third wave of Korean immigration to America since 1965 is often characterized by experts as college-educated professionals accompanied by families upon emigration from Korea. Their children, who are known as the one half (1.5) generation or the second generation, make up the present day Korean-American community in major cities, many aspects of which are critically analyzed by the younger generation of scholars in Part II of this book. The third wave of Korean immigrants, unlike the first wave of Korean laborers, is college-educated and its members were white-collar workers in Korea. However, they found that their lack of English proficiency hindered the full utilization of their knowledge and skills in the American economy and society. Therefore, many of them changed their careers and started small businesses or purchased existing businesses from retiring non-Korean businessmen. Thus, they were able to dominate certain types of business such as green groceries, dry cleaning, liquor stores and nail salons in American cities such as New York, Los Angeles, Chicago, and Washington.[13]

Korean immigrants who came to the United States during the third wave were young, married, and better educated than those

Korean-American Population in the Selected Areas, 2000 (Table 6)

Metropolitan Area	Population	Percent
Korean Population in the United States	*1,076,872*	*100%*
Los Angeles Metropolitan Area	257,975	24.0
New York Metropolitan Area	170,509	15.8
Washington Metropolitan Area	74,454	6.9
San Francisco Metropolitan Area	57,386	5.3
Chicago Metropolitan Area	46,256	4.3
Seattle Metropolitan Area	41,189	3.8
Total of above Six Metropolitan Areas	*647,769*	*60.15*

Source: Eui-Young Yu, "Korean Population in the United States," *International Journal of Korean Studies*, VI (1) (Spring/Summer 2002), p. 87.

who came through family reunification. Those who came to the U.S. through family connections were of lower socio-economic status than the general population of Korean immigrants in the same period. Almost one half (49.2%) of Korean immigrants received a B.A., B.S., or higher degree of education, according to Census 2000. The average income of Korean-Americans was $32,807 in 2000, which is a little lower than the $36,754 of White Americans.

The proportion of managerial jobs for Korean-Americans in 1990 was 15 percent for males and 9 percent for females as shown in Table 7. The proportion of Korean-American males in managerial jobs was 2 percent higher than that of all Americans, but 5 percent lower than that of Japanese-American male workers, while the number of Korean-American female workers in this category was much lower than the proportion of all Americans as well as that of Japanese and Chinese female workers. The proportion of professional jobs for Korean-Americans was 16 percent for males and 11 percent for females. It was 4 percent higher than that of all Americans, but 8 and 4 percent lower than that of both Chinese and Japanese male workers. In technical and sales jobs, the proportion of Korean-Americans was 29 percent for males and 25 percent for females in the same year. The proportion for all Americans was 15 percent for males and 16 percent for females, in contrast to 8 and 17 for Chinese workers, respectively, and 17 and 16 percent for Japanese workers. Thus the proportion of Korean-American workers was unusually high in 1990, due to the increasing number of those self-employed in small businesses. In service jobs, Korean-American male workers were employed in similar proportion to all Americans. Thus, a large proportion of Korean-Americans resided in urban areas, and engaged largely in small businesses as well as managerial and professional jobs. In the occupations of production/craft and operators, the proportions of Korean-American male workers were relatively lower than that of all Americans, though Chinese and Japanese male workers showed the same low percentages.[14]

Occupational Distribution by Sex: Selected Asian Americans Compared to All U.S. Workers, 1990; Left Male, Right Female in Percent (Table 7)

Occupation Male & Female	All USA		Chinese		Japanese		Filipino		Koreans		Vietnamese	
Managerial	13	11	15	15	20	14	10	10	15	9	5	7
Professional	12	17	24	17	20	19	12	20	16	11	13	9
Technical & Sales	15	16	18	17	17	16	15	16	29	25	18	17
Administrative Support	7	28	8	21	9	28	16	25	6	14	8	18
Service	10	17	19	14	9	14	16	17	10	20	12	19
Fish & Forest	4	1	1	1	4	1	2	1	1	1	2	1
Production & Craft	19	2	8	3	12	3	12	3	12	6	19	10
Operators	20	8	9	13	2	5	15	7	12	14	22	20

Sources: U.S. Bureau of Census, *Asian and Pacific Islanders in the United States*, CP-3-5, August 1993 in Norman R. Yetman, *Majority and Minority*, pp. 224 for 1990 data. The 2000 data is available in late 2003.

Korean-American Contributions to the United States

Recognizing the historical significance of the 100th anniversary of Korean emigration to the United States, the U.S. Senate passed S. RES. 185 at the second session of the 107th Congress on June 27, 2002. The resolution recognized that in December 1902, 56 men, 21 women, and 25 children left Korea and traveled across the Pacific Ocean on the *S.S. Gaelic* and landed in Honolulu. The early Korean-American community was united around the common goal of attaining freedom and independence for its colonized mother country. The members of the early Korean-American community served with distinction the Armed Forces of the United States during World War I, World War II, and the Korean Conflict.

In the early 1950s, thousands of Koreans, fleeing from war, poverty, and desolation, came to the United States seeking opportunities, like the waves of immigrants to America before them, have taken root and thrived in the U.S. through strong family ties, robust community support, and countless hours of hard work. Moreover, Korean immigration to the United States has invigorated business, church, and academic communities in the U.S. According to the 2000 U.S. Census, Korean-Americans own and operate 135,571 businesses across the United States, which have gross sales and receipts of $46,000,000,000 and employ 333,649 individuals with an annual payroll of $5,800,000,000.

Among the contributions of Korean-Americans to the United States include the invention of the first beating heart operation for coronary artery heart disease, the development of the nectarine, a 4-time Olympic gold medallist, and achievements in engineering, architecture, medicine, acting, singing, sculpture, and writing. Korean-Americans also play a crucial role in maintaining the strength and vitality of the United States-Korean partnership, which helps undergird peace and stability in the Asia-Pacific region and provides economic benefits to the people of the United States and Korea and to the rest of the world.

The House of Representatives also passed Resolution H. CON 297 at the 1st Session of the 107th Congress on September 25, 2002, honoring one hundred years of Korean immigration to the United States. This resolution was concurrent with the Senate's resolution, S. RES 185, submitted to the 2nd Session of the 107th Congress on November 30, 2001. A Proclamation by the President of the United States of America on the Centennial of Korean Immigration to the United States was announced on January 13, 2003. The President proclaimed:

> Today, Korean Americans live throughout the United States, representing one of our largest Asian-American populations. . . . we recognize the invaluable contributions of Korean Americans to our Nation's rich cultural diversity, economic

strength, and proud heritage. . . . The American and Korean people share a love of freedom and a dedication to peace. The United States was the first Western country to sign a treaty of commerce and amity with Korea in 1882, promising "perpetual peace and friendship" between our nations. Since that time, the United States has built a strong friendship with Korea – a friendship based on our common commitment to human dignity, prosperity, and democracy. In the coming months, more than 1 million Korean Americans throughout our Nation will celebrate the 100th anniversary of the arrival of the first Korean immigrants to the United States. During this time, we acknowledge and commend Korean Americans for their distinguished achievements in all sectors of life and for their important role building, defending, and sustaining the United States of America.

Conclusions

The Korean immigrants who came to the United States in the first wave from 1903 to 1924 worked ten hours a day with a meager salary of fifteen dollars a month or sixty-nine cents an hour. However, they were able to save some money to pay for their room and board and the rest of their money was allocated to support the nationalist movement and the provisional government in Shanghai, China. They organized the independence movement and fought for Korea's independence from Japanese colonial rule in Korea from 1910 to 1945. They were united to fight for freedom and peace in the Korean peninsula.

After the ban of Asian immigrants by the U.S. Immigration Act of 1924, which is known as the Oriental Exclusion Act, students from Asia were allowed to study in American colleges and universities. Thus, many Korean students with Japanese passports came to the U.S. to study at various academic institutions. Many of them returned home following Korea's liberation from Japanese colonial rule and participated in the establishment and administration of the Republic of Korea, when the student leaders of the Korean independence movement in the U.S. took up leadership and management positions in the liberated Korea.

Thus, the leadership of the Korean independence movement in America emerged from the student leaders when they were united and organized to expel Japanese colonial rule from Korea. However, factionalism was rampant among those student groups. Three major factions grew out of the independence movement. Some nationalist leaders, like An Ch'ang-Ho, approached Korean independence through the cultivation and education of the Korean people. Others, like Pak Yong-Man, advocated military means to fight and defeat Japanese colonial rule. Still others, like Syngman Rhee, approached the Korean independence movement by means of diplomacy and lobbying of the U.S. government to help achieve Korean liberation.

Rhee later became the first president of the Republic of Korea, in 1948, with the help of the United States Military Government, which ruled the southern part of Korea from 1945 to 1948. The U.S. decided to draw the 38th parallel line as a demarcation line in 1945, allowing the Soviet Union to take control of the northern part while the United States ruled the southern part. The original plan was to accept the surrender of Japanese armed forces by the occupying forces of the north and south of Korea; however, the division unfortunately became a permanent boundary between the two Koreas for more than half a century since the end of WWII.

The outbreak of the Korean War in 1950 saw more than one million U.S. armed forces eventually deployed to fight North Korean aggression. The casualties of the U.S. armed forces during the Korean War included 54,260 dead (of whom 33,665 were battle deaths), 92,134 wounded, and 8,176 listed as missing in action or prisoners of war. The post-Korean War immigration numbered 14,027 which included war brides, war orphans adopted by American families, and families of Koreans who had become permanent residents of the U.S. Following the passage of the Immigration and Nationality Act of 1965, which repealed the national origins quota system and gave priority to family reunification, the Korean-American population increased from fewer than 70,000 in 1970 to more than 1.5 million by 2002.

The Korean students who came to the United States in the 1950s and 1960s remained in America after receiving professional and advanced degrees to work in U.S. government agencies, teach at various academic institutions, and conduct research in scientific research institutes. Thousands of Korean professionals who became U.S. citizens following the passage of the 1965 Immigration and Nationality Act have now reached retirement age; however, their children, who received a much better education in the United States than their parents, are now working in mainstream American professions in academia, business and finance, law, media and communications, and scientific research.

However, Korean immigrants who came to the United States in the 1970s and 1980s encountered culture shock, communication problems due to language deficiencies, and alienation from mainstream America. Thus they created an enclave of Korean ethnic communities in many urban centers and they conduct their business among other Koreans. Because of communication problems, the first-generation Koreans do not participate in civic affairs or take part in political action groups. The Korean merchants who operate thousands of small businesses such as convenience stores, grocery stores, and green vegetable stands do not join the American Chamber of Commerce, which would integrate their businesses into mainstream American society.

Korean-Americans do not exercise their political power, though they contribute millions of dollars to the campaigns of presidential and Congressional candidates. Only 30% of Korean-Americans are registered to vote but only 23% of them regularly cast their ballot at election time. Koreans in America pay more attention to the national politics of Korea and support the candidate of their preference in Korean elections. However, the 1.5 and second generations of Korean-Americans are increasingly more active in American politics and work toward the empowerment of Korean-Americans. It is time for first generation Korean-Americans to donate their resources for the empowerment of the second generation Korean-Americans, so that they can run for office and engage in the American political process to realize their American dreams.

Notes

[1] Choy, Bong-Youn. *Koreans in America*. Chicago: Nelson-Hall, 1979.
Patterson, Wayne. *The Korean Frontiers in America: Immigration to Hawaii, 1896-1910*. Honolulu: University of Hawaii Press, 1988.
Kim, Won-yong. Chaemi Hanin Osipyon-sa (*A fifty-year history of the Koreans in America*). Reedley, Calif. Charles Ho Kim, 1959

[2] Patterson, *ibid.*

[3] Choe, Yong-ho. "A Brief History of Christ United Methodist Church, 1903-2003" in *Christ United Methodist Church, 1903-2003: A Pictorial History*. Honolulu: Christ Methodist Church, 2003. pp. 31-51.

[4] Cho, Chong-moo. *Profiles of Koreans in American Continent*. Seoul: Choson Ilbo Chulpan-sa. 1987. pp. 90-103.

[5] Choy, Bong-Youn. *Koreans in America*, pp. 141-160.

[6] Kim, Won-yong. *Ibid.*

[7] Kim, Han-Kyo. "The Korean Independence Movement in the United States: Syngman Rhee, An Ch'ang-Ho and Pak Yong-Man," *International Journal of Korean Studies*, V. VI, No. 1, (2002), 1-28.

[8] *Ibid.*

[9] *Ibid.*

[10] Hur, Won Moo, "Marginal Children of War: An Exploratory Study of Korean-American Children," *International Journal of Sociology of the Family*. 2(1972): 10-20.

[11] For an adopted Korean search identity, see Katy Robinson, *A Single SquarePicture: A Korean Adopted Search for Her Roots*. New York: Berkley Books, 2002.

[12] Hur. Won Moo. *The Korean-Americans*. Westport, CT: Greenwood Press, 1998. Also see "Korean Immigration to the United States, 1903-2003" in U.S. Immigration and Naturalization Service, Annual Report. Washington, D.C.: U.S. Government Printing Office, 2003.

[13] Marcus, Norland. "The Impact of Korean Immigration on the U.S. Economy," Research Paper for the IIE, 2003.

[14] Kim, Hugo Wheegook. "A Historical Overview of the Immigration to the United States and Political Participation of Asian Americans: A Perspective of Korean-Americans," East-West Research Institute Paper. Washington, D.C. 2003.

2. History of Korean Church: A Case Study of Christ United Methodist Church, 1903–2003

Yŏng-ho Ch'oe

In the Beginning

The origins of Christ United Methodist Church lie in the efforts of some of the earliest Korean immigrants to the Hawaiian Islands to organize worship services in cooperation with the Hawaii Methodist Mission. After working with the Methodist Mission superintendent, the Rev. George L. Pearson, a group led by Chung-Soo Ahn (An Chông-su) and U Pyŏng-gil (later known as Yun Pyŏng-gu) held its first Sunday service under the name of the Korean Methodist Mission on November 10, 1903. The Korean Methodist Mission, believed to have been located at the corner of River and Hotel Streets in downtown Honolulu, was not yet a fully organized church in 1903. Its establishment is nevertheless regarded as the founding of Christ United Methodist Church.

The participants in that first congregation were drawn from among the Korean immigrants who had begun to arrive on the Islands in January 1903 to work on Hawaii's sugar plantations. By the time organized immigration had ended in 1905, a little over 7,200 men, women, and children had made that journey. Of these, about 1,000 eventually returned to Korea for various reasons, and another 1,000 moved on to the mainland United States to seek better opportunities.

It is not known how many Koreans had accepted Christianity before coming to Hawaii. Estimates of the number of Koreans who might have attended church while they were still in Korea range from 400 to as many as one-third of all the immigrants. There is no way to prove any of these estimates, but the active role the church played in the initial stage of Korean immigration suggests that a considerable number of the immigrants had some contact with the church before departing Korea.

The difficult task of winning the Korean government's approval of immigration was solved with the help of the influential Presbyterian medical missionary Horace N. Allen, who had become a confidante of the Korean king and served as United States minister to Korea. When Koreans showed little interest in applying to work in Hawaii, recruiters sought the help of another American missionary, the Rev. George Heber Jones.

In a sermon given at the Naeri Methodist Church in Inchon, Jones urged his congregation to apply for work in Hawaii, where, he explained, agreeable weather and well-paying jobs awaited them. Jones's call moved many church members to respond favorably: a majority of the first group of the Korean immigrants (102 altogether), who arrived in Honolulu on January 13, 1903, were drawn from the congregation of Naeri Methodist Church. The group included Chung-Soo Ahn, Yee-Jay Kim (Kim Ûi-je), and at least fifty other members of the Naeri congregation. Ever faithful to their beliefs, they conducted worship service aboard their ship even while crossing the Pacific.

At a Honolulu pier, this first group of Korean immigrants was greeted by George L. Pearson, the superintendent of the Hawaii Methodist Mission. The second group of sixty-three that reached Honolulu on March 3, 1903 was led by Soon Hyun (Hyôn Sun), who was also a member of the Naeri Church.

The presence of so many Christians among the first immigrants no doubt prompted the creation of a church of their own soon after arrival. In a short time, Korean Christians could be found conducting worship services and proselytizing at various plantations, this even before American missionaries had begun to work with them. There are, for example, reports that soon after their arrival Chi-Pum Hong (Hong Ch'i-bôm), Chŏng-su Im, and Soon Hyun were proselytizing and leading worship services in Korean at Waialua and Kahuku, in accordance with the

American Methodist Church rules. Yee-Jay Kim is also reported to have led services at Mokuleia.

These Koreans worked with no denominational affiliation, but the Hawaii Methodist Mission, encouraged by their activism, began to show an interest in aiding and guiding them. The Rev. and Mrs. Richard H. Bimson wrote in their *Hawaii Mission of Methodist Church, 1855–1955* (p. 11): "Methodist work among the Koreans began in earnest, with the securing of a building for temporary quarters" in downtown Honolulu in September 1903.

Thereafter, other churches were organized in many parts of the Hawaiian Islands to propagate the Gospel among Koreans. Table 1 shows the Korean churches that had been established on various islands by 1914. In addition to these churches, as many as twenty-four smaller mission stations were scattered over the four main Hawaiian Islands.

Table 1. Korean Churches Established in the Hawaiian Islands, 1905–1914

Date Established	Location
April 1905	Ewa, Oahu
August 1905	Waipahu, Oahu
October 1905	Mokuleia, Oahu
November 1906	Lihue, Kauai
February 1907	Hilo, Hawaii
March 1907	Puunene, Maui
September 1907	Wailua, Kauai
May 1909	Wahiawa, Oahu
May 1911	Kahuku, Oahu
July 1911	Kona, Hawaii
August 1913	Papaaloa, Hawaii
June 1914	Honokaa, Hawaii

The Korean Methodist Mission had to await the arrival of Sŭng-ha Hong from Korea to lead its infant congregation. A pioneer Christian leader in Korea, Hong had served in the Namyang area, south of Inchon, before being dispatched to Hawaii, where he arrived in February 1904 to become the first preacher of the Korean Mission. In March 1904, not long after Hong took charge, the Mission rented a larger building at the corner of Emma and School Streets in Honolulu and began to hold church services there. A roster of church members apparently made around this time lists some twenty names and indicates eleven of them had been baptized in Korea. It is likely that at least some of these people constituted the founding members of the church.

On April 1, 1905, the Korean Methodist Mission was formally elevated to a fully organized church with the new name of Honolulu Korean Methodist Church. (Up until 1983, the church observed this date as its foundation date.) In addition to looking after the spiritual needs of its congregation, the church was actively engaged in proselytizing and dispatched Pyŏng-gu Yun, Kyo-dam Yi, and Hyŏng-jun Im to various plantations.

Unfortunately, Sŭng-ha Hong, a man of frail health, had a difficult time adjusting to the Hawaiian environment and was obliged to return to Korea in 1905. Following the departure of Hong, Chan-Ho Min was appointed as the second preacher for the Honolulu Korean Methodist Church in August 1905. A graduate of Paejae School in Seoul, Min received Gospel training and became a preacher before coming to Hawaii.

As the church struggled to secure a foundation for future growth, the Honolulu Korean Methodist Church, having no building of its own, held services in a rented one. The ambition to obtain its own building was finally fulfilled in August 1906, when the Hawaii Methodist Mission secured the Korean Compound on the corner of Punchbowl and Beretania Streets. The Korean Compound thus contained the Honolulu Korean Methodist Church as well as the Korean Boarding School for educating Korean youths.

With the reorganization of the Hawaii Methodist Mission in December 1905, the Mission began to dispatch Korean preachers.

Table 2 lists those preachers along with their previous affiliations in Korea and their assignments in Hawaii.

Table 2. Korean Methodist Preachers in Hawaii, 1905

Name	Church in Korea	Assigned Location
Chan-Ho Min	Chŏngdong Church, Seoul	Honolulu
Yee-Jay Kim	Naeri Church, Inchon	Waipahu, Oahu
Yŏng-sik Kim	Unknown	Ewa, Oahu
Chŏng-su Im	Namsanhyŏn Church, Pyongyang	Kahuku and Waialua, Oahu
Chi-Pum Hong	Namsanhyŏn Church, Pyongyang	Spreckelsville and Wailuku, Maui
Soon Hyun	Naeri Church, Inchon	Lihue and Hanamaulu, Kauai
Kyŏng-jik Yi	Tongdaemun Church, Seoul	Eleele and Koloa, Kauai
P'an-sôk Shin	Unknown	Hilo and Olaa, Hawaii
Chin-t'ae Ch'oe	Chŏngdong Church, Seoul	Kohala, Hawaii

Through the dedicated work of these preachers and others, the number of Korean church members increased by leaps and bounds in the islands of Hawaii. As a result, in 1905 Koreans could boast the largest average number of Sunday School attendees among all the Methodist churches in Hawaii: 605, as compared to 276 for Japanese and 64 for Caucasians. Moreover, Koreans constituted 64 percent of the total Methodist congregation in Hawaii, with about 10 percent of the Korean population in Hawaii being members of the Methodist Church.

Hawaii Methodist Mission and Arrival of Syngman Rhee
Through an agreement among Protestant missionaries of various denominations, the Methodists took charge of working with Koreans and Japanese while the Congregationalists did so with Hawaiians and Chinese. The Methodist missionaries were encouraged by the unusually quick and positive response shown by the Korean immigrants to their missionary efforts—certainly far more so than that of the Japanese and Chinese.

The presence of a substantial number of Koreans in Hawaii, coupled with an optimistic outlook of bringing them to God, encouraged the Hawaii Methodist Mission to invest significantly both spiritually and materially to work for the souls of Koreans in Hawaii. Securing the Korean Compound in 1906 was one part of such efforts. Here the Honolulu Korean Methodist Church was given a place to worship, and a Korean Boarding School was established for the education of Korean children.

In spite of the many good works done for Koreans by the Hawaii Methodist Mission, there were times when the relationship between the American missionaries and the Korean community became strained. Tensions arose when certain missionary leaders made public remarks that were downright offensive to the nationalistic sensibilities of the Korean people. In 1908, for example, the Rev. Merriman C. Harris, a former superintendent and long-time missionary in Japan, speaking to a public gathering in Honolulu, openly advocated Japanese control of Korea. According to the *Pacific Commercial Advertiser* (April 25, 1908), he even went so far as to state that the Japanese occupation of Korea "seems to be the hand of Providence working for the good of Korea." In the eyes of Koreans, the Rev. John W. Wadman, the incumbent superintendent of the Hawaii Methodist Mission, who had also served in Japan as a missionary for many years, proved himself no less insensitive by his words and behavior when he also openly favored Japanese rule over Korea. In 1912, when the Koreans in Hawaii were still seething in anger and resentment over the Japanese annexation of Korea two years earlier, Rev. Wadman accepted a donation of $750 from the Japanese consul general to be used for the education of Korean youths without prior consultation with Koreans. When Koreans in Hawaii learned of this, there were angry protests directed against the superintendent. They demanded that the money be returned immediately to the Japanese and that Rev. Wadman sever all ties with Koreans and leave Hawaii. To many Koreans, he became thereafter a *persona non grata*.

It was at this juncture that Dr. Syngman Rhee (Yi Sŭng-man) arrived in Hawaii in February 1913. For Superintendent Wadman, Syngman Rhee, a Methodist, was a godsend. With a widely known reputation as a young reformer in Korea, he had received the highest American education, earning an M.A. from Harvard and a Ph.D. from Princeton, and had served as secretary-general of the Seoul YMCA before coming to Hawaii. With his impeccable credentials and personal charisma, Rhee was immediately accepted as an important leader of the Korean community.

Hoping Rhee would mitigate the anger of the Korean community, Rev. Wadman appointed him as principal of the Korean Boarding School, putting him in charge of educating the Korean youths there. As soon as Rhee took over the Boarding School, he changed the name of the school to the Korean Central School and greatly expanded its activities. He even introduced a near-revolutionary education by admitting girls into his school, thus initiating coeducation for Koreans for the first time in Korea's history. His dedicated and innovative work under difficult conditions won him the high praises of the Methodist Mission and others. In his annual report of 1915, Rev. William H. Fry, the new superintendent of the Methodist Mission, extolled Rhee's works, saying they "have been the struggle of a real man of God." There was also tremendous support—moral and material—for Rhee's work on the part of the Korean community.

In the fateful year of 1915, the Korean community became deeply divided, and the impact of this division spilled over into the church community as well. The turmoil of 1915 began with a personal clash between two of the most important Korean leaders in Hawaii, Syngman Rhee and Young-Man Park (Pak Yong-man). But beneath the surface of personal conflict between these two powerful individuals were far more serious issues that deeply divided Koreans abroad. Prison cellmates as a result of their reform activities in Korea, Rhee and Park became "sworn brothers," pledging eternal brotherhood and cooperation. When Korea lost its sovereignty in 1910, they agreed to work together in Hawaii to regain independence from Japan. Soon after their arrival in Hawaii, however, their brotherhood, fell apart; instead, they became sworn enemies.

Open conflict came in early 1915 over control of the Korean National Association (KNA). Established in 1909, the KNA was a semi-government organization that claimed to represent the entire Korean community in Hawaii. Collecting a toll tax ($5.00 annually) from all adult Koreans, it commanded a large sum of regular income. Control of such an organization was absolutely vital for anyone with large political ambitions, such as Rhee and Park. In 1915, a dispute over monetary issues led the followers of Rhee to challenge the leadership of the KNA, then under the influence of Park. After violent encounters and police intervention, Rhee eventually gained dominance over the KNA. His victory, however, was achieved at a heavy price. The Korean community that had hitherto proudly demonstrated a strong solidarity was now irreparably torn asunder, and the animosity between the opposing camps would plague the community for decades to come.

Following the conflict over the KNA, Rhee also severed his ties to the Hawaii Methodist Mission. In 1915, he resigned as principal of the Korean Central School. One reason for his resignation had to do with fundamental differences over educational philosophies and objectives between Rhee and the Mission. The Methodist Mission wanted to educate Korean youths to be good United States citizens by inculcating them with American values. Rhee, on the other hand, wished to train them to become dedicated workers for Korean independence and future leaders of Korea. Moreover, Rhee opposed the centralization of the Methodist system that permitted interference in his work. Also, he resented that under the Methodist system Koreans could not own church properties in their own name. Leaving the Methodist Mission, he went on to establish his own nondenominational church, which in 1918 became the Korean Christian Church.

Syngman Rhee's departure from the Methodist Mission had serious repercussions, which caused a severe crisis in the Honolulu Korean Methodist Church. Many church members who were loyal to Rhee left the church to follow him, creating bitter sentiment on both sides. Still others became disillusioned and simply left the church altogether. By 1920, church membership had fallen from 170 to 70, a 60 percent decline.

Rancor caused by the KNA dispute also had an adverse effect on church work, making proselytizing among nonbelievers all the more difficult. For example, the Rev. Yu-sun Kim, who was assigned evangelistic duties in various plantations and villages, reported in 1919 that "the minds of the [Korean] people were so distracted with political agitation that it would be unwise for him to continue [any] longer in that work." In his 1919 annual report, the Mission superintendent wrote: "Aside from the political difficulties in which our Korean people seem to have been entangled for several years, there has been a decided lack of harmony in any Christian program that might be proposed from to time to time." Amid such turmoil, in 1916 the church adopted a new name, calling itself the First Korean Methodist Church.

Fort Street Church and a New Generation
In 1921, the First Korean Methodist Church bought a new site at 1520 Fort Street and the dedication service was conducted on January 10, 1922. According to Mary Hong Park, a daughter of the Rev. Han-Shik Hong and very familiar with the church in this period, the church building was originally built at the Punchbowl Street site and was later taken apart and reassembled at Fort Street in 1921. According to Mrs. Park, a parsonage and a guest house were later added behind the church, and the guest house frequently accommodated Korean students who were on their way to the mainland United States from Korea.

With the relocation of the church, the 1915 upheaval that had shaken the church and the Korean community began to subside. Under the leadership of the Rev. Sa-Yong Whang (Hwang Sa-yong) (1920–1923), the Rev. Soon Hyun (1923–1926), and the Rev. Han-Shik Hong (1926–1929), the church steadily grew, and membership increased from a mere 70 in 1920 to 168 in 1927. What is more striking, however, is the sharp rise in Sunday School attendance from 75 in 1920 to 250 in 1928. This indicates a steady growth of Christian faith in the younger generation.

The growth of the younger generation promised an optimistic future for the church while at the same time posing an unexpected problem. With great emphasis on education, increasing numbers of Koreans were seeking secondary and higher education for the younger generation. According to a Korean student yearbook, in 1939 seventeen Koreans graduated from the University of Hawaii and 123 from high schools. The yearbook also reports that the same year saw 87 Korean students enrolled at the University of Hawaii and 478 in high schools throughout the Islands, in addition to seven who matriculated at a teacher's college. Schooled in American educational institutions, the new generation of Koreans became increasingly less familiar with the Korean language and Korean traditions. As they became more intellectually sophisticated, the younger congregation sought dialogues and sermons that were intellectually more demanding. Without a formal Western education, however, most Korean ministers unfortunately did not have a full command of English at a sophisticated level and were often unable to meet the higher expectations of the younger generation. Cognizant of this problem, the First Korean Methodist Church made a formal request in 1928 to the district superintendent for a minister with these qualifications: one who had received an American education, could give English sermons, and would advocate Korean causes beyond the Korean community.

In 1930, the Methodist Mission found such a person in the Rev. Fritz Pyen (Pyôn Hong-gyu). Having received B.D. and Ph.D. degrees from Drew University, Rev. Pyen was appointed minister in charge of the First Korean Methodist Church in 1930. Of those Korean ministers who had served in Hawaii, he was the first to have received a formal American education and hold a theology degree. He led the Sunday service in Korean, repeating his sermon in English for those less familiar with the Korean language. He was greatly popular especially among the younger congregation. Unfortunately, however, Rev. Pyen served for only three years. In 1933, he left for Harbin, Manchuria, to engage in missionary work there. His departure was met with great disappointment on the part of the younger congregation.

One notable achievement in this period was the formal appointment in 1931 of two women workers—Dora Moon and Chung-Song Lee Ahn—as "local preachers" at the annual conference of Methodist churches. With their appointment, these two women were permitted to give sermons and to conduct funerals and other ceremonies. Their dedicated work among women was of great help not only to the church and its ministers but also to the advancement of the Korean women's cause in Hawaii. Dora Moon was also instrumental in organizing the Korean Missionary Society (Han'guk sôn'gyohoe) in 1932, which raised funds to assist various church works in Korea, such as supporting churches and the families of needy ministers.

The War Years
The surprise Japanese attack on Pearl Harbor on December 7, 1941, jolted Hawaii as it did the nation. The subsequent American declaration of war against Japan was greeted by Koreans as a golden opportunity to regain Korean independence. For Koreans in Hawaii, the well-being of the homeland they had left behind was foremost in their mind. When Korea lost its independence in 1910 upon Japan's forcible annexation, they no longer had a country to which to return. Their original dream of making a fortune in Hawaii and returning home with wealth was shattered. Instead, they directed much of their energy and resources toward recovering Korea's independence. From its foundation, the Korean First Methodist Church played a central role in such nationalistic endeavors. Many of its members were leaders of various political and social organizations in Hawaii, contributing significantly to advancing Korean causes. When news of natural disasters, such as floods and famine, reached them from Korea, the First Korean Methodist Church was invariably at the forefront in providing assistance.

During the war years, however, Koreans in Hawaii went

through an unfortunate experience. Immediately after the attack on Pearl Harbor, all of Hawaii was placed under martial law. In accordance with the Alien Registration Act of 1940, all Koreans, by virtue of the fact their homeland was under Japanese rule, were treated as enemy aliens. This was an unspeakable humiliation for Koreans. As long as they could remember, they had been fighting against Japanese militarism, and the ultimate defeat of Imperial Japan was their foremost goal. With a sense of outrage and sadness, Koreans in the United States campaigned vigorously to free themselves of enemy-alien status. As a result, in 1942 the United States Department of Justice formally announced Koreans among those who were exempted from registering as enemy aliens. With this ruling, Koreans escaped being sent to detention camps and other similar restrictions.

The military governor of Hawaii, however, refused to apply the Justice Department ruling to Koreans in the Islands and continued to require them to register as enemy aliens in spite of vehement protests by the Korean community. As enemy aliens, they were subject to restrictions such as curfew and limitations on employment and bank transactions. More unbearable than these restrictions, however, was the realization they were being treated as Japanese!

In spite of this humiliating discrimination, the Koreans in Hawaii never wavered in their support of the United States war effort. Members of the First Korean Methodist Church bought war bonds, engaged in periodic fund-raising, visited hospitals for wounded soldiers, and the like. More significant was the fact that as many as eighty-one young men from the Korean Methodist Church joined the United States armed forces. One of them, Lt. George S. H. Lee, a son of Dal-Young Lee, gave his life when he was killed in action on the European front in January 1945, only a few months before V-E day. On several occasions the church held special worship services to commemorate those on active duty and of course conducted a memorial service for Lt. Lee upon hearing the sad news of his death.

The war years also brought significant changes to the Korean community and the church. The influx of military personnel and the rise of war-related demands created new economic opportunities for Koreans in Hawaii. Many Koreans ran rooming houses and apartments, operated tailor and laundry shops, and started carpentry and other businesses. Through their resourceful entrepreneurship, many Koreans gained a secure economic foundation in Hawaii during the war years.

A New Church

By 1940, the First Korean Methodist Church exceeded 300 members. With the capacity of its church on Fort Street being only 200, it became clear that the growing congregation needed more space. In 1940, the decision was made to build a new church, and a committee was formed to handle the matter. It consisted of Won-Kiu Ahn (An Wôn-gyu), chair; Kwan-Doo Park (Pak Kwan-du), vice chair; Helen Park, finance chair; Hyŏng-shin Han; Wilha Chung; Hee-Kyung Lee Kwon; Chong-Soo Park; the Rev. Doo-Hwa Lim (Im Tu-hwa); and Superintendent William H. Fry.

The amount allocated for building the new church was $40,000, and of this total, the First Korean Methodist Church was to contribute $10,000, Superintendent Fry promised to raise $10,000, and the remaining $20,000 was to be funded by the Methodist Mission. A big campaign to raise the needed funds was launched on June 30, 1940, with a banquet hosted by the Women's Society for Christian Service. The outbreak of the Pacific War in 1941, however, interfered with the fundraising. With the new national priority of winning the war, fundraising work was slowed, but not completely stopped.

When the war ended in 1945 with an Allied victory, the campaign to build the new church resumed. In February 1947, a contract was signed to sell the Fort Street church and to purchase land at 1639 Keeaumoku Street. The Keeaumoku Street site was twice as large as the Fort Street property. Moreover, it was located right in the middle of the Makiki area in whose vicinities a large number of Koreans had established their residences during the war years and immediately following. In September 1949, a groundbreaking ceremony was conducted. The construction of the new sanctuary took only five months. On February 12, 1950, a dedication service was held for the new First Korean Methodist Church.

For the relocation and building of the church, the congregation participated in fundraising and other works with selfless dedication, responding enthusiastically to the call of the Rev. Euicho Chung, who had assumed the position of minister in charge in 1945. The total expenditures for moving into the new church were $64,793. To pay for this, the Hawaii Methodist Mission contributed $31,000, the Fort Street church was sold for $20,000, and the church congregation raised $14,317, leaving a surplus of more than $500.

A New Generation

The defeat of Japan in 1945 meant the liberation of Korea, which its people welcomed enthusiastically, anticipating a promising future. But Korea's division along the 38th parallel, followed by the emergence of two competing regimes and the outbreak of a tragic fratricidal war in 1950, shattered any optimism its people had held. As if to reflect the situation in Korea, the political climate within the Korean community in Hawaii fared no better. The rancor of the old political rivalry between the KNA and the Dongjihoe (organized and led by Syngman Rhee, who went on to become the first president of the Republic of Korea in the south in 1948) resurfaced in Hawaii. Unfortunately, the political turmoil adversely affected Korean churches in Hawaii as well.

One overriding wish of the elderly first-generation Koreans was to be able to visit, even if only once, the homeland they had left behind as young men and women. By the 1950s, there were not many survivors from the first wave of Korean immigrants to Hawaii, but the South Korean government refused to issue the necessary documents for travel to these elderly Koreans on the grounds that they had belonged to organizations that had opposed Syngman Rhee. Because many members of the First Methodist Church belonged to organizations such as the KNA and others that had competed against Rhee's group, they were unable to fulfill their long-cherished dream of returning home.

At the same time, the Korean community in Hawaii was witnessing a significant demographic shift as the number of first-generation Koreans who had immigrated to Hawaii in 1903–1905 steadily declined. This natural phenomenon was reflected in church membership as the number of members of the Korean-speaking congregation grew smaller while the English-speaking congregation continued to grow.

When the Rev. Euicho Chung resigned in 1951, a nation-wide search for a bilingual minister was conducted. When no qualified candidate was found within the Methodist organization, the church turned to the Rev. T. Samuel Lee (Yi Tong-jin), who for some years had worked as a missionary among Native Americans (the so-called American Indians) on the mainland. One problem with Rev. Lee's candidacy, however, was that he belonged to a Presbyterian church, not a Methodist one. Finding him to be the perfect candidate nevertheless, the First Korean Methodist Church desperately tried to secure his appointment. After careful negotiations, the Presbyterian Church of the United States in the end released Rev. Lee to the Methodist Church, allowing him to be appointed to the First Korean Methodist Church in 1952. (One of the reasons for his release is said to have been that some Presbyterian leaders felt the Methodists might have need of another "conversion" by a Presbyterian minister!)

Under the leadership of the Rev. Lee, the church made great strides. There was a big surge in the English-speaking congregation. In 1952, the average attendance at Sunday worship service was about 70 for those who spoke English and about 125 for those who spoke Korean. This situation, however, changed the following year when the English-speaking congregation began to exceed the size of the Korean congregation. As a result, the church leadership was increasingly taken over by the new generation of Korean-Americans.

The First Korean Methodist Church was blessed with many young men with exceptional talent and foresight who offered dedicated service to the church. To cite only a few of them, they included Herbert Choi (lawyer and later federal judge), Duke Choy (physician), Mary Whang Choy (community activist), Dora Kim Choi, Ellen Cha (church organist), Wilha Moon Chung, John Hahn, David Khil, Chan-Jay Kim (engineer), Esther Kim, Harriet Kim (a Japanese-American married to a Korean-American), You-Taik Kim (physician), Gladys Lee, Hyun-Moo Lee, Ida Lee, Kenneth Lee, Yoon-Ho Lee, Matthew Nahm, Mary Oh, Margaret Kwon Pai, Woon-Hark Paik, Kwan-Doo Park (architect), Helen Park (nurse), Esther Park (YWCA worker), Betty Hahn Sunwoo, Emma Shin Whang, John Woo, and Joseph Woo. Many of these Korean-Americans went on to become prominent leaders not just in the Korean community but in the larger Hawaii community as well. Also, among those who grew up in the church and went on to national and international prominence was Dr. Joseph D. Park (Pak Tal-cho), the famous chemist who developed Freon for refrigeration.

Another notable achievement made in this period was the achievement of financial independence for the first time in the history of the church. Since its inception, the church had relied on financial assistance in varying degrees from the Methodist Mission. But with the steady improvement of economic conditions among Koreans after the war, the church's financial outlook concomitantly brightened. By 1958, with an annual budget of $18,531, the church became more independent in fiscal matters, and at Rev. Lee's insistence, the church no longer sought financial aid from the Methodist Mission. With financial independence, in July 1958 the church was incorporated into an independent entity, and the deeds of all church properties were formally transferred to the church.

A New Name
The demographic change in the congregation created an unprecedented crisis during the 1960s. With the steady decline in number of first-generation Koreans, the church was dominated increasingly by the new generation of Korean-

Americans who spoke little or no Korean. After immigration from Korea had stopped in 1924, no significant number of new immigrants had arrived in Hawaii, and thus the days of the Korean-speaking congregation appeared to be numbered. The preponderance of the English-speaking congregation caused an unexpected problem for the church

In 1962, following the resignation of the Rev. T. Samuel Lee, the church was unable to find a qualified bilingual minister and was obliged to accept the Rev. Ray Bond as the minister in charge. For the first time in its history, the church came to be shepherded by a Caucasian who spoke no Korean and was unfamiliar with Korean culture and traditions. He was soon succeeded in turn by the Rev. Harry Pak (1963–1966), the Rev. Robert Fiske (1967–1969), and the Rev. Richard Isakson (1970), all of whom spoke no Korean (though Rev. Pak must have understood Korean). Since these ministers spoke no Korean, the Rev. Dae-Hee Park (Pak Tae-hûi) was appointed in 1962 as the Korean-speaking minister for the Korean congregation.

With the arrival of the Rev. Park, the ratio between the English- and Korean-speaking congregations began to shift once more. Owing to Rev. Park's energetic ministering, the number in the Korean-speaking congregation who attended Sunday worship service began to increase steadily (from 68 in August 1962 to 103 a year later). Under Rev. Park's dynamic leadership, the Korean-speaking congregation began to regain its vitality, creating an air of friendly competitiveness with the English-speaking congregation.

The Korean-speaking congregation was greatly assisted by the creation of the East-West Center at the University of Hawaii in 1960. Established by the federal government for the purpose of cultural and technical exchange between the United States and Asia, the East-West Center brought a large number of scholars and students from Asia to Hawaii every year. Since 1960, several dozen Koreans—mostly elite scholars and graduate students— have come to Hawaii each year in various programs sponsored by the East-West Center, and many of them have found in the First Korean Methodist Church a welcome place of worship and a home away from home. With the active participation of this new breed of Koreans in various church programs, the dynamic of the church underwent drastic changes, and the Korean-speaking congregation, which had only recently fallen into doldrums, suddenly found itself revitalized and rejuvenated. As a result, those who spoke Korean began to outnumber those who spoke only English.

Amidst these developments, the issue of changing the name of the church was brought forward. After the attack on Pearl Harbor, there had been a movement among those churches belonging to the Methodist Mission in Hawaii as a whole to do away with terms of ethnic identity in their names. All the Japanese and the Filipino churches had already adopted new names, discarding previous names that had identified their ethnicity. By 1960, the First Korean Methodist Church was the only church under Methodist jurisdiction in Hawaii that still maintained its ethnic name.

In 1963, the Board of the National Mission of Methodist Churches (headquartered in New York) sent a four-man study committee to look into the situation of the First Korean Methodist Church. In its recommendations, the committee urged the two groups—the English-speaking and the Korean-speaking—to interact with each other more so that the church could present itself as one united congregation, rather than two separate entities. The recommendations also included the suggestion that the church consider changing its name in such a way as to embrace all other ethnic groups within the local community. In other words, the Board of the National Mission was recommending the First Korean Methodist Church drop the term "Korean" and adopt a new name.

This recommendation touched off a storm of animated debate. While the English-speaking congregation in general favored the name change, the Korean-speaking group vehemently opposed it. Wishing to retain their ethnic identity, the Korean-speaking congregation—the elderly first-generation Koreans and their younger compatriots who had recently joined them—insisted upon keeping the old name. One of them went even so far as to challenge: "Can we not go to Heaven as Koreans?" Although this elderly learned man later took a more moderate position, the issue of abandoning the Korean name mobilized the Korean congregation to an animated opposition. The church in the end formed a study committee—five each from the English- and Korean-speaking congregations—to examine the issue of changing the name and to come up with recommendations. Chaired by Dr. Hee-Chang Chai, the committee included Herbert Choi, AeYoung Higuchi, Allen Paik, Helen Park, and Mathew Nahm from the English group and Hee-Chang Chai, Chŏng-min Ch'a, Chŏng-suk Ch'oe, Sun-do Kim, and Dr. Yu-taik Kim from the Korean group.

After deliberation, the committee came up with a report outlining the pros and cons of changing the church's name. The report, which favored the name change, emphasized the importance of opening a church that serves God to men and women of all nationalities without regard to ethnicity. It also raised the possibility that a church name that includes an exclusive identification with one ethnic group might discourage people of non-Korean background from attending. It urged the church to become more community oriented to its neighborhood and beyond, rather than remaining focused on one ethnic group. On the other hand, those opposed to the name change pointed out that it would be very unlikely for people of non-Korean background to join the church even if it were opened to them. They also pointed out that the numbers of the Korean-speaking congregation had been growing steadily over the past several years with the arrival of students from Korea (there were about 50 Korean students currently attending the church), and the name change might discourage these new attendees from participating in future church services. But more seriously, they pointed out that those Koreans who spoke no English would have no church to turn to if it were to change its name and that in such cases, their souls might be lost.

The committee report with the two opposing views was then put to a vote of the body of church members, name change requiring the approval of a two-thirds majority. In December 1964, mail ballots were sent out to all registered church members. The result favored the name change by the margin of 198 to 89. The matter was then referred to the quarterly conference on January 3, 1965, where the name change was approved by a vote of 27 to 11. The new name adopted at this time was Christ Methodist Church. With the adoption of the new name, the term "Korean" that had been dear to thousands of Koreans in Hawaii for more than sixty years was dropped, marking another turning point in the history of the church.

In 1968, when the Methodist churches in the United States were reorganized into the United Methodist churches, Christ Methodist Church accordingly changed its name to Christ United Methodist Church, as it remains today. In retrospect, it was highly ironic that the church changed its name from First Korean Methodist Church to Christ Methodist Church in 1965, because in that same year the United States adopted a new immigration law that brought a formal end to racial discrimination against admittance of Asian immigrants. With the enactment of the new immigration law in 1965, Hawaii witnessed the arrival of a new wave of Korean immigrants (as well as other Asian immigrants). Christ Methodist Church soon swelled with these new immigrants, most of whom spoke only Korean. As a result, the composition of the congregation reverted to mostly Korean-speaking church members, making the name change meaningless in reality.

In the meantime, changing the church's name did not bring with it the intended results. By removing the reference to ethnic identity, it was hoped that the church would become a place of worship for a multi-ethnic congregation. No such phenomenon took place. The church instead continued to thrive in the context of two different congregations under the leadership of the Rev. Harry Pak for the English speakers and the Rev. Dae-Hee Park for the Korean speakers. They even exhibited an air of rivalry, at least for a couple of years, after the name change.

The district superintendent, Frank E. Butterworth, who encouraged the concept of a multiracial church, attributed the failure of Christ Methodist Church to attract a non-Korean congregation even after the name change to the presence of two ministers who were both ethnically Korean. Against the wishes of the English-speaking congregation, the superintendent reassigned the Rev. Pak to a Hilo church on the Big Island in 1966 and appointed the Rev. Robert Fiske as the new minister in charge in 1967. The removal of the Rev. Pak was not well received by the English-speaking congregation, and many disappointed members opted to transfer to other churches, weakening the English congregation considerably. With a steady decline in its number, the English congregation decided to dissolve itself after holding its last worship service on June 10, 1973.

A New Beginning
Many of the Koreans who arrived in the second wave of immigration after 1965 had already accepted Christianity while in Korea and found in Christ United Methodist Church a convivial place to continue to worship. Others also increasingly turned to the church for its religious message as well as solace from the travails of immigrant life. Christ United Methodist Church welcomed them with open arms.

With the appointment of the Rev. Dae-Hee Park as the minister in charge in 1972, the confusion that had surrounded the future direction of the church was definitively settled. Name change notwithstanding, Christ United Methodist Church was to become a church of a largely Korean-speaking congregation as it witnessed an upsurge in membership consisting primarily of new immigrants from Korea. The church found a new mission, which was to work with the new immigrants struggling to put down roots in their newly adopted land. As the church became increasingly filled with Korean immigrants, its services and other programs also became increasingly Korea-oriented, following the practices of Korean Methodism, though it remained within the jurisdiction of the United Methodist Church of America.

Under Rev. Park's leadership, a number of important new programs were instituted to assist Korean immigrants. In running these programs, the church was blessed with the dedicated services of many Korean graduate students and scholars attending the University of Hawaii and the East-West Center as well as their wives. (Many of them went on to become important leaders in Korea, some rising to ministerial and other top positions in both the public and private sectors.) For the new immigrants, the church ran an English language program, assisted in the search for apartments and employment, helped to settle immigration issues, and provided counseling services, among other works. In addition, the church established a preschool so as to allow parents to be gainfully employed during the day, while also nurturing immigrant children in bicultural, bilingual education.

In 1970, the Korean Community School was set up to teach Korean language and culture to Korean youths on Saturday mornings, soon attracting as many as 200 students. Popular among the community people, as of this writing the Community School still actively runs its very useful program. When juvenile delinquency became a serious social problem in the Korean community in Hawaii, the Rev. Park organized the Korean Youth Program within the church in 1981 to provide various after-school programs for intermediate and high school students. It offered remedial English and other lessons, sports and recreational programs, as well as a counseling service, among other things. These programs were generally very successful, offering much-needed assistance to many struggling immigrants. After the departure of the Rev. Park in 1982, however, some of these programs were neglected. Not welcomed by the church, the Korean Youth Program was obliged to find a new home at the Honolulu YMCA, where it continued successfully for a number of years under the guidance of Yông-ho Choe and Duk-Hee Lee Murabayashi. The preschool gradually lost its original purpose of introducing bicultural values and traditions to children, and with time its facilities and equipment became so neglected that in 1990 the church concluded it could no longer continue its operation.

The Rev. Eung-Kyun Lee (Yi Ûng-gyun), who succeeded the Rev. Park in 1982, emphasized the spiritual aspects of Christian life and introduced some important new programs. Among the new immigrants recently joining the church were many not very familiar with the teachings of Christ and the church. Lee started a special Bible school for the lay members of the church. He reorganized the cell meeting (sokhoe) as an effective instrument of spiritual and social fellowship in a small-group neighborhood setting. In 1983, following the practice of churches in Korea, Christ United Methodist Church adopted a system whereby certain leading church members were elected to titular positions known as changno, kwônsa, and, chipsa.

With the rapid growth of the church, there was an increasing need to revive an English service. Among the congregation was a small number of people (mostly descendants of the early immigrants) who were more comfortable with English, and also the growing younger generation needed an English-speaking minister. Realizing this need, the Rev. Woong-Min Kim (Kim Ung-min), appointed as minister in charge in 1988, worked toward restoring the English service on a regular basis. With the appointment in 1990 of Ms. Unsil Lee, a recent graduate of Yale Divinity School, as a preacher for the English congregation, the English-speaking congregation was resurrected. Ever since, the English congregation has been gaining strength and vigor with increasing numbers of younger-generation Korean-Americans.

Centennial Sanctuary
With the influx of the new immigrants, there was a tremendous upsurge in church attendance and membership. With such vigorous growth, the church periodically encountered the

"joyful" problem of overcrowding. During the month of March 1980, the average attendance at Sunday service was 375, in addition to the 94 who attended Sunday School and 44 who attended youth classes. Encountering increasing difficulties with seating arrangements, in 1979, under Rev. Park's guidance, the church decided to expand the sanctuary and enlarge the seating capacity to 500 (at a cost of $205,230).

Hardly a decade had passed before the overcrowding problem once again posed a challenge. In 1988, soon after the Rev. Woong-Min Kim's arrival, the church once again concluded its space was insufficient. The church now embraced 700 regular adult members, 100 constituents, and 200 children—a total of 1,000 persons. An average of 600 adults along with 200 children and youth attended a typical Sunday service. Clearly, the existing facilities were inadequate to accommodate the growing church.

To deal with this and other problems, in December 1988 a Long Range Planning Committee was formed and charged with coming up with a proposal. In September 1989, this committee submitted a proposal to the Administrative Council recommending the construction of a new sanctuary that would serve as a meaningful commemoration of the centennial of the church's founding in November 2003. After approving the recommendation, the Administrative Council submitted it to the Church Conference, where members gave formal approval in December 1989. In January 1990, a Centennial Building Committee was formed and within three months, in March 1990, pledges of $1.7 million had already been made. In August 1993, Spencer Leineweber of the Spencer Architects was hired for its design, and in October 1996 a contract was signed with Allied Builder Systems to construct the church at a total cost of $5.7 million. On February 16, 1997, a groundbreaking service was held. A year and a half later, on September 6, 1998, a consecration service for the Centennial Sanctuary was conducted with great solemnity and cheer.

The task of building the Centennial Sanctuary was an arduous one. In addition to offering earnest prayers, virtually every church member gave generously of his or her mind and body — often by making generous monetary contributions to the extent of sacrificing his or her own material well-being. Most notable, however, is the farsighted and dynamic leadership displayed by the Rev. Woong-Min Kim, whose sagacious shepherding and unwavering faith in his flock enabled the congregation to overcome many obstacles and to dedicate itself to the successful completion of the Centennial Sanctuary. The magnificent Centennial Sanctuary now stands as a proud symbol of both the great successes and the generous blessings Christ United Methodist Church has met with over the past century.

The first Korean Protestant church established outside Korea, Christ United Methodist Church, under the guidance of the Rev. Eun-Chul Lee (Yi Ûn-ch'ôl), who became minister in charge in 2001, eagerly looks forward to meeting new challenges that the new century may bring forth.

3. The Korean Independence Movement in the United States: Syngman Rhee, An Ch'ang-Ho and Pak Yong-Man

Han-Kyo Kim

Prepared for presentation at the joint conference of International Council on Korean Studies and the Centennial Committee of the Korean Immigration to the U.S.A.
Fairview Marriott Hotel, Washington D.C.
August 16-18, 2002

Introduction

The purpose of this paper is to describe the national independence movement of the Korean residents in the United States and Hawaii before 1945 with emphasis on the roles played by its three most prominent leaders, Syngman Rhee, An Ch'ang-Ho and Pak Yong-Man. The first shipload of Korean emigrants came to Hawaii in 1903 largely for economic reasons. In the ensuing years, as Japan steadily made inroads into Korea, however, patriotic sentiments seized the Korean community. With the formal installation of the Japanese colonial regime in 1910, the restoration of sovereignty in their homeland became the primary political agenda of the Korea emigrants.

Early in the history of Korean emigrants, a number of local community leaders emerged in Hawaii and California and they, in time, came to rally around a few charismatic individuals of whom the best known were Rhee, An and Pak. There certainly were other outstanding activists who played key roles in the Korean independence movement in America, but they were either transients or their activities were not as sustained as those of the trio under study here.

Rhee, An and Pak were distinctly different in personal temperament and educational backgrounds although they were contemporaries and collaborated with one another at one time or another. More importantly, perhaps, their ideological outlooks and strategic designs were clearly divergent. Such divergence bred personal rivalries among them that led to serious divisions within the organizations of Korean emigrants in America and elsewhere in the world.

We will begin with a brief history of the Korean communities in America, followed by biographical sketches of the three leaders, focusing on their political activities in America before 1945. We will conclude with a few observations that help set the context for our review of the topic.

Korean Communities in America
The arrival of 121 Korean emigrants in Honolulu aboard the Gaelic on January 13, 1903 marks the beginning of the Korean community in the United States. In the next two years, 7,226 Koreans reached what was then the United States territory of Hawaii aboard 65 steamers. There were some women and children but most of these emigrants were adult male laborers headed for sugar and pineapple plantations on the Hawaiian islands.[1] In addition, there had been a few isolated cases of students and merchants making their way to the United States mainland beginning as early as 1880s, but the overwhelming majority of Korean emigrants were the farm workers brought over by the Hawaiian Sugar Planters Association through its agents in Korea.[2] In 1905, the flow of Koreans to Hawaii ceased when the Korean government bowed to pressure from the Japanese government that acted to protect the Japanese immigrant-laborers in Hawaii from competition.[3]

Common among these early emigrants was the desire for a better life with steady and lucrative jobs that the recruiting agents had promised. However, the reality they faced in Hawaii was much harsher---long hours of hard physical labor six days a week for meager wages, averaging from sixty-five to seventy cents a day.[4] Reports of higher wages and non-farm employment opportunities on the mainland enticed a sizable number to leave Hawaii---more than 1,000 in 1905-1910.⁵ It is then no surprise that "the early Korean immigrants had a weak national consciousness," pressed as they were by daily survival and adjustment problems.⁶

Before long, "the new life in a land of strange historical and cultural background made them feel a strong love for Korea and her people which inspired them to organize self-governing bodies on the Hawaiian farms."⁷ As early as 1905, a Friendship Association (Ch'inmok-hoe) was established on Ewa Plantation on Oahu Island that launched, in addition to a program of mutual aid, a boycott of Japanese goods. When Japan pressed Korea to appoint a Japanese diplomat as an honorary consul to protect Korean emigrants' interests in Hawaii, the presumed beneficiaries protested and asked for a Korean official instead, even at their own expense if necessary.⁸

Patriotic motives became clear when a special convention of Korean residents in Hawaii adopted, sometime in or before mid-July 1905, a petition addressed to President Theodore Roosevelt requesting his intervention on behalf of Korea's sovereign independence at the peace conference to end the Russo-Japanese War, and selected, as the representatives of "8,000 Korean residents" in Hawaii a local church pastor, Rev. Yun Pyong-gu, and a secret emissary from Seoul, Syngman Rhee.⁹

The Korean plea went unheeded. Japan took over Korea's foreign affairs and set up a quasi-colonial structure, a Residency-General, which steadily expanded its control over Korea's financial, judicial and military affairs. In 1907, Emperor Kojong of Korea was forced to abdicate in favor of his feeble-minded son and the last army units were dissolved.

Koreans in Hawaii and on the United States mainland held a joint protest rally against the so-called Protectorate Treaty of 1905 and passed a resolution condemning Japan's encroachment on Korea and vowed never to recognize Japanese authorities in

Korea or Japanese jurisdiction over the Koreans in the United States. Between December 1905 and September 1907, more than twenty organizations emerged and their stated purposes "included, without exception, resistance against the Japanese colonial policy and political independence for Korea."[10] These groups came together by September 1907 in the United Korean Society (Hanin Hapsong Hyophoe) headquartered in Honolulu.[11]

On America's West Coast, in the meantime, similar communal-cum-political organizations were formed: the Mutual Assistance Society (Kongnip Hyophoe) after 1905, with several local chapters in California, and the Great Unity Fatherland Protection Society (Taedong Poguk-hoe) in San Francisco. The Mutual Assistance Society publicly rejected Japan's offer of relief funds in the aftermath of the 1906 earthquake in San Francisco. Members of these organizations also attacked and killed Durham W. Stevens, a pro-Japanese American advisor to the Korean government.[12]

In a bold move to consolidate the patriotic efforts of all Koreans outside Korea, which was now under Japanese control, the Korean National Association (Tae Hanin Kungmin-hoe; "KNA" hereafter) was organized on February 1,1909 in San Francisco to represent all Korean interests in the United States, Siberia and Manchuria. On the United States mainland and Hawaii, KNA acted as a quasi-consular agency requiring all Korean residents to become its members and pay dues. At the news of Japan's annexation of Korea in 1910, the KNA held a large rally and adopted a resolution that called Japan an enemy nation and declared August 29, the date of the annexation treaty, a day of national humiliation. Most Korean political organizations in America were soon "consolidated" into the KNA.[13]

A few years after Korea had been placed under the firm and harsh rule of the Japanese Government-General, the Korean community in America went through a prolonged period of internal discord and realignment that was fueled, among others, by the schism between those supporting Pak Yong-Man and those backing Syngman Rhee. At the same time, new organizations came on the scene. The Korean Women's Association was organized in Honolulu in 1913, as the arrival of the "picture brides" were beginning to alter the lifestyle of the Koreans on the island.[14] Student and youth groups were formed for para-military training in Nebraska and elsewhere by Pak Yong-Man and others after 1909, while educational objectives were professed by An Ch'ang-Ho as he recruited the first members of the well-known Young Korean Academy (Hungsa-dan) in San Francisco in 1913.[15]

We should underscore here the pivotal roles played by various Korean Christian churches in meeting the communal as well as spiritual needs of the Korean emigrants from the very beginning of their life in the new world. The first church service was held on July 4, 1903. The Christian population among the Koreans in Hawaii, which numbered only 400 or so in 1905, gained, by 1918, approximately 2,800 new converts attending thirty-nine churches.[16] In California, church services began in Oakland in June 1914. In time, several churches of different denominations came to be established in other cities including Los Angeles, Chicago and New York. [17] These churches were "centers of the Korean community" where even non-Christians came for companionship and the discussion of various issues, including those that reflected their aspiration for national independence.[18] One example of the Korean congregations' nationalistic behavior was the controversy in 1912 over the acceptance of a $750 donation from the Japanese consul in Honolulu by American Methodist superintendent John W. Wadman, ostensibly to help poor Koreans. Despite Wadman's credible record as a pro-Korean sympathizer,[19] he was roundly denounced by Koreans for taking Japanese money.

The March First Movement of 1919 rekindled the flame of nationalism among Koreans in the United States. When World War I ended, the KNA planned to send a three-man delegation, which included Syngman Rhee, to the Peace Conference to plead the Korean cause. (It did not materialize due to the United States' refusal to issue necessary travel documents.) The news of the massive peaceful demonstrations and their brutal suppression by the Japanese in Korea took days to reach the Koreans in America. But by mid-March 1919, the KNA held a mass rally in San Francisco in support of the Movement and decided to establish a Korean Information Office headed by Philip Jaisohn (So Chae-p'il). Furthermore, the KNA chose to send its chairman, An Ch'ang-Ho to China in anticipation of the formation of a Korean provisional government.[20]

Shortly thereafter, "the First Korean Congress" was held in Philadelphia, April 14-16, 1919, under the leadership of Philip Jaisohn and Syngman Rhee. Approximately 150 Koreans, representing twenty-seven organizations from the United States and Mexico, gathered and passed resolutions containing a blueprint for the future Korean republic based on democratic principles and pledged to support the Korean provisional government in Shanghai as "a legitimate government of the Korean people." On the last day, the conferees marched, waving the Korean as well as the American flag, through the streets to Independence Hall and conducted an impressive ceremony that included the reading of the Korean Declaration of Independence by Rhee in the same room where the American Declaration had been signed.[21]

Clearly, the aim of the Korean Congress was to publicize the Korean cause and influence the American public. To that end, Jaisohn's information office started publishing pamphlets and a monthly magazine, the Korea Review. He also formed a League of the Friends of Korea to solicit active support from American sympathizers. By the fall of 1919, Syngman Rhee, as the head of the Korean Provisional Government ("KPG" hereafter), created a Korean Commission in Washington and appointed Kim Kyu-sik (Kiusic Kimm) to chair it. Its principal mission was to win friends especially among the members of the United States Congress. A few American lawmakers did speak in the halls of the United States Congress on Korea's behalf, although no formal action was taken.[22]

In addition to these public relations activities in the United States, the attention of Koreans in America was naturally focused on the rising tempo of patriotic activities in China and Siberia, where the majority of Korean activists were. There were three geographical centers of Korean exiles in Northeast Asia, Shanghai, the Chientao region of Manchuria, and the Maritime Province of Siberia. An Ch'ang-Ho was one of the first to arrive in Shanghai from America and he was instrumental in establishing Shanghai as the center of the independence movement and in getting KPG operations underway.[23] Syngman Rhee did not arrive in Shanghai until December 1920 to formally assume his duties as the president. A substantial portion of the funds that had been collected from Koreans in Hawaii and elsewhere in the United States was funneled to China. One source estimates that over $200,000 had been contributed by approximately 7,000 Koreans in the United States and Mexico for patriotic causes at this time, or roughly 30 dollars per person, one month's income. [24] Moreover, Pak Yong-Man, who vehemently opposed the KPG in Shanghai, perhaps for both policy and personal reasons, was active in northern China preparing for immediate military actions against Japan. Pak's followers in Hawaii gave him the financial and moral support for his campaign.[25] In short, the Korean communities in America provided two crucial ingredients to energize the independence movement in the period following the March First Movement: the leaders and financial resources.

By the end of 1921, however, the KPG lost much of its steam. An Ch'ang-Ho and a few other members of the cabinet resigned, voicing disagreement with Syngman Rhee, who in turn left abruptly for the United States. When the Washington Disarmament Conference met in 1921-1922, it was Jaisohn who submitted a petition signed by the representatives of various Korean groups in Korea asking for recognition of the Korean Provisional Government as the legitimate government of the

Korean people. The petition was never discussed due to strong Japanese objection.[26] When the League of Nations met in Geneva in 1933 to discuss Japan's invasion of Manchuria, Rhee journeyed there to mount a solitary campaign among the delegates and the journalists for international recognition of the KPG, but gained only occasional informal words of sympathy.[27] The KPG, in the meantime, won attention---and sympathy, at least from China---through individual acts of terrorism aimed at Japanese leaders, including its emperor in 1932. Kim Ku, a KPG leader allegedly operating with financial support from Korean residents in Hawaii, directed the bombing assaults.[28]

As Japan moved deeper into China, Rhee moved from Honolulu to Washington to resume an active diplomatic campaign for Korea's freedom. He foresaw an American war with Japan and issued a warning in the form of a book, Japan Inside Out, which was published in the summer of 1941. The gathering war clouds prompted the various Korean organizations including the KNA and the Comrade Society (Tongji-hoe)[29] to join forces and form the United Korean Committee ("UKC" hereafter) in April 1941 to give financial and spiritual support to the KPG. As the sole agent of the KPG, the UKC was to collect "independence contributions" and forward two-thirds of the revenue to the KPG. Rhee was chosen to chair the UKC, and was so approved subsequently by the KPG.[30]

After Pearl Harbor, the primary objective of the UKC was to secure formal diplomatic recognition of the KPG as the government of Korea, albeit in exile, and an ally of the United Nations against the Axis powers. Rhee, his advisors and a small staff met with or wrote to American officials, a Korean-American Council was formed to support the Korean endeavor, and a Korean Liberty Conference was held at a Washington hotel in 1942 on the anniversary of the March First Movement. [31] For a variety of reasons which we cannot discuss in this paper,[32] the United States rejected the repeated Korean pleas. A seven-man delegation headed by Rhee arrived in San Francisco in March 1945 to attend the first meeting of the United Nations

Organization but it was barred from the conference. World War II ended without an internationally recognized governmental entity representing the Korean people.

Having sketched the broad outline of the patriotic activities of the Korean community in America prior to 1945, we can now examine the contrasting records of the three leaders who led these activities.

Syngman Rhee Before 1945

Rhee was born in 1875, the only son of an impoverished descendant of Prince Yangnyong, the older brother of King Sejong of the Yi dynasty. Rhee's birthplace was a small village in Hwanghae Province, but his family moved to Seoul when he was only two years old. After a period of customary Confucian tutoring, Rhee enrolled in 1895 at Paeje School that was established by an American Methodist missionary and attracted young students interested in Western learning. He excelled in his studies, especially in English, and his speech at his graduation ceremony in 1898 was delivered in English---a feat that won praise from Korean and American dignitaries in attendance.[33]

It was a time when Korea was undergoing for the first time systematic political and cultural modernization. As an impressionable youth in his early twenties, Rhee plunged into the rough waters of politics by joining the Independence Club (Tongniip Hyophoe) and advocating frontal assaults on the ancient regime. His speeches inspired crowds to stage street demonstrations and his writings in the newly emerging journalistic publications demanded reforms. By the standards of the day, he was a radical.[34] After a brief period of triumph, Rhee was imprisoned on a charge of high treason and spent more than five and a half years behind bars. In his prison cell, he managed to write a book, The Spirit of Independence, exhorting fellow countrymen to do their patriotic duties and reform their society.[35] He also became a Christian and converted more than forty of his fellow inmates to join him.

As Japan was tightening its grip on Korea in the aftermath of the Russo-Japanese War, Rhee was released and, within a few months, headed for the United States under circumstances that have not been fully explained. It is said that his trip was arranged by two of Emperor Kojong's confidants, Min Yong-hwan and Han Kyu-sol, to solicit American intervention on Korea's behalf at the Portsmouth Peace Conference. Rhee and Rev. Yun Pyong-gu of Hawaii were able to secure a meeting with President Theodore Roosevelt, but their mission was a failure. Rhee then spent the next five years studying and earning academic degrees from George Washington University (B.A.), Harvard (M.A.) and Princeton (Ph.D.)---an impressive achievement in record time. When Japan formally annexed Korea, the first Korean with an American doctorate was on his way home to work at the Seoul YMCA.

His stay in Seoul did not last long, however. Feeling threatened by the mass arrest of Korean leaders in the so-called "105-man case," Rhee left for the United States for the second time in March 1912, ostensibly to attend a Methodist convention in Minneapolis. Several months after the church meeting, Rhee decided to move to Hawaii and open a new chapter of his life. For the next several years, he was engaged in running a church-operated school for Korean children, publishing a monthly magazine for Korean residents---the Korean Pacific Magazine (later, the Korean Pacific Weekly)---and in promoting evangelical works of church groups.

As he became more established as a leader in the Korean community, he also became involved in a bitter internecine power struggle with Pak Yong-Man, his erstwhile "sworn brother" and a fellow inmate in the Seoul prison. They were both energetic and ambitious and they shared patriotic devotion to Korea, but they were miles apart in their plans for recovering Korea's sovereign independence.

Pak advocated a direct military challenge to Japan and, to that end, training and establishing an army was the most urgent task.

Rhee, on the other hand, believed that the most effective way to defeat the Japanese colonial rule in Korea was to use diplomacy and propaganda means to secure the political support of major foreign powers and of the international community. If Pak considered Rhee's strategy somewhat uninspiring and irresolute, Rhee believed that Pak was too simplistic and misguided in his approach. Rhee had earlier visited Pak's military training bases in Nebraska and Hawaii perhaps to humor his younger comrade, but when the allocation of the limited resources of the KNA in Hawaii was at stake in mid-1915, the two protagonists became irreconcilably hostile to each other. Malicious rumors of embezzlement and corruption spread fanning ill will between them that escalated into physical confrontations, police intervention and litigation.[36]

The March First Movement transformed Rhee overnight from a local community activist in Hawaii into a national political leader with a revolutionary agenda. Independence movement leaders within Korea, in the Russian Maritime Province and in Shanghai all selected him as the top leader of the governments that they announced, although none of them used the title "president."[37] Why was he chosen to lead the government in exile? Presumably Rhee's past activities that had led to his imprisonment and later his meeting with the American president, his educational credentials and his residency in America were some of reasons for the fame and support that he enjoyed. His non-involvement in political jockeying among the contending personalities and groups in China and elsewhere in Asia may also have helped him seem more attractive.

Even before he went to Shanghai in late 1920 to assume his duties, Rhee wasted no time in representing himself---and acting---as "president," the title which his KPG colleagues formally conferred on him only later. He addressed a memorandum to the emperor of Japan announcing the creation of "a completely organized, self governed State" of Korea and the election of himself as "President of the Republic of Korea."[38] Similar notifications were sent to the governments of the United

States, Great Britain, France and Italy as well as to the presiding officer of the Versailles Peace Conference. He appointed Kim Kyu-sik to head a Korean Commission and started a fundraising campaign by selling bonds. At one point, he also signed a petition requesting that Korea be declared a mandate territory of the League of Nations as a means to ending Japan's domination of the peninsula. Rhee took all these actions without prior consultation with his colleagues in the KPG.

Rhee's sojourn in Shanghai failed to create unity in the KPG and his refusal to accommodate the left-leaning faction that included Yi Tong-hwi, a powerful advocate of an anti-Japanese military campaign, exacerbated the schism in Korean leadership. Moreover, Rhee's explanations for some of the controversial decisions he had made in Washington, such as the petition for a League mandate, failed to mollify his critics. After only six months in Shanghai, Rhee returned to the United States citing the need to attend to pressing diplomatic and financial problems for his departure. Back in Washington, Rhee teamed up with Jaisohn and others in an unsuccessful attempt to present the Korean case before the Washington Disarmament Conference, 1921-1922. In September 1922, the frustrated Rhee returned to Honolulu. His KPG presidency ended officially in 1925, when he was impeached by a one-vote margin for abandoning his office and for dereliction of duty in a hastily improvised impeachment proceeding in Shanghai.

For the next several years, Rhee remained mostly in Hawaii cultivating his political base, especially around the Comrade Society (Tongji-hoe) of which he was president for life. He traveled to Europe in 1932-1933 primarily to bring the Korean case before the League of Nations conference that met to discuss Japan's invasion of Manchuria. He was once again disappointed although his solo mission received some attention from the local press.[39] As Japan moved into China proper after 1937, Rhee foresaw a future conflict between Japan and the United States. He wrote Japan Inside Out, as mentioned earlier, to alert the Americans to the impending danger. He also moved back to

Washington and revived the long dormant Korean Commission, as both the UKC and the KPG commissioned Rhee to head a diplomatic mission and obtain formal recognition of the KPG.

During the war years, 1941-1945, Rhee became a familiar figure around Washington trying to win support from skeptical or unconcerned officials, politicians, journalists and other men of influence. A Korean Liberty Congress was convened in a downtown hotel as a publicity event. Proposals were submitted to the United States military for organizing guerrilla forces consisting of Korean fighters. Rhee also began sounding an alarm over the dangers coming from Soviet Communism. [40] These entreaties were largely ignored, including Rhee's attempt to attend the first United Nations conference in April 1945.

Two months after Japan's surrender, Rhee returned to Korea for the first time in 33 years. A discussion of his life and activities in the subsequent years is outside the scope of this study.

An Ch'ang-Ho

An Ch'ang-Ho was born in 1878 in South P'yongan Province to a poor farming family. He was the youngest of four children. Although his family lacked the social status of yangban, it nevertheless provided the young An with an education in the Confucian classics. In 1894, the fifteen-year old An witnessed firsthand the Sino-Japanese War, which brought destruction and misery to the hapless Korean civilians in the Pyongyang area. According to Yi Kwang-su, the popular literary figure of the 1920s who wrote a biography of An, the destruction caused by foreign armies fighting on Korean soil made the young An realize that Korea's own weakness was to be blamed.[41] He made his way to Seoul and began studying at a missionary school, Kuse Haktang. He also became a Christian.

In 1898, An joined the Independence Club and became active in Pyongyang, where he delivered a stirring speech denouncing bureaucratic corruption before a large crowd. When the reactionary government banned the Independence Club, An returned home and started a co-educational school in 1899 that he named Chomjin Hakkyo, or "gradual progress school," reflecting his belief in evolutionary change through education. Meanwhile, he decided to seek further education himself by going to the United States. He was encouraged in his decision by some American missionaries, including Rev. F.S. Miller, who officiated at An's wedding the day before the newlyweds left for America.

The Ans arrived in San Francisco on October 14, 1902 and landed jobs as live-in domestic helpers. An also sought opportunities for public school education, above all, to learn English, but the over-age Korean student was not welcome. He then made a decision "to forsake a formal education in America and to work towards strengthening the local Korean community."[42] No more than a dozen in number, Korean residents in San Francisco lacked internal harmony and, according to Yi Kwang-su, An witnessed a scuffle on the street between two Korean ginseng peddlers, an embarrassing experience that convinced him of the need to organize a fraternal society (Ch'immok-hoe). He visited with and persuaded fellow countrymen in the city to follow a civilized life style and to assist one another in becoming more respectable members of the community. He personally set an example by helping clean and beautify the homes of some Korean residents. It was a case of down-to-earth community work through patient person-to-person contact.[43]

In March 1904, An moved to Riverside, California, and took a job doing "schoolboy work," which entailed cooking, cleaning and other domestic chores. Some evenings, he studied English and the Bible. He also worked in fruit orchards with other Korean workers. In 1905, he moved back to San Francisco and organized the Mutual Assistance Association (Kongnip Hyophoe) to help Koreans arriving from Hawaii settle in and find employment. Within the next few years, local chapters of the Association, of which An was the president, were formed in Los Angeles, Riverside, Redlands and Rock Springs in Wyoming with a total membership of 600. [44] This Association also published a newspaper, the <u>United Korean</u> (<u>Kongnip Sinbo</u>), that reported---and denounced---Japanese acts of aggression against Korea.[45]

Early in 1907, An returned to Korea to see for himself what changes had taken place in his homeland and what he could do to stop the precipitous decline of the nation. On the way he stopped in Tokyo where he met Korean students, some of whom, such as Yi Kwang-su, were deeply impressed by him. Once in Korea, he gave speeches before students and intellectuals as well as the general public, in Seoul, Pyongyang and elsewhere. His themes included Christian principles, an exhortation not to sell land to the Japanese and a plea that everyone should do whatever he could, however small, for the country. The Japanese authorities kept a close watch on An's activities, which they suspected stirred up anti-Japanese sentiment. An also became friends with a number of individuals who were or soon would be key figures in journalistic and scholarly circles, such as Ch'oi Nam-son, Pak Un-sik, and Sin Ch'ae-ho.[46]

Sometime soon after his arrival in Korea, An established a secret organization, the New People's Association (Sinmin-hoe, "NPA" hereafter) whose professed purpose was "to renew our people,... to renew business...and to help establish a renewed, civilized and free nation by a renewed and united people." The membership of the NPA included journalists, youth and religious leaders, military officers, merchants and industrialists and members of the California-based Mutual Assistance Association. An talked Yang Ki-t'ak, a veteran newspaperman, into accepting the NPA presidency and he himself chose to work without an official title, concentrating on the recruitment of new members.[47]

An helped establish fourteen schools including the well-known Osan Middle School and Taesong Middle School, between 1907 and 1909. In order to establish a nationwide reputation for the latter school, which was meant to be a model for other schools, An invited Yun Ch'i-ho, the well respected educator and former high official, to serve as head of the school, while An himself actually operated it. Among the Taesong graduates were future activists in national independence movement, but it was ordered closed by the Japanese colonial government in 1913.[48]

An and the NPA were also involved in many other projects: a chain of book stores, publication of a magazine, The Youth (Sonyon) edited by Ch'oe Nam-son, a young students association, and a number of business ventures, including a ceramics factory, in keeping with An's idea of building educational, cultural and industrial foundations for a modern Korea. Apparently, An's ability to win friends and manage various voluntary organizations was intriguing enough for Japanese Resident-General Ito Hirobumi to invite An to a meeting in November 1907, where Ito allegedly floated the idea of An heading a Korean cabinet consisting of younger leaders. An summarily rejected the offer.[49] When Ito was assassinated by a Korean nationalist in 1909, An was suspected of involvement in the conspiracy and had to spend two months in a Japanese army prison.[50] By then, An knew that it was not safe for him to remain in Korea and decided to go into exile.

He slipped away aboard a Chinese salt carrier and landed in Weihaiwei in April 1910. A meeting with several of his comrades was held in Tsingtao in July to discuss the plans for restoring Korea's independence. The conferees were split between those advocating immediate military campaign and those, including An, in favor of a more gradual process of building up Korea's capabilities to win and keep its freedom, and no firm decision was reached. After Tsingtao, An traveled to Vladivostok, where he stayed a few months meeting Korean residents in the area and even visiting a potential site in Manchuria for a utopian Korean settlement. He made his way back to America via the trans-Siberian railway, Berlin and London, arriving in New York early in September 1911.[51]

For the next several years until 1919, An devoted himself to the works of Korean organizations in the United States, Hawaii and Mexico. He focused on strengthening and unifying the KNA, a project that led to his election, in late 1912, as chairman of the Central Congress of the KNA, a newly created top-level body, above the regional conferences of North America, Hawaii, Siberia and Manchuria. He traveled to Hawaii in 1915 to mediate an internal feud within the regional KNA that was caused by bitter rivalry between Syngman Rhee and Pak Yong-Man. He made a ten-month trip to Mexico, starting in October 1917, to help organize KNA branches especially in Merida, Yucatan, where hundreds of Koreans worked on sisal hemp farms under miserable conditions.[52]

At the same time, An undertook to organize a select group of patriotic young men into a fraternal society for moral and intellectual development; the Young Korean Academy (Hungsadan) was formally established on May 13, 1913, in San Francisco with 35 original members in attendance. An personally conducted rigorous interviews whenever possible before inviting new members to join the Academy and he took pains to have all eight provinces of Korea represented in the Academy's membership in order to avoid any suspicion of regional favoritism.[53] In time, local chapters of the Academy came to be organized in China and Korea itself, providing An a dependable base of support for his nationalist campaign.

True to his conviction that Koreans should build up their economic muscle, An made a sustained effort during his second sojourn in the United States to establish a business corporation, North American Industrial Company (Pungmi Sirop Chusik Hoesa), as a first step. Common stock was sold to Koreans in America and Mexico, with many shares going to members of the Young Korean Academy, and by 1918, $70,000 had been raised. The company first undertook commercial potato farming, and switched to rice cultivation later, but the venture was largely unsuccessful.[54]

At the conclusion of the armistice in 1918, An called a KNA meeting that resolved to submit a petition to the Paris peace conference. He also took steps to raise funds for the diplomatic activities. But he was not optimistic about the chances for success; he continued to hold the view that Koreans should first build a firm foundation for independence. While KNA leaders were still discussing their plans for the peace conference, the March First Movement erupted in Korea. An first received the news via Shanghai and he promptly notified various regional KNA conferences and individual leaders such as Syngman Rhee and Philip Jaisohn. Under An's leadership, the Central Congress of the KNA passed resolutions to mount diplomatic and public information campaigns for American support which Jaisohn and Rhee were to conduct on the East Coast. The Central Congress also decided to raise funds and urged all Korean residents to contribute a minimum of $10 for the month of March and one twentieth of their monthly income thereafter. An personally traveled extensively in California to solicit "independence contributions." He was also selected to go to Shanghai as a representative of the KNA and participate in the establishment of a Korean provisional government.[55]

An arrived in Shanghai via Hong Kong May 25, 1919 and stayed in China, mostly in Shanghai, for the next five and a half years until November 1924. Even before his arrival, An had already been selected by those pressing for the immediate establishment of a provisional government to assume the post of Minister of Home Affairs. An, however, preferred, a more gradual process of various individuals and groups cooperating, perhaps, to form an united political party and declined the cabinet post. But he was eventually persuaded to join the government as acting premier and he helped reorganize the government (KPG) from a parliamentary cabinet system to a presidential system. Armed with the modest funds he had brought with him, An patiently convinced suspicious rivals to compromise and keep the façade of a functioning KPG under Syngman Rhee as the first president--until 1921.[56]

The contentious exiles could not, however, long refrain from going their separate ways. The incumbent of the second highest office, Premier Yi Tong-hwi, resigned and left Shanghai in early 1921, shattering any hope for continuation of a functioning KPG. An himself resigned in May 1921 as KPG's labor department superintendent, a modest title that he had allowed himself to take after giving up the acting premiership. Freed of formal KPG ties, An tried anew his campaign to construct a political organization of national unity. After months of painstaking preparations, he organized a conference of national representatives of all Koreans from various geographical areas and of all political persuasions. On January 3, 1923, the conference opened in the French concession area of Shanghai with approximately 160 attendees representing over seventy organizations. An opened the session and he tried for the next six months to hammer out a common strategy for the independence movement. The future of the KPG was one of the hotly debated issues but the discussion of three options---to keep the status quo, to reform it, or to abandon it in favor of a new organization---became deadlocked without any resolution.[57]

An was more successful in organizing the Far Eastern Branch of the Young Korean Academy. He recruited new members, including Yi Kwang-su, who helped him write and disseminate his "Epistle to My Compatriots" (Tongp'o ege kohanun gul) that encapsulated An's political ideas. He also visited northern China in search for a suitable piece of land to build an ideal community---a life long dream of An. Turning to education, another long standing interest of his, An established in March 1924 a school in Nanjing, Tongmyong Institute, to help prepare Korean students for college education in Europe, America or China.[58] An then left Shanghai to return to his family and comrades in America.

An's stay in America was relatively short this time and he was busy visiting and thanking his supporters and conferring with the Young Korean Academy members in California. He also toured the Midwest and the East Coast of the United States. He stopped for varying lengths of time in Chicago, South Bend, Detroit, Kansas City, Princeton and New York to give speeches and meet with students including Paek Nak-chun, Ho Chong, Chang Tok-su, Kim To-yon and others. A young Columbia student, Chang Ni-uk accompanied him part of the way. He also met Philip Jaisohn twice in the course of 1925. Early in 1926, An had to leave the United States primarily because he could not extend his visa to stay longer. He sailed to China via Australia and Hong Kong, arriving in Shanghai in mid-May.

Upon arrival in Shanghai, An was informed that he was elected premier of the KPG but he declined. Instead, he endorsed a new venture by the Young Korean Academy to publish a magazine, Tongkwang (Eastern Light) in Korea. At the same time, he planned to create a Great Independence Party (Tae Tongnip Tang) and to continue exploring the chances for the model community project. With these in mind, he visited Beijing in the fall and went on to Manchuria. While visiting the Jilin area in southeastern Manchuria, he delivered a speech before a large crowd that apparently included the young Kim Il Sung, according to sources in North Korea.[59] The lecture meeting was broken up when Chinese police moved in and arrested dozens of people, including An, presumably at the request of Japanese authorities in the area. He was released, however, after a twenty-day detention, and went on to visit northern Manchuria before returning to Shanghai. His continuing interest in a model community site was part of the reasons for his trip to the Philippines in 1929, where he was impressed by the open and more democratic American colonial policy, as compared to the Japanese behavior in Korea.[60]

An was one of the 28 founding members of the Korean Independence Party (Han'guk Tongnip Tang) that was established on January 25, 1930; other co-founders included Yi Tong-nyong, Kim Tu-bong, Yun Ki-sop, Cho So-ang and Cho Wan-gu. Kim Ku, the future leader of the KPG, was also involved in the party.[61] The formation of the party that brought together various non-Communist nationalists at this time may have been an attempt to keep the moribund KPG alive. The exiled group, however, won the respect and support from the Chinese when two young KPG supporters hurled bombs at the procession of the Japanese emperor in January 1932, and at high Japanese officials in Shanghai three months later. The two attacks were directed by Kim Ku who used $1,000 sent to him by his supporters in Hawaii.[62] In the aftermath of the second attack, the Japanese police conducted a massive search for the presumed accomplices and An fell into their hands.

An was taken to Korea in June 1932. The fifty four-year old prisoner, in failing health, was charged with violation of the infamous Peace Preservation Law and was sentenced to four years in prison. Paroled after three years, An visited a few friends in Seoul and elsewhere and retired to a cottage on a secluded hillside in his home province of South P'yongan. He was re-arrested a little over two years later when scores of his friends, including Yi Kwang-su, were jailed by the Japanese thought police only days before the Marco Polo Bridge Incident that eventually led to World War II in Asia. Six months later, the gravely ill An was transferred to the University Hospital in Seoul, where he died on March 10, 1938 at age 59.

Pak Yong-Man

Pak Yong-Man was born July 2, 1881 to a yangban family of military tradition in a rural town in Kangwon province. The only son of his parents, Pak was orphaned at an early age and was raised by his uncle, Pak Hui-byong. When his uncle moved to Seoul and began studying English, Pak Yong-Man enrolled at a Japanese language school. When his uncle went to Japan to study, Yong-Man once again followed and he graduated from a middle school and studied politics at Keio Gijuku for a couple of years. His uncle also introduced him to Pak Yong-hyo (no relation), a prominent reform advocate in exile in Japan, and the latter may have influenced the young Pak with reformist ideas. The budding political activist returned home, perhaps in 1897, and became involved in a peasant right movement, hwalpin-tang ("Help the Indigent Party"), the People's Assembly (Manmin kongdong-hoe) and a protest movement of Poan-hoe against a Japanese demand for Korean farm lands. He was also active in the Christian youth group that gathered at Sangdong Church in Seoul and became well known to some of the American missionaries. Although details on his life in this period remain murky, we know that he was imprisoned twice by the conservative Korean government, each time for several months at least. During his second stay in prison, he and

Syngman Rhee, a fellow inmate, became "sworn brothers."[63] It was Pak who smuggled the manuscript of Rhee's The Spirit of Independence out of prison and out of Korea to the United States.[64]

Released from prison some time in 1904, Pak followed his uncle to Sonch'on, South P'yongan Province and taught Korean, Japanese, arithmetic and Chinese classics at a local private school. for a short time. Pak, together with several other students, left for the United States, presumably in late 1904.[65] Landing in San Francisco, Pak and his party made their way to Nebraska where railroad construction work was easily available. At one point, however, Pak joined his uncle Hui-byong who had arrived in the United States in 1905 and operated an employment agency in Denver, Colorado. While in Denver, Pak organized a conference of thirty-six "patriotic" Koreans from various parts of the United States partly to publicize the Korean cause to the Republic National Convention that met there in June 1908. The Korean conference also made the decision to establish a military school as a step toward an armed struggle against Japan.[66]

Following the death of Pak Hui-byong, Pak Yong-Man returned to Nebraska and enrolled at the University of Nebraska. He also set up "The Young Korean Military School" in a rented farm at Kearny, Nebraska, in the summer of 1909; a year later the school moved to the campus of Hastings College. About thirty students registered for a summer program of farm work and training that included, besides military drills, learning etiquette, American history, English and Korean. Pak himself prepared a primer for Korean lessons. The school project was partially financed by an assessment levied on the members of the Korean Resident Association of Nebraska that was first organized in 1909. The military school, or program, produced its first "graduating class" of thirteen students in 1912 and remained in operation until 1915.[67]

Pak Yong-Man, in the meantime, was busy not only with his own college education[68] but also with a year of journalist work in

San Francisco as the editor of <u>Hapsong sinmun</u> (renamed <u>Sinhan minbo</u> later), a newspaper published by the North American Regional Headquarters of the KNA. He published an essay, "On a Universal Draft System," in the paper and stressed the patriotic duty of everyone to serve in the military as well as to pay an assessment. Pak's journalist career continued in Hawaii beginning in December 1912, when he became the editor of <u>Sin Han'guk-po</u> (renamed <u>Kungmin-po</u> or <u>The Korean National Herald</u> later) published by the Hawaiian Regional Conference of the KNA.[69]

Hawaii provided Pak an opportunity to expand his military training project. He established the Korean Military Corporation in June 1913 at Ahuimanu, Oahu, and a Korean Military Academy in August. The Academy enrolled some 124 students who had been soldiers in Korea before they emigrated to Hawaii; they worked ten or more hours a day on a pineapple farm but spent their "spare" time in military training. The project, however, did not last long and it came to an end by late 1917. Financial difficulty was a reason for its closing as well as opposition from United States government sources responding to complaints by the Japanese. Moreover, Pak had to cope with growing opposition from within the Korean community, especially from Syngman Rhee and his supporters, who considered the project too costly and unrealistic.[70]

When World War I ended, Pak "published a declaration of independence in the name of the Korean nation, the first declaration of its kind." [71] He also organized a Korean Independence League (Tongnip-dan) in March 1919 as a military training school and the League functioned as his support group even when he was away. Pak, in the meantime, decided to go to the Northeast Asia because it was the logical place to wage the campaign against Japanese colonialism. He joined the United States Siberian Expeditionary Forces as an intelligence officer and left Hawaii on board a United States transport in May 1919.[72] While in Siberia, Pak worked together with a Comintern agent named Wurin in a Sino-Russian Joint Propaganda Department headed by the latter.[73] After the American expedition ended, Pak remained in the area. Although he had been offered the post of foreign minister in the Korean Provisional Government in Shanghai, he declined it in part because Syngman Rhee was selected the head of the KPG. Instead, he organized a "Military Unification Conference" in Beijing in April 1921 that was attended by Sin Ch'ae-ho, a nationalist historian, and Kim Ch'ang-suk, a Confucian activist, and others representing groups in Manchuria, Siberia and Hawaii. Apart from issuing a demand for the dissolution of the KPG and a call for a conference of national representatives, the conference was not otherwise productive.[74]

Pak's activities in subsequent years can only be stated in tentative terms because little verifiable information is available. He is said to have contacted Korean leaders in Manchuria to explore the chances for collaboration in setting up a military base. He also allegedly worked with a few Chinese warlords in northern China including Wu Peifu, Feng Yuxiang, and Chang Zuoxiang to consider Mongolia as a possible site for a military base. Incredible as it may sound, Pak at one point allegedly conferred with the Japanese on anti-Communist measures, and he had entered Korea on a Chinese passport.[75] We do know that Pak made a trip to Hawaii in 1925 to raise funds from his supporters. We also know that Pak was assassinated by a Korean youth, a member of Uiyol-dan, the left-leaning terrorist group, in 1928 under circumstances that are not clear.[76]

Concluding Comments

By way of conclusion, three broad observations are offered. (I) The independence movement of Koreans in the United States before 1945 had peaks and valleys that reflected the political changes surrounding Korea. (II) The three most influential leaders of Koreans in the United States provide sharp contrasts in personal attributes and political ideas and these differences had a negative impact on the movement. (III) The Korean community in the United States has displayed a high degree of patriotic devotion and commitment, despite dispiriting setbacks.

(I) Patriotic activities of the Korean emigrants in America surged in three periods, each of which witnessed major changes in political circumstances facing Korea: 1905-1910, 1919-1921, and 1941-1945.

The years between 1905 and 1910 saw the initial organization of the newly arrived Korean emigrants. Several thousands of farm laborers made up the majority of the emigrants and they lacked the financial and educational background necessary to adapt to their new environment. Local mutual aid groups and churches were first formed and provided opportunities for cooperation and community life during this period.

These were the years of accelerated and ruthless intrusion of Japanese power into Korea leading to the final extinction of the Korean empire. In response, the Korean groups and churches in America became politicized and energized. A national consciousness developed and sacrifices, mostly, but not confined to, monetary contributions were made for the sake of patriotic causes. Sundry social and civic organizations came together in the Korean National Association that had branches even in Manchuria, the Russian Maritime Province and Mexico. Active, if inconclusive, discussions on regaining national sovereignty took place. Once Japan's colonial rule became a fait accompli, however, the sense of urgency in the activities of Koreans overseas subsided.

The second period, 1919-1921, was comprised of the immediate post-World War I years that kindled the flames of nationalism in various parts of the world, including Korea. The March First Movement touched the heart of every Korean living in America. They rallied, demonstrated, and lobbied for support from the United States and the victorious allies. The KNA and other Korean organizations mobilized their members and collected funds for these purposes.

At the same time, Koreans in America took part in the formation and operation of the Korean Provisional Government in

Shanghai. An Ch'ang-Ho, Syngman Rhee and a few others went to China from the United States and played key roles. Rhee was active in Washington, before and after his brief China trip, as the president of the KPG in making diplomatic contacts and in raising funds. Pak Yong-Man refused participation in the KPG but he, too, rushed to China to prepare an active anti-Japanese campaign. All three of them enjoyed the moral and financial support of their friends and supporters in America. The flurry of activity touched off by the March First Movement subsided eventually, especially after An's resignation from the KPG in 1921.

By 1941, both An and Pak were gone but Rhee resuscitated the long-dormant Korean Commission in Washington, D.C. and waged a steady diplomatic and publicity campaign to gain a sympathetic hearing from the United States government. With the prospect of Korea's liberation in sight at long last, Koreans were anxious to join the fighting ranks of the allies and prepare for an independent fatherland. However, they had at best only limited success. Furthermore, their cause was marred by internecine feuds.[77]

It is not easy to point to any tangible and direct consequences of the Korean endeavors in America during the war years. But the presence of Korean residents on American soil and the expressions of their aspiration did not go unrecognized at the conferences at Cairo, Yalta and Potsdam. Above all, Koreans in the United States---despite the disunity among them--- undoubtedly had the satisfaction of having remained faithful to their nationalist cause.

(II) The root cause for the internal discord among the Koreans must be attributed to the inability of Syngman Rhee, An Ch'ang-Ho and Pak Yong-Man to work together for the common end that they sought with passion. The marked divergences and contrasts in family and educational background, in personality, and in political and policy priorities among the three leaders ultimately prevented them from agreeing on a common approach and, consequently, splintered and weakened the nationalist movement.

The families of both Rhee and Pak belonged to the yangban class, while An was born into a commoner's family. All three received a traditional Confucian education in their early years, but Rhee and Pak completed formal university educations in America, while An had only occasional instruction in English and Bible studies. We are reminded of these social and educational differences when we read about the contrast between the aristocratic behavior ascribed to Rhee and the plebian style to An.[78] We should also remember that An and, to a lesser degree, Pak, worked as common laborers at different times of their American experiences, but the same cannot be said about Rhee. Those who knew An recollected that he was personable and helpful, particularly to those in need.[79]

Rhee's relationship to An was never close or warm, although they worked together to establish the KPG as a functioning organization and An reportedly defended Rhee to those in Shanghai who criticized Rhee. For one thing, Rhee and An lived and worked mostly in different parts of the United States, An in California and Rhee in Hawaii or Washington. In contrast, Rhee and Pak had maintained a close but turbulent relationship especially after they both moved to Hawaii. They attracted devoted followers and competed for political and financial support in a geographically confined area. After 1915, rivalry between these two strong-willed individuals became intense, turning their "sworn brotherhood" into sworn animosity. The underlying cause was their disagreement over the best strategy to recover Korea's independence.

Put in simple terms, Pak advocated a direct military campaign to fight for independence. In preparation for such a campaign, a universal draft system would have to be instituted, and military training, particularly for the officers corps, should be supported by all patriotic Koreans. He set up training camps in Nebraska and Hawaii and he was busy until his death trying to set up a new, perhaps larger, base somewhere in northern China or Mongolia in collaboration with Chinese warlords. The primary purpose of his last visit to Hawaii in 1925 was to raise funds for the project. He apparently had no qualms about working with either the Bolsheviks or the right-wing militarists, as long as they could help him fight the Japanese.

Rhee, on the other hand, realized that Koreans could not defeat the Japanese in an open contest of arms. International support, particularly from major Western powers, was a sine qua non in order to force the Japanese out of Korea. Diplomacy and public relations were the most logical tools for this strategy. Of course, in order to win foreign support, Koreans must prove themselves worthy of such assistance. Education and social reforms based on democratic principles would create an enlightened and civilized society that would ultimately win the respect and support of the international community. To that end, Korea should follow the Western democratic model and eschew Communism.

An's record shows a two-pronged strategy to build Korea's national power: education and economic development. He established schools in Korea and in China. He also started business enterprises in Korea and the United States. He stressed education not only for its pragmatic application, but also for its promise to effect moral regeneration. Honesty, sincerity and industry were the virtues that the members of the Young Korean Academy were to strive for under his leadership. Although he did not categorically reject the military campaign strategy that he at times seemed to endorse while in China, his counsel to his friends and supporters was to transcend personal or ideological differences, and unite and work together for the long haul toward independence.

In terms of both personal temperament and political priorities, it appears that An was the best qualified to serve as peacemaker between Rhee and Pak. An indeed tried---unsuccessfully---his hand in personal mediation by going to Hawaii in 1915.[80] Had he succeeded, he could have brought together Rhee's sophistication and knowledge of the world affairs with Pak's dynamic energy for their common cause and may have prepared the Korean community in America better to face the avalanche of events in the 1940s. Pak's untimely and tragic death and An's own painful but heroic end foreclosed a potentially promising opportunity for Koreans to emerge as a united nation within and outside Korea as the thousands of Koreans in America had hoped for over forty years.

It is truly remarkable that the Korean community in America, numbering only in the thousands and for the most part struggling to eke out a living during the initial stages of their settlement, was able to support not only the succession of nationalist programs in the United States but also anti-Japanese activities elsewhere in the world as well. They were largely from the less privileged socio-economic classes in their home country, which then was unable to protect or assist them in any way. Virtually cast away in a strange land without advance preparation, these Koreans survived and retained their emotional ties to their distant homeland for four decades or more.

Called upon by their leaders to support various diplomatic, propaganda and educational activities in the cause of Korea's independence, these immigrants responded with substantial financial contributions, although their aggregate sum cannot be ascertained. Time and again, the KPG and other organizations in China looked toward their compatriots in the United States for money to help finance their patriotic campaigns. Geography dictated a division of labor among the nationalist Koreans overseas, assigning financial responsibility to those in America.[81] It was not an easy burdens to bear.

With the benefit of historical hindsight, it is tempting to speculate what the Koreans in America could have accomplished with a more united leadership at the top: Could they have secured a better hearing for their cause in the capitals of the allied powers in World War II and altered the course of history for their homeland after 1945?

Endnotes

[1] Bong-youn Choy, Koreans in America (Chicago: Nelson-Hall, 1979), pp. 75-77; Hyung-chan Kim and Wayne Patterson, compils. and eds. The Koreans in America, 1882-1974, A Chronology and Fact Book (Dobbs Ferry, N.Y.: Oceana Publications, 1974), pp. 2-6.

[2] Yu Kil-chun, So Chae-pil, Yun Ch'i-ho are examples of early Korean students who had come before the waves of farm laborers. Choy, pp. 71-72. For details on the Hawaiian Sugar Planters Association and its project to bring in Korean workers to balance off the Japanese who had arrived earlier, see Wayne Patterson, The Korean Frontier in America: Immigration to Hawaii, 1896-1910 (Honolulu: University of Hawaii Press, 1988), especially chaps. 6-9.

[3] Ibid., chap. 13.

[4] Choy, pp. 94-96. The monthly income was $16 for men and $12.50 for women in Hawaii.

[5] Ibid., p.76.

[6] Yo-jun Yun, "Early History of Korean Immigration to America," in Hyung-chan Kim, ed. The Korean Diaspora (Santa Barbara, CA: ABC-Clio, 1977), p. 37.

[7] Ibid.

[8] Ibid., pp. 37-38.

[9] Yu Yong-ik, Yi Sung-man ui salm kwa kkum [The Life and Dream of Syngman Rhee] (Seoul: The Joong Ang Ilbo-sa, 1996), pp. 38-44.

[10] Choy, p. 143; Hyung-chan Kim, "Korean Community Organizations in America: Their Characteristics and Problems," in Hyung-chan Kim, The Korean Diaspora, p. 70.

[11] Ibid. Also see Warren Y. Kim [Kim Won-yong], Koreans In America (Seoul: Po Chin Chai Printing Co., 1971), pp. 50-51. Warren Kim gives a different English translation of the name of this organization: the Korean Consolidated Association.

[12] Choy, pp. 143-144. Stevens was on his way from Seoul to Washington D.C. His defense of Japanese policy in Korea aroused the anger of Koreans in San Francisco and when he refused to retract his pro-Japanese remarks, Chang In-hwan of the Great Unity Fatherland Protection Society shot him. The Korean community in California and Hawaii hired lawyers and provided the defense fund for Chang's trial; Chang was sentenced to a 25-year prison term but was released after ten years. Ibid., pp. 146-149; Hyung-chan Kim," Korean Community Organizations..." in Hyung-chan Kim, The Korean Diaspora, pp. 70-71.

[13] Choy, p. 115; Hyung-chan Kim, "Korean Community Organizations …," in The Korean Diaspora, p. 71.

[14] Kim and Patterson, The Koreans in America, p.20. The first "picture bride," Sara Choe, arrived in November 1910. Eventually more than 800 of them came to Hawaii. Choy, pp. 88-89.

[15] Kim and Patterson, The Koreans in America, pp. 19-20; Choy, pp. 116-117. Kim and Patterson translate Hungsa-dan as "Corps for the Advancement of Individuals."

[16] Kim and Patterson, pp. 3-4; Hyung-chan Kim, "The History and Role the Church in the Korean American Community," in Hyung-chan Kim, The Korean Diaspora, pp. 50-51.

[17] Ibid., pp. 57-58.

[18] Choy, pp. 257-258.

[19] It was Wadman who helped secure a letter of introduction for Rev. Yun Pyong-gu to meet President Theodore Roosevelt in 1905. Wadman was instrumental for the development of the Methodist church in the Korean community; see Hyung-chan Kim, "…The Church in the Korean American Community," in Hyung-chan Kim, "The Korean Diaspora", pp. 51-52.

[20] Choy, pp. 153-154.

[21] Ibid., pp. 154-156; Yu Yong-ik, Yi Sung-man ui …, pp. 134-140. For a detailed account on the First Korean Congress see Chong-Sik Lee, The Politics of Korean Nationalism (Berkeley: University of California Press, 1963), pp. 142-144.

[22] Ibid., pp. 144-145.

[23] An had reservations about creating an exile government at this time and he was reluctant to accept a high position in the government. Nevertheless, An patiently persuaded opposing factions and personalities to compromise in the interest of unity and set the provisional government in motion; ibid., pp. 131-137.

[24] See Choy, p. 158. However, the basis for these figures cannot be verified although they may be within possible ranges.

[25] Pak Yong-Man had been designated as the minister of foreign affairs in the provisional government but he did not work in that capacity very long, if any time at all. Chong-Sik Lee, The Politics of Korean Nationalism, pp. 174-176.

[26] Choy, pp. 159-160.

[27] Yu Yong-ik, Yi Sung-man ui …, pp. 174-176.

[28] Choy, pp. 167-168.

[29] Syngman Rhee had organized Tongji-hoe in Hawaii in July 1921 as his own political support group. Ibid., 118-119.

[30] Ibid., pp. 170-172.

[31] Yu Yong-ik, Yi Sung-man ui …, pp. 194-196.

[32] Han Kil-su, the controversial head of a Sino-Korean People's League, is often mentioned as Rhee's archrival who sabotaged the UKC's work thereby

giving the impression to the American policy makers that the Koreans were hopelessly divided. Alger Hiss and his alleged pro-Soviet orientation is also mentioned as a contributing factor for the unsympathetic decisions of the State Department, of which Hiss was a key official, see ibid., pp.198-205. This writer holds the view that the United States had no coherent Korea policy and was merely treading water in the turbulent sea of world politics.

[33] Unless noted otherwise, most of the biographical information on Rhee are from Yu Yong-ik, op. cit.

[34] A recent study on Rhee calls him a radical, see Chong-Sik Lee, Syngman Rhee: The Prison Years of a Young Radical (Seoul: The Yonsei University Press, 2001), 208 pp.

[35] An English translation of the full text is now available: Syngman Rhee, The Spirit of Independence: A Primer of Korean Modernization and Reform, translated by Han-Kyo Kim (Honolulu: The University of Hawaii Press, 2001), 305 pp. For a comprehensive study of Rhee's activities in prison, see Yu Yong-ik, Cholmun nalui Yi Sungman (Youthful Syngman Rhee) (Seoul: The Yonsei University Press, 2002), 511 pp.

[36] For an account of the Rhee-Pak conflict, see Kingsley K. Lyu, "Korean nationalist Activities in Hawaii and the Continental United States, 1900-1945, Part I: 1900-1919," in Amerasia Journal (published by the Asian American Studies Center, University of California, Los Angeles), vol. 4, no. 1, 1977, pp. 65-85. Lyu is very critical of Rhee's tactics. A more spiteful account is in Dae-sook Suh, ed. The Writings of Henry Cu Kim: Autobiograhy with Commentaries on Syngman Rhee, Pak Yong-man, and Chong Sun-man (Honolulu: Center for Korean Studies,University of Hawaii, and University of Hawaii Press, 1987).

[37] The formal titles varied from "Director of the State and Foreign Affairs" (announced March 21, 1919, by the Siberian group), to "Prime Minister" (April 11 by the Shanghai group), and to "Chief Executive" (April 23 by the group in Seoul). Yu, Yi Sung-man ui ... p.142.

[38] See a photo copy of the memorandum sent to the Japanese emperor: ibid., p.149.

[39] Rhee contacted diplomats from major countries, and targeted Chinese representatives in particular but could not get much beyond repudiation of Japanese imperialist expansion, and no support for raising the Korean issue at the conference. While he was in Geneva, he met an Austrian woman, Francesca Donner, whom he married in New York in 1934.

[40] See a reference to Rhee's letter to President Roosevelt dated May 15, 1943 in Yu, Yi Sung-man ui ... p. 246. On February 4, 1945, Rhee wrote to the Undersecretary of the State, Joseph Grew, urging a prompt recognition of the KPG to thwart the Soviet plans for a communist regime in Korea, ibid.

[41] Yi Kwang-su, Tosan An Ch'ang-ho [Tosan is An's nom de plume] (Seoul: Hungsa-dan Ch'ulp'anbu, 1998), pp. 7-8. This is the fourth printing of

the third edition. The same biography was published in 1947 by Tosan kinyom saop-hoe without revealing the author's identity.

[42] Hyung-chan Kim, Tosan Ahn Ch'ang-ho: A Profile of a Prophetic Patriot (Seoul: Tosan Memorial Foundation and others, 1996), p. 32.

[43] Ibid., p.32; Yi Kwang-su, pp. 15-16.

[44] Hyung-chan Kim, Tosan Ahn Ch'ang-Ho, p.41.

[45] Ibid. It is said that the newspaper circulated even in Korea despite Japanese attempts to suppress it.

[46] Ibid., pp. 51-54.

[47] Ibid., 56-59.

[48] Ibid., 59-64.

[49] Ibid., pp. 65-70.

[50] Ibid., pp. 70-71. An was released not only because he was not a party to the assassination conspiracy but also because the Japanese were still hoping that he would turn a collaborator.

[51] An probably had to wait in Vladivostok for a remittance of travel fund from his wife in America. See ibid., pp. 72-77.

[52] Ibid., pp. 85-89, 96-121. Also see Tosan An Ch'ang-ho Sonsaeng Kinyom Saop-hoe [An Ch'angho Memorial Foundation], Sunan ui minjok ul wihayo: Tosan An Ch'angho ui saeng'ae [In the service of the suffering nation: the life of An Ch'ang-ho] (Seoul: Tosan An Ch'angho Sonsaeng Kinyom Saop-hoe, 1999), Chronology, pp.232-259.

[53] Hyung-chan Kim, Tosan Ahn Ch'ang-Ho, pp. 89-96. For a putative verbatim record of An's close questioning of a prospective Academy member, see Yi Kwang-su, pp. 164-205.

[54] Hyung-chan Kim, Tosan Ahn Ch'ang-Ho, pp. 84-85, 123-124.

[55] Ibid., pp. 121-130. It is interesting to note that Hyung-chan Kim speculates that An would have declined any active participation in the planning of the March First Movement had he been in Korea, ibid., p.130.

[56] Ibid., pp. 135-162. An is credited for having constructed an underground communication system to keep in contact with nationalist activists in Korea. He also took on a diplomatic task of conferring with visiting United States congressmen seeking American help for the Korean cause.

[57] Ibid., pp. 180-186.

[58] Ibid., pp.186-204.

[59] Ibid., p.233 and Endnotes 61, 62 and 64 on p. 317.

[60] Ibid., pp. 235-237.

[61] Ibid., p.238. Also see Kim Ku, Paekpom Ilchi: The Aitobiography of Kim Ku, translated by Jongsoo Lee (Lanham, MD: University Press of America, 2000), p. 227.

[62] Hyung-chan Kim, Tosan Ahn Ch'ang-ho, pp. 244-245.

[63] So Yong-sok, "Pak Yong-man ui sasang kwa minjok undong: Nationalistic Movement and Thought of Yong-Man Park," Hyopsong

Nonch'ong, published by Wonsim University, No. 13 (September 2001), pp. 24-25.

64 See "The Translator's Introduction" by Han-Kyo Kim, and "Postscript" by Pak Yong-man, in Syngman Rhee, The Spirit of Independence, pp.13 and 27-28.

65 Yu Il-han and Chong Han-kyung (Henry Chung) traveled with Pak Yong-man. Pak also took Syngman Rhee's six-year old son, Pong-su, to America. So Yong-sik, p.27.

66 Dae-Sook Suh, ed. The Writings of Henry Cu Kim, pp. 256-260; So Yong-sik, pp. 27-28

67 Ibid., pp. 29-30; Dae-Sook Suh, pp. 262-263. Some of the information in these two sources are ambiguous or inconsistent and require scrutiny and additional data. Henry Cu Kim recalled that "some 100 students" enrolled in the Young Korean Military Academy but Yu Yong-ik has a more plausible number of "about 30," Yu Yong-ik, Yi Sung-man ui ..., p. 128.

68 Henry Cu Kim noted that Pak received " a B.A. degree in political science with a minor in military science" in 1912, see Dae-Sook Suh, p.189.

69In early February1913, Syngman Rhee arrived in Hawaii, apparently at Pak's urging, see ibid., p. 190.pp.Also see Yu Yong-ik, Yi Sung-man ui ..., p. 130.

70 Ibid., pp. 130-131. Henry Cu Kim recounts the details of the Pak-Rhee dispute in Dae-Sook Suh, pp. 190-196.

71Ibid., p. 273. What Pak said in the "declaration of independence" is unknown and I have not seen any reference to this declaration in other sources.

72 Kingsley K. Liu, p. 73.

73 Chong-Sik Lee, The Politics of Korean Nationalism, p. 175.

74 Ibid., pp. 151 and 175; Son Po-gi, "Pak Yong-man," in Han'guk kundae inmul paekin son (One Hundred Koreans in Modern History), published by Sin dong-a, January 1970,p..216. Lee gives the dates of April 17 and 24 for the conference, but Son states that it met in June 1919.

75 Dae-Sook Suh,pp. 273-276. See also Suh's own comments on Pak's activities in the 1920s in ibid., xiv-xv.

76 Son Po-gi, p. 216; Dae-Sook Suh, 276.

77 Koreans in the United States were able to gain a special status different from that of the Japanese during World War II. About 20 Koreans received training and worked for the Office of Strategic Services during the war. See Yu Yong-ik, Yi Sung-man ui ..., p. 196. Rhee's Korean Commission had a rival group headed by Kim Won-yong (Warren Kim) and sanctioned by the United Korean Committee operating in the wartime Washington, see Choy, pp.178-181.

78 A long-time supporter of Rhee, Ho Chong, contrasted An and Rhee in these terms, see Hyung-chan Kim, Tosan Ahn Ch'ang-ho, pp. 210-211.

79 Easurk Emsen Charr who came to America in 1904 as a small child and met An on several occasions writes how An bought a three-piece suit and

helped find a job for him in San Francisco; see Easurk Emsen Charr, <u>The Golden Mountain: The Autobiography of a Korean Immigrant, 1895-1960</u>, edited and with an introduction by Wayne Patterson, Second Edition (Urbana, IL: University of Illinois Press, 1996), pp.142-149.

[80] Hyung-chan Kim, <u>Tosan Ahn Ch'ang-ho</u>, pp. 102-105.

[81] A policy proposal submitted by Pak Yong-Man to his supporters in the Korean Independence League in July 1925 contains an explicit statement of this division of labor: "The actual campaign of the independence movement shall be entrusted to the Korean residents in the Far East, and the Korean residents in Hawaii shall provide financial support to the movement and promote education for children." See Warren Kim, pp. 63-64.

PART II.

THE PRESENT

4. The Dawn of a New Generation: The Historical Evolution of Inter-Generational Conflict and Cooperation in Korean-American Organizational Politics

Angie Y. Chung[1]

There has been an abundance of literature written on Korean immigrant entrepreneurship and immigrant adaptation processes in the U.S. within the past couple of decades but a relative scarcity of material that has looked at the political and organizational development of Koreatown. Although several works have touched on the structure of business-related associations (Min 1996; Park 1997), contemporary research on the impact of inter-generational relations on community-based organizations and Korean-American political structures is still relatively sparse. However, earlier works by Ilsoo Kim (Kim 1981) and Bong Youn Choy (Choy 1979) and more recent studies by 1.5 generation scholars like Edward T. Chang (Chang 1988; Chang 1999) and Edward J.W. Park (Park 1998; Park 1999a) have contributed to our current understandings of ethnic politics by focusing on different aspects of Korean and Korean-American leadership.

Drawing on these previous works and my own research data, the purpose of this article is to trace the historical evolution of Korean-American organizations in Los Angeles within the context of ethnic power structures and to explore the various dimensions of inter-organizational conflict and cooperation as

[1] The author would like to thank Bill Yoon, Edward Chang, Ye Hyun Chung, Min Zhou, Walter R. Allen, Edward J.W. Park, Minjeong Kim, and the book reviewers for their comments and support during this study. The research was assisted by a fellowship from the International Migration Program of the Social Science Research Council (with funds provided by the Andrew W. Mellon Foundation), resources from the Center for Comparative Immigration Studies, and a grant from the Institute of American Cultures and UCLA Asian American Studies Center. Special thanks to KIWA and KYCC for their assistance with the research. Direct correspondence to: Dr. Angie Y. Chung, Department of Sociology, University at Albany, 1400 Washington Avenue, Albany, NY 12222; aychung@albany.edu.

they have affected community politics in the post-1992 Los Angeles Riots era. While I argue that ethnic political structures in Koreatown have been formatively shaped by a variety of cultural, structural, and historical forces, my work emphasizes the central presence of what I call the traditional "ethnic elite"[2] in influencing community discourse and determining the lines of conflict and cooperation in ethnic politics. In this study, "ethnic elite" refers to individuals and groups that occupy a higher status within the political infrastructures of an ethnic community because of their greater access to the human, financial, and/or social capital resources[3] of that community.

My own research draws on multiple methodological techniques, including ethnographic fieldwork, face-to-face interviews, participant observation, small-scale surveys, and analyses of secondary data.[4] The interview sample collected between 1997 and 2001 includes a total of 60 interviewees, including affiliates of two 1.5/2nd generation Korean-American organizations—the Korean Youth and Community Center (KYCC) and the Korean Immigrant Workers Advocates (KIWA)[5], as well as a variety of other organizational representatives, church leaders, academics, youth, and immigrant business owners from various

---

[2] My investigation of hierarchies within ethnic communities is certainly not an attempt to claim that certain groups within the Korean-American community have been completely empowered by their class or gender privilege. Instead, my use of the term "ethnic elite" is meant to imply that this privilege is only relative to others within the community yet still marginalized in respect to white elite powerholders of the U.S. Indeed, in some ways, the differential distribution of power and resources within the ethnic community may be partly attributed to larger mainstream hierarchies. As such, I attempt to broaden current understandings of empowerment based on the differential access of indigenous groups to valued networks, resources and institutions within both the ethnic community and mainstream society.

[3] Social capital refers to the resources and benefits to which individuals and groups have access by being part of an ethnic-based social network.

[4] The author would like to thank Min Zhou, Walter R. Allen, Edward J.W. Park, John Horton, Abel Valenzuela, Jr., and the book editors for their comments and support during this study. The research was assisted by a fellowship from the International Migration Program of the Social Science Research Council with funds provided by the Andrew W. Mellon Foundation and a research grant from the Institute of American Cultures and UCLA Asian American Studies Center. Direct correspondence to: Dr. Angie Y. Chung, Department of Sociology, SS340, University at Albany, 1400 Washington Avenue, Albany, NY 12222; koreana_99@yahoo.com.

[5] KYCC is a non-profit social service agency assisting economically disadvantaged youths and their families, as well as a variety of other health, advocacy, community, business, housing, and employment-related services. KIWA has worked to organize, empower, and advocate for workers in the Koreatown community through legal assistance, protest demonstrations, educational seminars, and other political activities.

generational backgrounds. In addition, I draw on field observations gathered as a part-time volunteer intern for KIWA and KYCC.

Although my research includes interviews with 1st generation leadership and studies by immigrant scholars, the data relies heavily on the voices of newer generations of leadership among the 1.5 and 2nd generation. However, the hopes of this author is to contribute to the current dialogue on the political emergence of 1.5/2nd generation ethnic organizations by maintaining a balanced understanding of both the old and new waves of political leadership that have come to shape Korean-American politics today.

The Historical Development of Ethnic Organization Structures in Koreatown

Koreatown politics in the early years of its formation offer many parallels with that of other Asian immigrant enclaves in terms of its autonomous development from the rest of American society. Within the context of cultural and political isolation, Korean immigrants were able to build the foundations for ethnic political solidarity around their common experiences as immigrants, particularly in the 1970s and 1980s when the relatively small population was struggling with similar language and cultural disadvantages, marginal ethnic status in American society, spatial isolation in urban neighborhoods, and a common political cause directed against Japanese colonialism of Korea (1910-1943) (Choy 1979; Kim 1981; Takaki 1989; Yang 1982). Yet even beyond the immigration experience, the collective consciousness of the Korean immigrant community had been formatively shaped by a fierce sense of nationalistic pride and unity (as well as a deeply-seated suspicion of outsiders), stemming from a long history of oppression under colonial rule and foreign occupation in the homeland (*Ibid.*).

Whereas other immigrant populations like the Chinese community have built their political loyalties around native regional and linguistic differences, Korean immigrants in the U.S. have been bonded by the relative ethnic and cultural homogeneity of their native country. Instead, political power has been organized around other interests. In the case of Los Angeles, the development of community power structures has rested in the hands of three general elite groups – namely, church leaders, business owners, and several Seoul government-linked organizations (i.e. Korean Federation) – whose position have been strengthened and legitimated by key institutions like the Korean media and the General Consulate (Chang 1999; Park 1998). Although other groups have been instrumental behind the scenes, the upper ranks of organizational hierarchies have been generally dominated by older immigrant males from middle-class backgrounds.

Korean newspapers are replete with reports of political conflicts and alleged misconduct among the ranks of community leadership even today – a by-product of internal struggles for individual status and prestige ("Problems of the Korean-American..." 1992a; "Problems of the Korean-American..." 1992b). Based on my research and interviews, I attribute this quality of Korean immigrant politics to several external factors. First, the underlying influence of Confucianism with its emphasis on individual status and hierarchies as well as Korea's short historical experience with democratic rule has been pivotal in intensifying tensions over organizational control and individual competition for presidential positions. Culturally and politically isolated from mainstream America, community-based organizations have also relied heavily on financial resources garnered from within the Korean immigrant community, which aggravates internal resource competition and makes accountability for individual expenditures more difficult to monitor.

In his works on Korean-American church leadership, Pyong Gap Min (Min 2000) offers another compelling explanation for internal conflicts based on structural inequalities that middle- to upper-class Koreans encounter upon immigrating to the U.S. According to Min, presidential titles take on particular significance for Korean immigrants from privileged backgrounds, who while able to compensate for downward income and occupational mobility through small enterprise, are unable to recover their high social status through American organizations as a result of language/ cultural barriers and discrimination. As one 2nd generation male put it, "[With] the first generation, their status is tied to a title. If Dr. _____ didn't have that title, he's just like any other doctor." Thus, leadership positions in ethnic institutions like churches and political organizations help such members to make up for lost status upon immigration.

Despite these tensions, the overall level of ethnic political solidarity in the early stages of Korean immigrant settlement may be considered relatively strong and stable, particularly when we compare it to Korean-American politics today. Aside from personal struggles for leadership status, overt political conflicts among Korean immigrant institutions during this early period were minimized in the interests of mutual assistance, solidarity against mainstream indifference, and ethnic immigrant-based needs. Furthermore, the virtually uncontested concentration of power among the three aforementioned branches of the ethnic elite provided a stabilizing, albeit hegemonic, force over the political development of the ethnic community. Members of the ethnic elite generally dominated community discourse, leaving little room for major political dissent by internally marginalized groups like women and immigrant workers.

While the ethnic elite have been able to maintain relative control over Koreatown politics, a combination of structural and demographic changes in recent decades have laid the foundations for major changes within the political infrastructures of the Los Angeles Korean-American community that have significantly weakened their uncontested stronghold over local affairs. For one, although the community did not fully emerge until after the passage of the 1965 Immigration Act, the Korean-American population has since expanded and experienced rapid upward mobility and residential dispersal into outlying suburban neighborhoods of Los Angeles and Orange Counties, such as Fullerton, Garden Grove, and Glendale—despite the continuing presence of Korean-owned businesses and other ethnic institutions in Koreatown. Reflecting broader trends throughout Los Angeles County and California more generally, this outward movement has been accompanied by the massive influx of Latino residents and workers into the traditional ethnic enclave of Koreatown, which has transformed the neighborhood into a multi-ethnic community. Moreover, as the population matures, younger generations of leadership with new visions of political empowerment have emerged to contest the traditional values of the old ethnic elite. The leadership has been further inspired by political events in Korea, including the rise of anti-government student/labor movements in the past few decades and more recent interest in North Korea-South Korea reunification.

The combined effects of residential dispersal, class divisions, racial diversification, and generational shifts have prompted structural and ideological transformations that set the stages for major political upheavals within the community. In particular, contemporary studies have focused on three specific events throughout the 1980s and 1990s as playing pivotal roles in shaking the foundations of traditional ethnic power structures in Koreatown and re-shaping the dynamics of inter-organizational conflict and cooperation. These events include the 1980 Kwangju rebellions in South Korea (Chang 1988)[6], the Korean-Black conflicts of the 1980s (Chang 1996; Cheng and Espiritu 1989; Freer 1994; Park 1996; Yoon 1997) and early 1990s[7], and the 1992 Los Angeles Riots (Baldassare 1994; Cho 1993; Kim 1993). The first two events were critical in planting the seeds of ideological dissent against the pro-Seoul and pro-U.S. ethnic elite and setting in motion a generational shift in power that

---

[6] The Kwangju rebellions began as a major uprising among pro-democratic student leaders against military dictatorship in Korea in May of 1980 and ended as "one of the bloodiest struggles in modern Korean history."

[7] The Korean-Black conflicts refer to tensions that arose between Korean immigrant entrepreneurs and African-American patrons and activists regarding their treatment of minority customers in Los Angeles and other major cities across the nation.

would shape the community's response to the 1992 Los Angeles Riots. However, it was the climactic eruption of the 1992 Riots that had the most far-reaching effects because of its profound sentimental and financial consequences on the Korean-American communities in Los Angeles and across the nation.

Sparked by the acquittal of police officers accused of beating up a Black motorist, the 1992 Los Angeles Riots involved five days of rioting among mostly disempowered Blacks and Latinos, which among other things, resulted in the massive destruction of Korean-owned small businesses throughout Koreatown and South Central (Hazen 1992; Ong and Hee 1993; "Riots Effects...." 1996). The Riots inflicted severe psychological and financial ruins on the immigrant business owners and workers of Koreatown, who lost their lifetime investments and sole means of livelihood in a matter of days. Furthermore, the victims were left to recover on their own as a result of language and cultural barriers that prevented them from effectively drawing on mainstream institutional support (Korean-American Inter-Agency Council 1993). Because the event has received relatively wide coverage in current scholarly literature, I will limit the details of my discussion to four major consequences of the 1992 Riots on ethnic political solidarity.

United by a collective sense of loss, helplessness, and abandonment from American powerholders, the 1992 Los Angeles Riots was initially formative in strengthening a sense of ethnic consciousness among future generations of leadership and in rekindling political solidarity among Koreans in the U.S., regardless of their status, location, or background (Chang 1999; Kim 1993; Min 1996). Secondly, the L.A. Riots conferred greater power to those who were best situated to seek outside financial support in the rebuilding process and to communicate the grievances and perspectives of Korean-Americans to mainstream society – namely, native-born and native-reared Korean-American leaders (Park 1998; Park 1999a). At the same time, this new leadership also brought with it new politically liberal and Americanized ideologies about the situation of the Korean-

American community in the U.S. that often clashed with those of the traditional ethnic elite, leading to periods of conflict amidst ethnic solidarity (*Ibid.*). Finally, by placing the Korean-American community in the public spotlight, the 1992 Riots helped to unleash an influx of outside resources and institutional networks, which substantially expanded the outreach of more established 1.5/2nd generation organizations and provided internally marginalized ethnic organizations the opportunity to build a progressive base within the ethnic community. As I will discuss, these four developments would restructure the dynamics of inter-group opposition and cooperation among Korean-American organizations in Los Angeles.

The Various Dimensions of Inter-Generational Conflict in Korean-American Politics

Based on current scholarly literature and interviews with different generations of leadership, I find that the roots of inter-generational tensions in Korean-American community politics may be attributed to several factors related to the divergent cultural values of the leadership, dissimilarities in organizational structures, language barriers, differential sources of empowerment and larger structural constraints faced by the community as a whole. These factors shape almost every aspect of political life—from day-to-day interactions among community leaders to organizational strategies on various political issues to more large-scale collective efforts within the ethnic community.

The most obvious area of conflict arises from incongruities between the traditional Korean belief systems of 1st generation leadership and the more Americanized perspectives of 2nd generation leaders. As mentioned earlier, immigrant politics have been formatively shaped by Confucian values that place greater emphasis on the importance of hierarchy in inter-personal relationships. Until the 20th century, Korean society was organized around a caste-like hierarchy between the *"yangban* (upper-class elite)" and *"ssangnom* (lower-class)," in which age, education, gender and social status dictated the nature of social roles and interaction – elements of which have carried over into Korean immigrant politics today. In this light, newer immigrant leaders interpret the assertive, critical, or informal mannerisms of younger, native-born Americans toward older immigrants as signs of insolence or, at best, ignorance about their cultural roots and cherished value systems. Driven by both Confucian ideals and the middle-class "American Dream," the values of the ethnic elite are firmly based on the belief that money determines control and legitimacy in the political arena (Chung 2001). At the same time, immigrant leaders have criticized younger generations of leadership for compromising or sacrificing the interests of Korean immigrants in order to further their own political agendas in America ("A Cause for Korean-American..." 1994; Park 1999a).

In stark contrast, the Americanized values of younger, native-born/native-reared Korean-Americans are generally centered on concepts of democratic rule and equal opportunity (although how this plays out in the individual political perspectives and actions of liberal and conservative leadership varies considerably). More informed interviewees have expressed disdain or disillusionment with the alleged nepotistic and corrupt practices of the ethnic elite leadership, which they hear about or read about in ethnic newspapers. Furthermore, most do not subscribe to the deferential values of Korean immigrants, arguing that immigrant leaders are easy to criticize the hard work of 2nd generation leaders while actually doing little of the grunt work themselves. In this light, one female interviewee points out that in America, respect is earned and not automatically given. More liberal factions also criticize such beliefs as legitimizing the marginalization and subordination of women and other racial minorities. While capitalism is certainly an underlying part of conservative American values, some argue from the pragmatic stance that preoccupation with financial interests demonstrates lack of understanding of political processes in the U.S.

In this respect, one should not underestimate the significance of language barriers not only in stifling the lines of communication that might help to mediate cultural clashes between generations of leadership, but also, in shaping the power dynamics of inter-generational relationships in different contexts. To explain, language may act as an important medium through which groups are able to protect their specific interests – from something as simple as understanding information passed in public proceedings to acquiring political legitimacy or representation within specific settings to gaining general access to ethnic or mainstream institutions. An ideal example of the power of language is demonstrated in my case study on a multi-ethnic public safety coalition called the Koreatown and West Adams Public Safety Association (Chung 2001). [8]   In this particular case, I documented how 1.5 generation Korean leaders began to wield greater political influence within KOWAPSA upon incorporating non-Korean-speaking leaders into the organization, while non-English-speaking Korean immigrants were inadvertently phased out of the organization because of language barriers. Although this particular situation suggests otherwise, my interviews nevertheless indicate that 1.5 generation leaders have generally played a critical role in bridging the cultural gap and mediating power struggles between different generations of leadership because of their bilingual skills and bi-cultural orientations.

Incompatible cultural systems may also help to explain the difficulties Korean/Korean-American organizations and inter-generational coalitions have experienced in either incorporating leaders of different generational status or working with others on collaborative projects. Despite efforts to enhance inter-generational solidarity in the aftermath of the riots, the absence of an institutional infrastructure that can involve younger generations on an equal level have been a major hindrance in the formation of ethnic political solidarity (Chang 1999). Chang (1999) makes a clear distinction between 1st and 2nd generation Korean-American organizational structures with the former

---

[8] KOWAPSA was initially established in March, 1994 by first-generation Korean leaders from the Koreatown community, who after a series of lengthy negotiations, incorporated upwardly-mobile African American and Anglo residents of the West Adams neighborhood associations. The official purpose of the organization is to oversee the construction of a new community policing substation between the borders of West Adams and Koreatown.

being based on a more autocratic and hierarchical style of leadership and the latter on a more democratic model of organization-building. He argues that immigrant organizations have largely failed in their efforts to include native-born generations in the post-Riot era, because they often relegate such members to menial tasks within the organization. My interviews confirm that individual interactions and coalitional efforts between both parties are often strained by such incompatibilities in organizational style. For instance, a common complaint among younger, more Americanized interviewees was that immigrant leaders tended to join projects in order to enjoy the public spotlight while assigning the brunt of the workload to younger members. As one 2nd generation activist complained, "How do you work with the 1st generation organizations where their understanding of 'let's work together' means 'I will work the whole thing and you just do the work for me?'"

Aside from simple value differences, these cultural conflicts are also indicative of larger inequalities in the social structures of both the ethnic community and mainstream society. One of the main sources of inter-generational conflict stems from intensified competition for resources and political representation within both ethnic and mainstream societies. The origins of this conflict are two-fold: For one, the politics of ethnic solidarity in the U.S. operates in such a manner that regardless of internal differences, Korean-Americans – and in many cases, Asian-Americans in general – must compete with each other for the same limited resources and political representation, because of the way many mainstream resources are oftentimes allocated through the lens of race and/or ethnicity.

Second, the differential empowerment of 1st generation immigrants and 2nd generation Korean-Americans suggests not only that each side has something that the other side doesn't, but also, that each side *lacks* something that the other has. Such inequality is indicative of the marginal social status of Korean-Americans in different strata of ethnic and mainstream social structures. In the case of 1st generation immigrants, lower nativity status in addition to language and cultural barriers prevents them from developing valuable social and institutional ties with mainstream institutions – thus, excluding them from the benefits of political representation, mainstream resources, and outside institutional support. Although certainly empowered by their access to these very networks particularly in the post-Riots era, 2nd generation leaders do not have the same capacity to mobilize the abundant resources and networks of the ethnic community, which continue to maintain substantial value in a society that places limitations on what ethnic organizations can do.

All in all, the origins of political and ideological tensions between the 1st generation and the 2nd generation arise from both pragmatic and sentimental attachments to different imagined ethnic communities – one based on a homeland-oriented construction of the ethnic community and the other straddling the boundaries of both ethnic-America and American citizenship. From a pragmatic perspective, each side is best situated to represent different constituencies within the larger community but is most empowered within his or her respective political sphere. For instance, Korean immigrants would not tend to fare as well in a political arena in which English is the dominant language, social networks with American institutions are vital to daily operations, and prestige is determined by American norms of leadership. The same can be said for 2nd generation leaders situated within a homeland-based ethnic power structure. Furthermore, intense disagreements about where Korean-Americans should direct their time, money, and attention (i.e. homeland politics or American politics) also stem from strong emotional and psychological connections to these different imagined communities. Depending on how ethnic politics is spatially conceptualized, Korean-American leaders have utilized different strategies for participating in U.S. politics, empowering the Korean-American community, and relating to other racial minority groups, among other things (Chang 1996; Park 1999a).

The Complexities of "New" Korean-American Organizations in Post-1992 Los Angeles

Although inter-generational relations have certainly been a defining feature of contemporary community politics, the lines of inter-organizational conflict and cooperation are not always based on generational status. Differential empowerment may create the conditions not only for inter-generational conflict, but also, inter-generational dependency, such that some 1.5/2nd generation organizations must still work within the constraints of immigrant power structures. Even organizations like KIWA that have drawn negative attention from the ethnic elite and the Korean media have built a visible base of support within the broader immigrant population.[9] Furthermore, relations *among* 1.5 and 2nd generation leaders – although more stable than relations with 1st generation leaders – are still subject to the fragmentary effects of ideological dissonance and resource competition. If anything, it is more useful to conceptualize the foundations of political loyalties as being organized around relations with the traditional ethnic elite leadership as partly determined by the organization's political agenda.

My research shows that as opposed to simply supplanting one ethnic power structure with another, generational transitions in the political leadership of the ethnic community have resulted in the diversification of ethnic organizational structures that continue to operate in relation to traditional immigrant hierarchies – whether it be in a cooperative or oppositional manner. In the aftermath of the 1992 Riots, two specific types of 1.5/2nd generation organizations have assumed positions of prominence and played critical roles within Korean-American politics – namely, social service agencies and political advocacy groups. The few works that have been done on contemporary organizations in Koreatown have noted the rise of several 1.5/2nd generation organizations, including political organizations, such as the Korean-American Coalition (KAC), the Korean-American Democratic Committee (KADC), and the

---

[9] In the case of KIWA, this base of immigrant support is primarily composed of immigrant workers and progressive activists.

Korean-American Republican Association (KARA); social service agencies like the Korean Youth and Community Center (KYCC), the Korean Health, Education, Information, and Research Center (KHEIR), and the Korean-American Family Service Center (KAFSC); and advocacy groups, such as the Korean Immigrant Workers Advocates (KIWA) (Chang 1999; Park 1998). Korean-American leaders have also become involved with important alliances, such as the Multi-Cultural Collaborative (MCC) and the Asian/Pacific- Americans for a New Los Angeles (APANLA). Relative to immigrant organizations of the past, 1.5 and 2nd generation Korean-American organizations have become more heterogeneous in terms of internal structure, service provision, political visions and ideologies, support networks and their relationship with the traditional ethnic elite, partly as a result of greater access to resources and heightened political visibility after the 1992 Riots.

At the crossroads of inter-generational conflict and cooperation, 1.5/2nd generation ethnic organizations have situated themselves in different positions within the organizational structures of Koreatown, depending on how they have negotiated their relations with traditional immigrant powerholders. In general, my study (Chung, forthcoming) has found that most 1.5/2nd generation Korean-American organizations fall somewhere in a continuum between two ideal types of ethnic community-based organizations. On the one hand are those organizations that have established relatively stable (albeit not conflict-free) relations with immigrant elite groups, partly because they share certain fundamental ethnic-class values (e.g. middle-class American Dream) and also rely on them to a certain degree for political legitimacy, resources and other kinds of support from the immigrant-based population. On the other hand, we have also witnessed the recent emergence of more progressive and ideologically driven organizations whose values are more oppositional than coinciding with those of the ethnic elite and who must therefore draw on stronger networks outside the ethnic community, including transnational, Asian American, or labor-based organizations.

While they have certainly made inroads in terms of enhancing generational solidarity through intra-generational coalitions like the Korean-American Inter-Agency Council (KAIAC)[10], more subtle power differentials continue to play out even among 1.5/2nd generation ethnic organizations. Part of this difference has to do with where these organizations primarily derive their resources and support within the ethnic community and mainstream society. An organization's main base of support is determined by its leadership (including the executive director and governing board), the political agenda of the organization, the historical origins of its emergence, and the population on which it relies for most of its programs. Those who have stronger networks with the ethnic elite leadership as well as mainstream corporations and governmental institutions have tended to wield greater influence over political affairs than do those with weaker networks in these areas. My observation of alliances and political interactions among different 1.5/2nd generation organizational leaders indicates that how resources are distributed and collaborative strategies are formulated depend largely on who has the strongest influence over these types of intra-generational efforts. Of course, other features, such as the strength of the organization's leadership (i.e., the executive director), also factor into the power equation, but nevertheless, organizational support networks lay the foundations for determining status in ethnic hierarchies.

I would like to add a note that other ethnic communities have also played an increasingly crucial role in the development of Korean-American politics, especially in light of the demographic shifts and political events mentioned earlier that opened the doors of the community to the outside world. In particular, as new generations of leadership arise, ethnic community politics is more likely to be influenced by the growing presence of Latinos from the local neighborhoods of Koreatown to the larger governmental structures of Los Angeles and even California.

---

[10] KAIAC is a coalition of 1.5/2nd generation Korean American organizations that was established in the aftermath of the 1992 Riots in an effort to coordinate collective resources and prevent conflict over future "turf issues."

According to the 1990 U.S. Census, Latinos constitute more than half of Koreatown's residential population – a demographic trend that has had variable impact on newly emerging Korean-American organizations. Among the current generation, organizational responses have varied with some groups maintaining minimal contact with the Latino population, others establishing inter-organizational linkages and coalitions with other Latino groups, and still others incorporating Latinos as clientele and staff members. As of yet, however, the overall influence of the Latino community on the power structures of the Korean-American community may still be considered negligible, because of their language barriers, vulnerabilities as "non-citizens," insufficient socioeconomic resources, and minimal capacity to organize politically, among other obstacles.

Conclusion

As the tragedies of the 1992 Los Angeles Riots begin to fade into the distant memories of our past, our community may either choose to forget the mistakes that led up to this key turning point in Korean-American history or find ways to grow collectively from what we have learned. In particular, we must ask ourselves how we can change in order to find greater political empowerment both as a community in itself as well as a community embedded within the broader American society. In many respects, both generations of leadership have made significant headway, yet history shows how this progress has been riddled with periods of conflict amidst cooperation and inequality amidst solidarity.

In the earlier years of its political formation, the ethnic power structures of Koreatown were governed by the three branches of the ethnic elite – namely, church leaders, business owners, and certain homeland-linked organizational presidents – whose authority both ensured stability and stifled opposition from marginalized groups. Within the context of various structural and demographic shifts, the Kwangju Rebellions, the Korean-Black conflicts, and the 1992 Los Angeles Riots opened the doors of opportunity by challenging the pro-Seoul, pro-U.S. ideologies of the ethnic elite, increasing representation among 1.5 and 2nd generation organizations, and opening the doors to mainstream society and its abundant resources. This transformation brought about a significant shift in community power structures that ultimately heightened inter-generational conflict and introduced new forms of internal inequality based on traditional hierarchies and organizational partisanship. At the same time, new ethnic organizations have shown significant resilience and dynamism by adapting their political strategies to these internal hierarchies and drawing on alternative sources of support. Hence, ethnic politics in Koreatown is shown to be characterized by fluctuating periods of inter-group tension as well as ethnic solidarity.

What are the implications of these findings on current literature? Traditional studies on assimilation argue that immigrant adaptation is a uni-directional straight-line process, whereby immigrants begin on the peripheries of the ethnic enclave economy but are eventually able to achieve full cultural and socioeconomic integration into mainstream social structures over generations by foregoing most ethnic affiliations (Gordon 1964). From the perspective of ethnic politics, this would be manifested by the simple transferal of power from the 1st generation to the 2nd generation, the increasing fragmentation of political leadership, and eventually, the dissolution of ethnic politics as we know it (Abelmann and Lie 1995). Instead, my research finds that ethnic ties are still critical to the political development and individual progress of Korean-Americans by consolidating crucial resources and networks that each generation lacks but the other has. In simplest terms, the 1st generation is best able to mobilize the resources and networks of the immigrant population, whereas the 1.5 and 2nd generation are well situated to tap into non-co-ethnic networks and mainstream institutions.

At the same time, ethnic politics is much more complex in that it is characterized by significant heterogeneity and inequality both within and across different generations of political leadership. On the one hand, one may argue that it is this diversity of political perspectives that makes for a rich and fruitful dialogue in the political arena by bringing a voice to both the empowered and the marginalized. At the same time, I would contend that the ultimate goal would be not only to negotiate the vast cultural differences that divide our political leadership but also, to find a way to maximize the effective use of our ethnic and mainstream resources in such a way that power is granted to all groups within the ethnic community and not only its powerholders, both new and old. Only in this way can the Korean-American community rightfully begin to demand full equality and respect within the broader American society.

References

_____ . 1994. "A Cause for Korean-American Celebration -- and Controversy." *Los Angeles Times*, (13 May), B-3.

Abelmann, Nancy and John Lie. 1995. *Blue Dreams: Korean-Americans and the Los Angeles Riots*. Cambridge, MA: Harvard University Press.

Baldassare, Mark. 1994. *Los Angeles Riots: Lessons for the Urban Future*. Boulder, CO: Westview Press.

Chang, Edward T. 1988. ""Korean Community Politics in Los Angeles: The Impact of the Kwangju Uprising." *Amerasia Journal* 14 (1): 51-67.

_____ . 1996. "Toward Understanding Korean and African American Relations." *OAH Magazine of History*: 67-70.

_____ . 1999. "The Post-Los Angeles Riot Korean-American Community: Challenges and Prospects." *Korean and Korean-American Studies Bulletin* 10 (1-2): 6-26.

Cheng, Lucie and Yen Espiritu. 1989. "Korean Businesses in Black and Hispanic Neighborhoods: A Study on Intergroup Relations." *Sociological Perspectives* 32 (4): 521-34.

Cho, Sumi K. 1993. "Korean-Americans Vs. African Americans: Conflict and Construction." Pp. 196-211 in *Reading Rodney King, Reading Urban Uprising*, edited by Robert G. Williams. New York, NY: Routledge.

Choy, Bong-youn. 1979. *Koreans in America*. Chicago, IL: Nelson-Hall.

Chung, Angie Y. 2001. "The Powers That Bind: A Case Study of the Collective Bases of Coalition-Building in Post-Civil Unrest Los Angeles." *Urban Affairs Review* 37 (2): 205-26.

_____ . Forthcoming. "Social Capital Strategies and the Ethnic Elite: Explaining Ethnic Political Solidarity in Post-1992 Koreatown." Under Review.

Freer, Regina. 1994. "Black-Korean Conflict." Pp. 175-203 in *The Los Angeles Riots: Lessons for the Urban Future*, edited by Mark Baldassare. Boulder, CO: Westview Press.

Gordon, Milton. 1964. *Assimilation in American Life: The Role of Race, Religion, and National Origins*. New York, NY: Oxford University Press.

Hazen, Don. 1992. *Inside the Los Angeles Riots: What Really Happened and Why It Will Happen Again*. New York, NY: Institute for Alternative Journalism.

Kim, Elaine H. 1993. "Home Is Where the *Han* Is: A Korean-American Perspective on the Los Angeles Upheavals." Pp. 215-35 in *Reading Rodney King, Reading Urban Uprising*, edited by Robert G. Williams. New York, NY: Routledge.

Kim, Ilsoo. 1981. *New Urban Immigrants: The Korean Community in New York*. Princeton, NJ: Princeton University Press.

Korean-American Inter-Agency Council. 1993. *Korean-American Inter-Agency Council Press Packet*. Los Angeles, CA

Min, Pyong G. 1996. *Caught in the Middle: Korean Communities in New York and Los Angeles*. Berkeley, CA: University of California Press.

_____ . 2000. "The Structure and Social Functions of Korean Immigrant Churches in the United States." Pp. 372-91 in *Contemporary Asian America: A Multidisciplinary Reader*, edited by Min Zhou and James V. Gatewood. New York, NY: New York University Press.

Ong, Paul and Suzanne Hee. 1993. *Losses in the Los Angeles Civil Unrest.* Los Angeles, CA: UCLA Center for Pacific Rim Studies.

Park, Edward J. W. 1998. "Competing Visions: Political Formation of Korean-Americans in Los Angeles, 1992-1997." *Amerasia Journal* 24 (1): 41-57.

_____ . 1999a. "Friends or Enemies?: Generational Politics in the Korean-American Community in Los Angeles." *Qualitative Sociology* 22 (2): 161-75.

Park, Kyeyoung. 1996. "Use and Abuse of Race and Culture: Black-Korean Tension in America." *American Anthropologist* 98 (3): 492-99.

_____ . 1997. *The Korean-American Dream: Immigrants and Small Business in New York City.* Ithaca, NY: Cornell University Press.

_____ . 1992a. Problems of the Korean-American Community: Irresponsible Operation of Organizations. *Korea Times,* (8 April), A7.

_____ . 1992b. Problems of the Korean-American Community: Mismanagement of Donations. *Korea Times,* (9 April), A-9.

_____ . 1996. Riots' Effects Are Still Smoldering in Koreatown. *Los Angeles Times,* (29 April), A-1.

Takaki, Ronald T. 1989. *Strangers From a Different Shore.* New York, NY: Penguin Books.

Yang, Eun S. 1982. "Koreans in America, 1903-1945." Pp. 5-22 in *Koreans in Los Angeles: Prospects and Promises,* edited by Eui-Young Yu, Earl H. Phillips, and Eun S. Yang. Los Angeles, CA: Center for Korean-American and Korean Studies.

Yoon, In Jin. 1997. *On My Own: Korean Businesses and Race Relations in America.* Chicago, IL: University of Chicago Press.

5. In the Name of the Family: Gender and Immigrant Small Business Ownership

Eunju Lee

> I now come in five days a week. Sometimes I tend the cash register. For most of the time, I oversee employees on displaying, pricing, and doing inventories of stock.... My presence is still needed here for the store is still new. This is a fast-moving, cash business.... If the owner keeps an eye on the business, it certainly gets more profitable.

- Mrs. Kim, Wife of a New Jersey grocery owner

Although young and energetic, Mrs. Kim was nonetheless tired of putting long hours into her family's grocery business, which remains open from eight in the morning to eight at night, seven days a week. She was looking forward to cutting back her workload. About a year and a half ago, the Kim family relocated to New Jersey and started a new store in a middle-class neighborhood, tucked away in a strip mall. Employing eight full-time workers, the new store has been doing well enough over the last year for Mrs. Kim to take the weekend off. Even with the five days per week schedule, she spends more than sixty hours per week at the store. Still, this is quite an improvement compared to her early days of marriage, when she worked seven days a week at the family's first store in Brooklyn.

Mrs. Kim's story typifies the experiences of thousands of wives who are working in Korean immigrant businesses. First, she worked for wages and contributed to the household income before the family decided to open its own business. Without her wages, it would have been much more difficult to save money for start-up capital. Second, her unpaid and committed labor has been crucial for the store to remain competitive all these years. To make her labor available, Mrs. Kim even sent her first-born child to Korea to be raised by his grandparents. The savings in labor costs had enabled the Kim family to maximize profits, which were later used to purchase a bigger store. Third, as the store remains profitable, she plans to take a lesser role in its day-to-day operation. She hopes to pay more attention to her kids. Finally, despite her past and present contributions to the family business, she is not the owner. Her husband is registered as the sole owner. Since she does not share the business ownership with her husband, she, like thousands of immigrant wives working in their family businesses, is "officially" considered as a family worker.

In the literature of immigrant entrepreneurship, women like Mrs. Kim receive little attention because their ties to businesses are informal, complicated, and fluid. While these women are sometimes considered as self-employed for analytical purposes (Sanders and Nee, 1996), the significance of their presence is largely limited to their role as a source of family labor.

The significance of family labor is not in dispute. Research consistently emphasizes that family labor allows the immigrant small business to remain competitive by reducing operating costs and increasing profitability through invisible layers of benefits. Particularly since many immigrant businesses are likely to operate without paid employees (Light et al., 1994), family labor becomes crucial to their survival. Sanders and Nee best capture its significance in the following:

> The family supports self-employment by furnishing labor and enabling the pooling of financial resources... [T]he ability to rely on family labor significantly reduces operating costs. Because they have a greater stake in the success of the business, family workers are more productive than non-family labor when hourly wages are low. Furthermore, family labor can be trusted to handle sensitive transactions in which the risk of opportunism and malfeasance is high (Sander and

Nee, 1996, p. 233).

The problem is that under the banner of family labor women's contributions, especially those of wives of the owners, have become minimized and distorted. As the case of Mrs. Kim demonstrates, the wives are not just family workers. Treating these women as a source of family labor grossly oversimplifies the extent of their contributions to immigrant small businesses.

Interestingly, surprisingly few empirical studies are available on the subject despite the wide recognition of the importance of family labor. To the best of my knowledge, only one study has given serious attention to the subject, focusing on children's labor in Chinese takeout restaurants (Song, 1997). Beyond its customary nodes, the literature is largely devoid of further discussion of family labor. If the subject is mentioned, it is in the context of the family as in the above. Because family labor is conceptualized as a resource derived from the family, the natural tendency of this view is to examine the *family*, not family labor itself. Consequently, the nature and utilization of family *labor* in immigrant small businesses remain largely unexamined.

The current theorization of family labor tends to focus on its utility and thus fails to see the connection between ownership and family labor. Scholars pay little attention to the subtle reality that who provides family labor is determined by the identity of the owner. Only by realizing the connection between the source of family labor and the ownership of the business can we begin to question the gendered nature of family labor and its connection to patriarchal gender relations in immigrant families. Phizacklea (1988) summarizes the essence of the problem in the following: "What is usually glossed over in the literature is the extent to which this 'family' and 'community' labour is female and subordinated to very similar patriarchal control mechanisms in the workplace as in the home" (p. 31).

There is considerable evidence that this pattern of the husband as owner and the wife as family worker prevails in Korean immigrant businesses. Yoon (1997) found that 50 percent of his Chicago sample and 70 percent of the L.A. sample had wives working in the stores. Young's study (1983) of the early years of Korean green grocers documents the critical role of owners' wives in these businesses. Although these studies recognize the wives' roles in businesses, they fail to see the underlying gender dynamics that produced uneven paths in immigrant small business ownership. Gender is a missing link in our current conceptualization of family labor in immigrant small business ownership.

This paper argues that the current thinking on immigrant small business ownership is largely based on the experiences of men who are officially recognized as owners and that gender profoundly shapes the decisions and outcomes related to immigrant small business ownership. In its examination of the processes of opening a small business among Korean immigrants, it asks why and how Korean women assume the role of family workers while their husbands become owners of small businesses. By doing so, it demonstrates how patriarchal gender relations are the key to an understanding of the making of Korean small business owners.

Korean Immigrants in the New York City Metropolitan Area
From the turn of the century to the present, New York City has witnessed the influx of immigrants of many nationalities and the subsequent formation of diverse ethnic communities within its environment. Despite its long history as the most prominent city for receiving immigrants, however, Korean immigrants were virtually nonexistent in New York City until the late 1960s (I. Kim, 1981). Historically, Asian immigration was limited to the West Coast and Hawaii, where a small number of different Asian groups entered in succession to avoid the hostility and restriction of native-born whites (Cheng and Bonacich, 1984). Thus, few Asians settled on the East Coast until recently, with the exception of the residents of a few Chinatowns in major cities.

The growth of various Asian ethnic communities in New York City and its surrounding areas has been generated by immigrants arriving after the 1965 Immigration Reform (Wong, 1986). With the influx of new immigrants, the New York City metropolitan area has recently emerged as one of the regions most heavily populated by Asians (Kitano and Daniel, 1995).[1] Within a little more than thirty years of immigration, the population of Koreans in the New York metropolitan area has dramatically increased, from a few thousand in the late 1960s to more than 100,000 in 2000. According to the 2000 Census, the New York – New Jersey CMSA contains the second largest Korean population after Los Angeles,[2] totaling 170,509.

The influx of Korean immigrants has been accompanied by Koreans entering retail and service businesses. In just three decades, the presence of Korean-run businesses like dry-cleaning stores, produce and fish markets, and nail salons have become ubiquitous. According to one estimate, in 1990 at least 30 percent of Korean immigrants in New York were self-employed or worked as family workers in small businesses (Light and Roach, 1996). Some scholars report even higher rates of small business ownership based on surveys (Min, 1996; Light and Bonacich, 1988).

As of the late 1990s, it was estimated that Koreans owned and operated 350 garment manufacturing firms; 3,000 grocery stores (including liquor); 2,000 dry cleaners; 800 fish markets; 2,500 nail salons, and 1,400 retail produce stores in the New York City metropolitan area.[3] There are numerous other types of businesses

---

1. Even old Chinatowns were revived after the 1965 immigration reform. Zhou's study (1989) demonstrates that despite its long history, New York City's Chinatown was in decline before 1965. Without the influx of new immigrants, it would not have remained as a viable community.

2. These two communities contained almost 37 percent of Korean immigrants in 1980 (Sakong, 1990).

3. There are several sources for these numbers. First, Goldberg (1995) reports that "1,400 produce stores; 3,500 groceries [including liquor]; 2,000 dry cleaners; 800 seafood stores; and 1,300 nail salons" are owned by Koreans (p. 45). The estimates of ethnic business associations are similar to these numbers (*Korean Times*, 15 April, 25 May, and 25 July 1996). Based on his interviews with leaders of Korean business associations, Min (1996) reports

in which Korean immigrants are found in large numbers,[4] totaling up to more than 9,500 stores, according to various sources (Min, 1996; Goldberg, 1995). This figure truly demonstrates both the extent and the selectivity of entrepreneurship among Korean immigrants.

Data and Methodology
The primary concern of this study is to gain insights on how gender shapes the process of opening and running small businesses among Korean immigrants in the New York City metropolitan area. For this end, I adopted a method of ethnographic fieldwork, which lasted about nine months between 1997 and 1998. The fieldwork consists of in-depth interviews with owners and their family members and observations at the seventy Korean-owned small businesses and visiting Korean business associations and talking with informers. I also attended events and functions related to Korean small businesses such as an annual banquet for nail salon owners and workers.

Recognizing there are variations and differences in the processes and outcomes of small business ownership by industry, this study largely selected businesses belonging in the following three industries: produce and grocery retail stores, dry cleaning services, and nail salons. These three industries are not only considered "flagship" industries for Korean immigrants at present, and readily recognized as the emblems of Korean immigrant entrepreneurship, but together they amount to more than 7,000 businesses. By limiting the participating businesses to

---

there were 2,200 import retail and wholesale businesses; 1,500 dry cleaners; 400 nail salons; 350 garment manufacturers; 2,950 produce and grocery/liquor retail stores owned by Koreans in 1991. The estimate for nail salons is based on the numbers provided by two Korean nail salon associations.

4. Based on interviews with leaders of business associations, Min (1996) estimates that 15,000 businesses are operated and owned by Koreans in the area. This number includes import retail and wholesale, and clothing, shoe, and jewelry retail. The number is only an estimate and may not include members of most recent business associations. For example, the recently formed Korean One-Hour Photo Association claims 250 members.

those in three industries, I hoped to closely observe patterns in the processes and outcomes of ownership within each industry.

Given the sheer number of the businesses in these three industries, I employed two strategies for selecting the study sample. First, I chose areas where all three types of businesses could be easily located. Second, these areas should be scattered around the metropolitan areas reflecting variations in the characteristics of clients such as income and race. In the end, ten such areas were targeted.

Over the course of the fieldwork, I visited about ninety-five businesses, seventy of which were included in the final sample. Those not included in the study sample fell into the following three situations: (1) the owner was not Korean; (2) the owner was rarely present at the store, leaving much of the day-to-day operation to the Korean manager; and (3) the owner refused to participate. Except for twelve cases in the third category,[5] other situations turned out to be very useful. At a number of businesses belonging in the first two categories, I was able to talk to non-Korean owners, Korean managers, or non-Korean workers.

The in-depth interviews with the owner and his/her spouse were conducted in Korean and took place at the business, focusing on the experiences of each owner and his/her spouse, including the detailed accounts of the process of opening their own business, the daily routines of running the business, and roles and responsibilities both at the business and at home. When both the wife and husband are present at the business, one person became the primary respondent and the other became the secondary based on their availability and accessibility. At most of the participating businesses, I also collected observational data that recorded interactions between the husband and the wife, workers and the owners, and, to a lesser extent, customers and owners. In most cases, business owners and their family members welcomed

---

5. In my fieldwork notebook, I kept a short description of these stores. However, I missed two or three.

and accepted my presence largely because of my "insider" status. Consequently, I was able to observe these interactions in natural settings.

Patterns of Running Korean Small Businesses
When gender is brought into the discussion of immigrant small business ownership and family labor, it creates opportunities for new inquiries. Instead of accepting the status quo, new inquiries raise questions of why and how. For example, why are women such as Mrs. Kim not considered owners? What is the typical arrangement of using family labor in Korean businesses? What is the practice of treating wives as family workers based on? How do men and women accept this practice? As the first step to answer these questions, this section examines how gender determines men and women's status in immigrant small business by looking at the relationships between patterns of family involvement and ownership.

As the phrase "all in the family" sums up (Awanohara, 1991), both media and academia present an image of family members harmoniously working together to sustain a family business. Most Korean businesses do not fit into this popular model of operation; the reality is more complex. Regardless of the family's involvement, Korean businesses depend upon paid employees as much as they do on the family. Typically, a married couple runs a business together with and without the help of paid employees. It appears that there are three types of family involvement in the operation of Korean businesses: all in the family, no family labor, married couple operation.

"All in the Family" Operation
Despite the popular image of an immigrant business in which all family members are working together to keep the business going, this type of family labor utilization is not as prevalent as we are led to believe. In Korean small businesses, children and extended family members have a diminished role in day-to-day operations. In fact, the interview data and the fieldwork experience suggest that this pattern is far less prevalent than businesses that operate without involvement of any family member.

About 15 percent of the businesses in the sample (eleven out of seventy stores) had a kin member (other than the owner's spouse) working at the business.[6] The business involvement of kin is arranged under a number of different circumstances. One such circumstance involves on-the-job training of recently arrived relatives, who spend months or sometimes years working for a family member's business. Indeed, many of the owners in the study were themselves at one time the newly arrived kin who benefited from this situation. Korean owners help kin by hiring them, but it is not always to the owners' benefit.

Another circumstance for kin involvement seems to be hardship. Even with hard work and long hours, not all businesses become prosperous. A few owners, struggling to survive, received help from extended family members. In one case, a mother worked in her daughter's tiny dry-cleaning drop-off store. When her daughter left the store to get some coffee, the mother confided in me how much she disliked working there. She felt that she had no choice but to help her daughter, who was divorced and had few resources. If she could, she would rather watch her grandchildren.

Finally, there is the "all in the family" style of operation where multiple family members – siblings or adult children – work together at one business. Only three cases in the sample of 70 businesses are qualified as true "all in the family" operations. Interestingly, these three cases were found in the produce/grocery industry, which is considered the most labor intensive, even by Korean immigrants well known for their willingness to work hard.

Not coincidentally, all three had an aging patriarchal father registered as owner. At the Lee family grocery in New Jersey, the male head of the family runs the store with help from his wife and

---

6. Yoon's (1997) survey of Korean business owners in Chicago also shows the figure at 11 percent.

his three adult children. While he firmly believes that working together is in the best interest of his family, his family members were simply following his wishes. His daughter, who would like to find another job, quipped, "my father is the boss" responding to a question on work hours of various family members. She indicated that he is the one who determines how the business should run. It is questionable how profitable it is to fully mobilize family members. The following response from a young man, working as "manager" at the store owned by his father further demonstrates that patriarchal family relations are at the center of this type of business operation:

> Even on Sundays, I attend church only in the morning and work in the afternoon. Since my old father is working, it is difficult for me to rest.... My father oversees most of the business transactions including restaurant supplies. He is experienced and has a control of this business, so the business is doing well. He wants me to inherit this store.... I do not want to disappoint him but I am not sure this is what I want to do.

In general, Korean immigrants do not depend upon their dependent children as a significant source of help. While children's help is not unheard of,[7] their labor contributions are quite limited in the overall scheme of the business operation, unlike children of Chinese immigrants in the takeout businesses in Song's (1997) study. Why, then, are Korean immigrants different from the Chinese immigrants? First, unlike owners in Chinese take-away businesses, many Korean owners are largely of middle-class origin and most have a basic understanding of English. Thus, they do not depend on their kids as translators. Second, Korean parents, many of whom are college graduates, seem to put the highest priority on children's education. Finally, having

---

7. It is known that some children do provide more than token help often during their teen years or in college. Their labor contributions are substantial on weekends or during school vacations. However, I did not encounter such cases in my sample.

children work after school is more logistically difficult for Korean business owners since their stores are not located in the same neighborhoods as their homes.

Korean immigrant owners tend to view occasional help by older children as more an expression of their filial gratitude than a real source of help. One couple, running a dry-cleaning shop, allowed their teenage children to help with bagging finished clothes, and to communicate with customers on weekends. The wife explained that asking children for help is "a way of teaching kids to appreciate how hard the parents have to work in this country to provide better opportunities for them."

No Family Labor
A significant minority of the Korean businesses in the study did not have any family member involved in the business. They were most likely to rely on paid help. This somewhat unexpected trend is not limited to the study sample, however. During fieldwork, I frequented many Korean-owned businesses that did not fall into the scope of my research and were not included in the final sample of seventy businesses. The variety of business choices available to Korean immigrants was impressive. Among these businesses were a stationery store, a one-hour photo shop, a corner coffee shop, and a Dunkin' Donuts franchise. Equally surprising was the diversity of business practices. While family labor remains an important part of the typical Korean-owned small business, there was an increasing trend to run businesses exclusively with paid help. In a few such cases, owners were not even present for most of the business hours but left the day-to-day operation to hired Korean managers.

Out of seventy stores in the sample, twenty-six were run without the involvement of any family member. Most of the owners in this type of operation were married and some had grown children or other extended family members living in the New York metropolitan area. Thus, the non-involvement of family members was not due to the lack of their availability.

The businesses without family workers were concentrated in the nail salon industry where a majority of the owners are women. The absence of family is not limited to the nail salon industry, however. I found that both small and large grocery stores and a few of the dry-cleaning stores operated with no family worker. Without the family's help, these businesses depended on paid employees, both Korean and non-Korean. Paid employees have been an important part of Korean immigrant businesses from very early on. In this sense, Korean small businesses are characteristically different from the typical immigrant small business that has no paid employee (Light et al., 1994).

Running a business without the involvement of a spouse or other family member is certainly not the norm, but nonetheless is a growing trend. Further, the fact that this practice is prevalent among women-owned businesses such as nail salons suggests that reliance on family labor is indeed tied to ownership of the business.

Married Couple Operations
In about of the half of the businesses (thirty-three out of seventy), both the husband and the wife were involved. With or without paid employees, this is the most typical arrangement for Korean small businesses, though again, many of these businesses did have paid employees. In fact, the figure from the study sample underestimates the prevalence of married couple operations. The purposive inclusion of women-owned nail salons and small dry-cleaning drop-off stores in the study arbitrarily lowered the representation of businesses that would fit into this category. Inferring from other studies and field experience, this type of operation is applicable to more than 60 percent of all Korean small businesses.

Most of the wives in this situation were as involved as their husbands in the day-to-day tasks of running their business. About three quarters of the wives in this group worked more than five days a week. A few couples commuted together morning and evening, indicating identical work hours. Regardless of the degree of involvement, however, these wives were officially considered as family workers since none of them was registered as owner.

The official designation of these wives as family workers tends to see their contributions as serving limited outcomes: *e.g.*, saving the cost of labor and providing a source of trusted help. Interviews with these women, however, indicate that the extent of their contributions is far greater. The responsibilities of most wives were as comprehensive as those of their husbands and were carved out to fit into a larger scheme of business operation.

While these wives fulfilled different tasks than their husbands, depending on the industry they were in, they had a comprehensive grasp of their businesses. This is why the presence of the wife is more than just a source of labor. Having another person in charge allows the immigrant small business to operate efficiently with a limited workforce, and can further enable them to expand beyond one store. In one case in the study, a couple that ran a dry-cleaning store with two part-time workers was able to buy a coin-operated laundry mart a few blocks away from their main store. They did not hire a new worker for the laundry mart, but continued to manage both stores between the two of them. While the husband goes out to check the machines at the laundry, the wife stays at the main store.

Even for thriving businesses, where saving on labor costs is not a paramount concern, the complementary roles of the wives are important to the operation. One of the more established produce stores employed a full-time cashier. The owner's wife comes in for a few hours a day just to take care of banking and paperwork. However, on Mondays, when the regular cashier is off, the wife works twelve hours on the cash register. She would like to hire a part-time cashier to work on Mondays, but that has not been easy. Meanwhile, she continues to fill in to smooth the business operation.

The following case may best illustrate the typical experiences of wives working in the businesses owned by their husbands. Mrs.

Hong has adapted her work schedule to cope with the demands of running a retail fish business. Her husband normally starts his weekday around 3 a.m., leaving his Brooklyn home for a trip to the Fulton Fish Market.[8] He arrives at his store in Queens between 7:30 and 8:30 a.m. and with two Latino workers, prepares the fish for the day's sale. Mrs. Hong arrives at the store around 9 a.m. and works until around 7 p.m. She runs the store much of the day on her own, working at the cash register and supervising the two workers while her husband rests in the back. From 4 p.m. until 7 p.m., the business is the most brisk, and all four, two workers and Mrs. Hong and Mr. Hong, work nonstop. On most evenings, she heads for home before her husband, leaving the responsibilities of closing to her husband. Although she and her husband are physically in the store at the same time, each has a different clock to follow and different tasks to perform.

In a majority of the businesses, the experiences of these "family workers" were similar to that of Mrs. Hong. Just like their husbands, they had multiple responsibilities and oversaw the overall operation of their businesses. Wives like Mrs. Hong are not family workers in a strict sense. They may not be legal owners, but they were certainly *de facto* co-owners.

Husbands as Owners and Wives as Family Workers
Married couples ran a majority of Korean businesses, where the husband is considered as owner and the wife as family worker. Even when multiple family members worked jointly in the business, ownership belonged to the male head of the household – the husband, the father of the family. The profile of the study sample reveals no surprises in this regard. Men were sole legal owners of all groceries, except for one, which had been incorporated. The same was true for the full-size dry-cleaning stores, except one that a widowed mother and her married son operated together. Drop-off shops and nail salons were the exceptions, with women largely retaining ownership.

---

8. The wholesale fish market located at the edge of downtown Manhattan near the restored Seaport Museum area.

The concept of the family business is central to understanding why the man becomes the owner in a business run by a married couple. The practice is palatable to immigrants because of its tacit assumptions that both the husband and the wife are working for the sake of the family business and that legality of ownership is largely a matter of paperwork. What, then, is a family business and how is it different from "other" businesses?

To cite one owner, "a family business should at least make profits equivalent to good salaries for two people, the husband and the wife." Other owners used the term in English since no similar term could be found in Korean to refer to businesses run by married couples. Interestingly, some respondents seemed to use the term, "family business" to make a distinction from "a woman's business" although they did not seem to believe that there was such thing as "a man's business."

On the surface, the distinction seems to be based on how much income the business can generate. Some male owners regarded women-owned businesses as insufficient to produce a decent income and support the whole family. On average, the women-owned stores required smaller start-up capital and generated fewer profits than the men-owned stores. However, about a half of the women-owned nail salons were quite successful, so they defied the immigrants' characterization of "a woman's business" in terms of business volume and profits. In fact, some fancy nail salons in the study were located in wealthy neighborhoods of Manhattan and they were often bigger than some groceries in the study. As some nail salon owners unwittingly acknowledged, the income generated by their business was the primary source for the family's living. According to informants, many nail salons have reached a level of a success coveted by many immigrant businesses.

The real basis for this distinction is simple. The difference between a family business and a woman's business really rests on whether the male head of the family owns and is involved in the business. As long as a woman is the sole owner and in charge of a store, it becomes a woman's business no matter how profitable it is. In contrast, if the husband is involved in the operation of a business in any extent, the store is perceived as a family business. Groceries, dry-cleaning stores, and fish markets were considered family businesses while nail salons were generally viewed as women's businesses.

Under the banner of the family business, it becomes legitimate for the husband to claim the ownership of the business and solicit support from his wife. This is not to say that the wife is not eager to offer her help. In fact, many of the wives were willing partners even before their family businesses were open. They continued to provide various forms of support and endured double burdens of responsibilities at home and at work. In contrast to the wives in family businesses, the husbands were largely removed from women-owned businesses. As the table summarizes, only male owners in family businesses call upon their wives for assistance.

Table 5.1 Utilization of Family Labor by Industry and Gender of Legal Owner

	Nail		Groceries		Dry Cleaning		Other	
Owner' Gender	M	W	M	W	M	W	M	W
Extended		2	5			3		1
No family labor		15	5		3	3		
Spouse	4		12		14		4	

Notes: M for Male Owner and W for Women Owner

Four nail salons listing men as legal owners are particularly intriguing examples of how the Korean immigrant community legitimizes male authority and perceives women's roles in immigrant business. All of these male owners are the husbands of women who actually run the salons and who have worked for many years as manicurists. The women were physically present during most of the store's operating hours and provided services to customers. Mrs. Park is one of them. When I asked her about her husband's responsibilities, she was quite amused and explained as follows:

> My husband helps me out here and there. He provides rides to the employees of this salon before and after work. Nowadays, if you want to attract workers to a store in Brooklyn you have to offer pick-up and drop-off services. The subway ride takes too long and the workers often carry cash. During the day, he is busy with Nail Salon Association's affairs and South Korean politics.... While he is out, he sometimes shops for nail supplies.

Apparently, after providing the morning rides to her and her workers,[9] he rarely spent time in the store. Her husband was not, in fact, involved in South Korean politics or the New York Korean Nail Salon Association in any meaningful way at all. What he did outside the store was rather vague and was largely limited to socializing with other Koreans. This imaginary "political" work, however, was their way of rationalizing his absence from the store, while still justifying his authority.

As in the other three cases, Mr. Park legally owns the business although he is only marginally involved in the store's daily operation. Mr. Park has a nail license, but he has never practiced the trade.[10] Mrs. Park, on the other hand, is proficient in all the

---

9. Providing rides is not required, but is considered a way of attracting and retaining good workers for salons located in less desirable neighborhoods. This is sometimes a necessary precaution since workers are paid in cash and many have long subway rides home to Queens late in the evening.

10. New York State requires a license for anyone working in nail salons. After hours of training, one must pass a written exam administered in Korean. Before the legislation became effective in 1994, New York State allowed a temporary reprieve for those who could provide documentation on work experience. Mr. Park attained the license through this process with false documentation.

required skills for nail service and knows her customers by their first names. Her familiarity with the routine and manners indicate that she was the *de facto* owner of this thriving store. She worked in the very same store as manicurist for many years until the previous owner – her boss at the time – offered to sell the store to her two years ago. When the deal came through, her husband was registered as the owner.

This Brooklyn nail salon was one of the businesses that initially responded to the pilot survey. Mr. Park filled out the survey, both his information and hers. Interestingly, he listed his wife as manager and minimized her role while embellishing his daily responsibilities. As the Parks' case demonstrates, the wife's status as the source of family labor (or elevated status of "manager") in her husband-owned store has little to do with her true responsibilities and contributions. Instead, it is dictated by the way the husband exercises his authority and power by assuming ownership. To put it simply, when the husband becomes the owner, his wife automatically becomes the family worker. When the wife becomes the owner, however, her husband never becomes the family worker in a Korean small business. This would undermine his authority if he were to assume the subordinate role of "family worker."

Ownership and Patriarchal Gender Relations
The common practice of husband ownership of a family business is not a just a matter of paperwork. Not only does it reflect the cultural customs of Korean immigrants, but it also reveals men and women's deep-seated values regarding family relations. Only when these issues are examined, can one understand why the wives abstain from claiming ownership to which they are more than entitled. Some may easily dismiss their decision as cultural. Rather than simply some long-held, seemingly "cultural" attitude of deference, however, this arrangement is a product of patriarchal gender relations that has been reconfigured in the new social context of immigrant family business.

Basis of Ownership

While it is reasonable to assume that men's ownership of family businesses is based on their ownership of a previous store, their role in capital accumulation, or training and experience, it appears that the claim of ownership is not related to whether it is legitimated by such requirements. In fact, several cases showed the opposite.

Many of the Korean immigrants came to the United States as a family unit since marriage likely preceded immigration (see Chapter 3). As Park's (1997) study and others have demonstrated, marriage is a prerequisite for Korean immigrants to open a small business. In fact, in my study sample, only one case among the businesses operated by married couples showed that the husband opened his first business with his brothers before getting married. Thus, previous ownership outside or prior to marriage is unlikely.

In addition, claiming ownership bears little relation to how the start-up capital has been raised. In some cases, wives borrowed or received large sums of money from their families to secure start-up capital or to purchase the new business. Such was the case in Hannah's experience:

> As newlyweds, we came to New York for our college degrees but soon found juggling work and study too difficult. After a year of trying, we decided to make money first and then go back to school full-time. My parents in Korea were not keen on the idea, but they sent us a large sum of money for the start-up. It was like a dowry for my marriage since I had a simple wedding with no reception. My husband's family could not provide much.... After finding a small produce store in Bronx, my husband took care of the paperwork with a lawyer....

Finally, both men and women build experiences by working in Korean small businesses before opening their stores or sometimes accumulate extensive knowledge over a quick period through prearranged on-the-job training. It is possible that men will acquire a more thorough knowledge of the business because their responsibilities assigned as workers expose them to several dimensions of the business operation. However, these differences in training and experience for men and women are marginal since the knowledge required to run typical immigrant small businesses is often minimal.

Claiming legal ownership has less to do with legitimate grounds but more to do with cultural customs that largely put the authority with the husbands. As Hannah's experience exemplifies, it is common among Korean immigrants that husbands take charge of navigating through the bureaucratic and legal systems. This navigation lends Korean men a power to decide who should be listed as owner. Korean custom allows men to assume ownership without inviting their spouses, even though some men acknowledged that their wives are "partners." At the same time, the customs do not encourage women to step up and demand their share of the ownership unless the marriage does not work out.[11]

The following case illustrates that claiming ownership in a Korean-owned business defies a common business sense but indicates how immigrants live by their own sets of rules. Mrs. Lee operates a Manhattan grocery. Before she opened this store with her husband, she worked at her uncle's grocery for a number of years. After marriage, both she and her husband put their savings together as start-up money for this store. The store was profitable, so her husband recently purchased a second store, where he spends most of his time. He continues to deliver produce items to both stores and checks in with his wife everyday. The wife manages the store with help from two workers while working the cash register. She may act as owner and certainly, feels entitled to the ownership of this store. However, the business permit posted

11. Dr. Min of Queens College of New York informed me that sometimes women have to go through a long legal battle to claim their shares in divorce proceedings because of the legal ownership status.

above the entrance door clearly listed her husband as the legal owner.

Power in Marriage

The real reason why men are listed as owners of the businesses over which their wives have an equal claim is that husbands exercise power and authority in Korean marriages. Korean society has been well known for its strong adherence to Confucian ideology, and patriarchal gender relations are part of its rigid values. Confucian values subordinates women, wives in particular, to men; these values are deeply ingrained in Korean social institutions, from family laws to property ownership. While Korea's rapid transition into an advanced industrial society has provided platforms for changing these values, the changes have been slow. For example, only in recent years are mothers allowed to contest custody of their children during divorce proceedings.

The immigrant owners and their wives in the study belong to the so-called "old" generation who grew up under the strong influence of the Confucian ideology.[12] Many of these wives attended college but few expected to have a career or to enjoy equal power with their husbands. On the other hand, men were taught to hold onto the authority as the father and husband.

Few of the wives working in family businesses had egalitarian relationships with their husbands. In some marriages, power seemed to be clearly in the hand of the husbands. One husband, who did not allow me to talk to his wife, claimed that he makes decisions, including the purchase of the current business, and dismissed his wife's experiences as insignificant.

Even in less male-dominant marriages, men and women did not see themselves as equal partners. Not surprisingly, wives took

12. Young generations of Koreans, especially those under the age of 35, grew up after Korea began to reap the benefits of rapid industrialization and modernization.

care of many of the household responsibilities but most did not seem to demand that their husbands share the burdens. This does not mean, however, that wives had no desire to have egalitarian relationships with their husbands. Their desire was indirectly indicated in praises of women's equality in America or in wishes for their daughters' future. It seemed that the best they could hope for was maintaining a stable, yet respectable, marriage.

A desire to maintain a stable marriage not riddled by conflicts and tension was a major concern for the wives working in their family businesses. The most revealing evidence of power differentials in marriage came from their efforts to appease their husbands by avoiding conflicts and reducing tensions. One of the most difficult challenges, as many of these wives have cited, was to make their husband feel in charge of the business. One wife explained it this way:

> Sometimes, I hold my tongue even if I want to correct what he does. I know about this business as much as he does. How many Korean immigrants ran dry-cleaning businesses in Korea? We all learned here [in America].... To boost my husband's morale, I let him make decisions.... He used to work in a company and had a number of employees under him. Now he has only me. He needs to feel that he is in charge.

Another wife described why it was better for her husband to spend time away from their store:

> I used to get into arguments with my husband over small things. Since we spend so much time together, we still argue.... However, I learned that it was not worth to fight most of the time, especially over small matters. He gets mad at me afterward... When he is stressed, I now encourage him to go out and play golf.

Others used similar tactics, sending their husbands for lunch with friends or to play golf. Interestingly, some wives described their husbands as being like impatient children who had to be pleased. It almost seemed that they were conscious of the unequal privileges enjoyed by their husbands. The wives appeared to feel entitled to deride their husbands a little through such observations, while he was out of earshot.

Breadwinner and Homemaker
The majority of the women did not have regular wage work after marriage in Korea, but they seemed to accept working outside the home as requisite to immigrant life in the United States. Mrs. Kang, who was working in her family grocery business, articulates this common immigrant mantra:

> Back in Korea, I knew that most Korean immigrants ran small businesses for living in the United States. I did not work in Korea outside the home, but understood that once we are in the States things would have to change. Women have to work in America! Without their help, families cannot sustain a good lifestyle. [Emphasis added]

Like this wife, both women and men working in family businesses frequently describe wives' roles as "helping out." This word choice is interesting. As in English, the Korean term for "helping out" does not mean taking the primary responsibility. It indicates that while immigrants may accept the new roles upon immigration they continue to view the extent of the wife's role as somewhat supplementary to that of the husband's. Even more interesting is that Mrs. Kang, like many wives in the study, does not just help out, but works around the clock. Her view may not reflect the true nature of her work; it nonetheless represents perceptions of immigrant wives working in family businesses.

The transition into immigrant life has been challenging for both Korean women and men. Women, in particular, were thrust into a new role of making a living upon immigration. Willingly or not, all of the women interviewed accepted this task at one point or another by taking a wage job. With the opening of a family business, the wives were called upon to assist their husbands. Despite their transition from housewife to wage worker and to family worker, few wavered from the belief that the husband should be the primary breadwinner. While many wives were committed to their family businesses, they also viewed their role as secondary. By deferring the ownership to their husbands, women seemed to send the signal that the primary responsibility of supporting the family rests on men's shoulders.

The view that the husband should be the primary breadwinner also provides a rationale for men to claim ownership. It was important for male owners to view themselves as ultimately in charge of their businesses not only for the sake of authority, but also out of genuine conviction that these businesses were the lifelines for their families. The realities of immigrant family business force many wives to stay involved in business as much as their husbands were. Ideally, men would have their wives to cut back their hours. For these men, their wives' diminished roles in business symbolize the ultimate success of their immigrant life. Some owners took great pride in having their wives work only part time or mostly spend time taking care of children and home nowadays. The situation in which wives can work part time and spend more time with the children wouldn't have been possible at all without their contributions in the first place. However, it seems that men get to take the credit for it.

Maternal Guilt and Coping with Double Burdens
The decision to enter small business may have spurred the adaptive behaviors of immigrants, but it does not necessarily transform gender relations. The women and men in the study entered the unknown territory of small business without much change in their values and attitudes toward social expectations for women and men. Despite their new economic activities, wives were not exempt from traditional responsibilities at home. In other words, they were still expected to fulfill their roles as mother and wife.

Since their husbands cannot be counted on, these wives call upon their children, female relatives, and sometimes paid help to share their burdens at home. At the time of the interview, twelve of the seventy families had a parent residing with them. Many more families have relied on their parents at some point over the years. In some cases, when parents were not available, wives hired other Korean elderly women or sometimes Latino immigrant women as live-in help. Another way of coping was to teach their children self-care. Children as young as nine or ten years of age were eating dinner – often prepared by their mothers in advance – by themselves and staying home without supervision until their parents got home late.

While juggling responsibilities between home and business, many women – especially mothers of young children – felt a deep sense of guilt toward their children. One woman running a dry-cleaning drop-off store made the following criticism toward herself and other Koreans:

> We [Korean immigrants] say that we immigrated to the United States for the sake of the children. Look at us, however. We are just too busy to run a business, and our children are growing up without us. We don't know who their friends are and how they spend time…. The only thing we say to them is study hard!

The maternal guilt toward children is the primary reason why many wives were hoping to cut back their work in the future. Only a few in the study, like Mrs. Paik, were so lucky. My visit to her family store coincided with her work hours, which had been reduced to about four hours a day for five days a week. She noted that I would have missed her if I had come in later and she shared her experience:

> We opened our first store about fifteen years ago and I worked all seven days. The business was good and there was literally just enough time for a

bathroom break. It was grueling work.... After working like animals for two or three years, I had my first child. When the child was born, my mother came to the States, and stayed with us and took care of the baby and housework.... I was back at work in a month. I look back on those years and cannot believe we lived like that.... Now I stay with my kids until they leave for school and get here around 10 am. I leave for home around 1 or 2 p.m. so I can be there when my kids get home.... We bought a house on Long Island so that the kids can have a nice place to live. What is the point of buying a nice house if you are not going to be there to enjoy it? At least, I should be there for my children.

Her guilt toward her children is apparent and she tries to make up for all those years that her three children grew up without their parents. She seriously cut back her work hours only two years ago. Besides, she believes that her husband's long hours make up for both of them. When I asked him about how he spends time with his children, he proudly commented that he now has a "family night." The definition of his family night is being at home for dinner every Wednesday.

While a strict linear relationship cannot be drawn, a general pattern seems to exist between the years of business and the decrease in the wife's involvement in business. Her contributions are the greatest during the initial few years of the business establishment. Immigrants in small business are aware that the initial couple of years are the most critical to the success of the business. As immigrants primarily rely on informal sources of financing, they are under huge pressure to pay a "personal mortgage" on time or pay back the loan from relatives as soon as possible. If the stores succeed in generating enough profits, many wives would not hesitate cutting back the time they spend at work and diverting their attention to their homes.

Conclusion

While scholars generally recognize the significance of the family to the establishment and success of immigrant small businesses, few have considered the gendered nature of family labor. This chapter examined how family labor is utilized in immigrant small businesses. It demonstrated that the most prevalent type of operation in Korean small businesses is a business run by a married couple. Although a married couple runs a business together, the husband assumes the ownership and the wife becomes the source of "family labor."

Under the rationalization of "family businesses," wives of small business owners are obliged to provide their help to their husbands with little change in their conjugal relationships. In contrast to family businesses, women-owned businesses did not count on help from husbands. To put it simply, the husbands do not function as family workers. This shows that family labor is largely a euphemism for unpaid labor by owners' wives.

Given the complexity of women's roles in immigrant small business, the terms "family worker" or "family labor" seem less than adequate to capture the nature of women's contributions to immigrant businesses. More often than not, wives working in their family businesses are *de facto* co-owners (Young, 1983). I suggest that future discussions on family labor in immigrant small businesses should consider the following points. First, we need to recognize the term "family labor" as somewhat of a misnomer. While children (Song, 1997) or kin sometimes provide help, wives of immigrant owners are the primary source of family labor. We need to differentiate the roles of other family members and the wife of the owner in immigrant small business. To use the term "family labor" or "family worker" to capture wives' role in immigrant small business grossly minimizes the degree of their contributions.

Second, reliance on family labor is neither universal nor constant. Patterns of its utilization indicate that the type of immigrant small business is an important indicator for the degree of family members' business involvement. For example, while nail salons

147

are labor-intensive, they rarely rely on family workers. As for dry cleaners, married couples are often sufficient to function as the primary operational unit with one or no paid worker. Thus, while family labor plays an important role in Korean immigrant businesses or any small business, it is nonetheless replaceable.

Finally, we need to recognize that family labor is a gendered resource. It is important to understand the link between ownership and family labor in the context of patriarchal gender relations. The concept of family labor masks the reality in which immigrant men become owners while immigrant women become family workers. As feminist scholars have pointed out, without accounting for women's unpaid work, it is not possible to fully understand women's status in the workplace. Women's family labor in immigrant businesses is such an example.

This study shows that men's claim of ownership is an affirmation of their authority and power in their family. Few Korean immigrant couples had egalitarian relationships despite women's participation in business. Even though Korean men and women left their home county behind and they found the ways of adapting to the new environment, their adaptive behaviors still reflect the values of the old country.

One of these values they seemed to hold on to is the belief that husbands should be primary breadwinners. This belief is part of the reason why both men and women readily accept the practice of registering only the husband as owner. In contrast to the view of husband as primary breadwinner, the role of wife is generally described as "helping out" despite the reality that most wives were as equally involved in the business as their husbands were. By holding on to these traditional gender roles, these wives hoped to relieve themselves from demands of running family businesses. Despite participation in the workforce and in family business, the wives did not gain much power in marriage. Without this reward, they have no real motives to remain involved in family businesses except to sustain their viability. The findings of this chapter support previous studies arguing that for Korean

148

immigrants, changes in gender roles are not always accompanied by women's employment (Chang, 1995; Um, 1992). I also argued that real changes in conjugal relations would be more difficult for couples operating businesses together since the husband was likely to exercise his authority over his wife both at home and at work.

6. Korean Immigrant Women's Work in the Nail Salon Industry: Gender, Race and Class in the Service Sector

Miliann Kang

Acknowledgements

I would like to thank the Centennial Committee and Prof. Ilpyong Kim for inviting me to contribute to this volume. This article was originally published in the journal, Gender and Society, Dec. 2003 under the title, "The Managed Hand: The Commercialization of Bodies and Emotions in Korean Immigrant-owned Nail Salons," and is reprinted here with permission from Sage Publications. Thanks to Liann Kang, Wi Jo Kang, Nora Choi-Lee, Jung-hwa Hwang, Eunja Lee, Eunju Lee and especially Jiwon Lee, for research assistance. Catherine Berheide, C.N. Le, Jennifer Lee, Sara Lee, Susan Walzer and Chris Bose, Minjeong Kim and the G & S anonymous reviewers offered valuable comments and suggestions. My dissertation committee at New York University, Craig Calhoun, Jeff Goodwin, and Ruth Horowitz, and readers, Troy Duster and Kathleen Gerson, guided the theory and research design. Funding was provided in part by New York University, Skidmore College and Grinnell College. This study was awarded the Cheryl Allyn Miller award for research on women and work by Sociologists for Women in Society.

Abstract

Korean immigrant women have established an innovative entrepreneurial niche that provides a significant source of small business ownership and employment, and contributes to the economic prosperity of the Korean-American community. These establishments forge novel forms of interaction in both majority and minority neighborhoods while providing a former luxury item to a diverse racial and class population. This ethnographic study of service interactions in Korean immigrant women-owned nail salons in New York City introduces the concept "body labor" to designate a type of gendered work that involves the management of emotions in body-related service provision. I explore variation in the performance of body labor caused by the intersection of the gendered processes of beauty service work with the racialized and class-specific service expectations of diverse customers. These patterns demonstrate how Korean immigrant women learn to provide different kinds of services according to the race and class of their customers, and in so doing, they both challenge and reproduce existing forms of inequality within U.S. society.

Key Words: Korean women, immigrant women's work, body labor, emotional labor, gendered work, intersections of race, gender and class

Introduction
By focusing upon the case study of Korean immigrant manicurists and their relations with racially and socio-economically diverse female customers in New York City nail salons, this study highlights Korean women's economic contribution to the Korean-American community through their entrepreneurship and employment in this service niche. This contribution has been largely neglected in the scholarship on Korean immigrants in the United States. This study also broadens the study of immigrant women's work by illuminating the gender, race and class dimensions in the performance of emotional labor in beauty service jobs by introducing the concept of "body labor," the provision of body-related services and the management of feelings that accompanies it.

The last decade witnessed a turn toward "Bringing Bodies Back In" (Frank 1990) to theory and research in sociology and feminist scholarship. What can be gained by "bringing the body back in" to the study of emotional labor, and more broadly, of gendered work? What are the dimensions of body labor, and what factors explain the variation in the quality and quantity of its performance? An embodied perspective on gendered work highlights the feminization of the body-related service sector and the proliferation of intricate practices of enhancing the appearance of the female body. A race, gender and class perspective highlights the increasing role of working-class immigrant women in filling body-related service jobs and the racialized meanings that shape the processes of emotional management among service workers.

This study compares nail salons in three racially and socio-economically diverse settings, employing participant observation and in-depth interviews (N=62) in the tradition of feminist ethnography and the extended case method. After providing a brief overview of the case study of Korean-owned nail salons in New York City, the data presentation maps out the physical and emotional dimensions of body labor in three different nail salons and explains patterns of variation according to the race and class of the clientele and neighborhood.

In addition to contributing original empirical research on Korean immigrant women's work in the new and expanding niches of body service work, this article broadens the scholarship on emotional labor by addressing its performance by racial-ethnic and immigrant women in the global service economy. It demonstrates how the gendered processes of physical and emotional labor in nail salon work are seeped with race and class meanings that reinforce broader structures of inequality and ideologies of difference between women.

Background of the Study
In order to provide context for this study, I describe the development of nail salons as a niche for Korean immigrant women's work, focusing on the dynamics of race, ethnicity and immigration. As one of the few arenas in which immigrant and native-born women encounter each other in regular, sustained, physical contact, Korean immigrant female-owned nail salons in New York City illuminate the complex performance and

production of race, gender and class as they are constructed in feminized work sites in the global service economy. Since the early 1980s, Korean women in New York City have pioneered this new ethnic niche of more than 2,000 Korean-owned nail salons throughout the metropolitan area, or approximately 70 percent of the total, as estimated by the Korean-American Nail Association of New York. Each salon employs an average of five workers, suggesting an occupational niche of roughly 10,000 women. While the New York State licensing bureau does not keep track of nail salon licenses by ethnic group, their figures reveal an overall 41 percent growth in the nail industry (from 7,562 licensed nail technicians in 1996 to 10,684 in 2000) in NYC, Westchester, and Nassau. These numbers undercount a sizable number of women who do not possess licenses or legal working status. While exact figures accounting for the income generated by these salons is not available, one Korean journalist estimated that the economic contribution of the nail salons to the prosperity of the Korean-American community rivals that of grocery stores. Nonetheless, the hard work of Korean immigrant women in establishing and operating these salons has been neglected in much of the scholarship on Korean immigrants in the U.S.

While concentrating on Korean immigrant women, this study examines both race and ethnicity as salient categories of analysis. I designate the salon owners and workers according to ethnicity, but I recognize shared racial positions that push not only Korean but other Asian immigrant women into this niche. For example, in New York, there is a significant presence of Chinese and Vietnamese as well as Korean-owned nail salons, and on the West Coast, the niche is almost solely dominated by Vietnamese women (www.nailsmag.com). Common factors such as limited English language ability, unrecognized professional credentials from their countries of origin, undocumented immigration status, and co-ethnic resources in the form of labor, start-up capital and social networks, explain why Asian immigrant women of various ethnic groups cluster in the nail salon industry. Similarities across Asian ethnic groups include not only the human capital of the women themselves but the conditions of the labor market and the U.S. racial hierarchy that they encounter. Through their shared race, gender and class locations, Asian women have been coveted as productive and docile workers, whose "nimble fingers" (Ong 1987) make them desirable and exploitable in an increasingly feminized, impoverished and unprotected labor force (Cheng and Bonacich 1984; Hu-DeHart 1999). Racialized perceptions of Asian women as skilled in detailed handiwork and massage further contribute to customers' preference for their manicuring services, as evidenced by the fact that many customers racially identify the salons as owned by Asians or "Orientals," as opposed to by specific ethnic group.

In sum, because it would be methodologically unsound to generalize findings based on a limited sample of *Korean* women to include all *Asian* immigrant women in the nail industry, this study maintains ethnicity as the significant category for describing the workers and owners, but frames differences between the customers and variation in service interactions according to race. Thus, I discuss the different dimensions of Korean-immigrant women's performance of body labor performance through the integrative lens of race, gender and class rather than a more specific focus on Korean ethnicity.[1]

Theoretical Framework
Emotional Labor in Body-Service Work: Race, Gender and Class Intersections
Work on the body requires not only physical labor but extensive emotional management, or what Hochschild's seminal work describes as emotional labor (1983). The concept of body labor makes two important contributions to the study of emotional labor: 1) it explores the embodied dimensions of emotional labor; and 2) it investigates the intersections of race, gender and class in shaping its performance. By bringing together an embodied analysis of emotional labor with an integrative race, gender and class perspective, I show how this case study of nail salon work re-theorizes emotional labor to have greater

applicability to gendered occupations dominated by racialized immigrant women.

Building upon Hochschilds' work, studies of emotional labor have illuminated the increasing prevalence of emotional management in specific occupations and industries, the gendered composition of the emotional labor force, wage discrimination, burnout and other occupational health issues (Hall 1993; Leidner 1999; Lively 2000; Wharton 1999). Steinberg and Figart (1997) provide a comprehensive overview of the field that examines both qualitative case studies of the contours of emotional labor in specific work sites and quantitative investigations of its prevalence and its impact on job satisfaction and compensation. Despite the many dimensions of emotional labor that have been addressed by feminist scholars, the body-related contours of emotional labor as it manifests in low-wage service work dominated by racial-ethnic women, particularly in the beauty industry have yet to be examined in-depth.

While the study of beauty and the beauty industry presents a rich opportunity to explore the emotional work involved in servicing female bodies, this literature has focused attention almost exclusively on the experiences of middle-class White women consumers and their physical and psychological exploitation by the male-dominated beauty industry (Banner 1983; Bordo 1993; Chapkis 1986), neglecting the substandard working conditions, unequal power relations, and complex emotional lives of the women who provide these services. Several excellent ethnographies of beauty salons (Furman 1997; Gimlan 1996) have explored the dimensions of class and age in beauty shop culture, but they have not addressed the experiences of women of color as either customers or body service workers. Studies of the bodies of women of color, while illuminating cultural representations of racialized bodies as inferior and exotic (Hooks 1990) and the politics of body alteration, particularly regarding hair (Banks 2000; Rooks 1996) have also neglected the actual interactions between consumers and providers of body-related services and the hierarchies that govern these exchanges.

In addition to neglecting emotional work in body-service jobs, the literature on emotional labor has framed the processes of interactive service work primarily through a gender lens and paid less attention to the cross-cutting influences of gender, race and class. Hochschild's original case study of flight attendants and subsequent applications to other female-dominated occupations have emphasized the gendered employment experiences of native-born White women as paralegals (Pierce 1995), nannies and au pairs (Macdonald 1996), fast food and insurance sales (Leidner 1993) and police officers (Martin 1999). My research expands this research not only in its empirical focus on immigrant women of color in its analysis of emotional labor not only as gendered work but through the theoretical framework of race, gender and class as "interactive systems" and "interlocking categories of experience" (Anderson and Collins 2001:xii). This framework critiques additive models that append race and class to the experiences of White, middle-class women and instead highlights the simultaneity and reciprocity of race, gender and class in patterns of social relations and in the lives of individuals. Thus, I demonstrate that different expectations or "feeling rules" (Hochschild 1983, x) shape the performance of emotional labor by women according to the racial and class context.

Drawing from Hochschild's definition of emotional labor, I incorporate this intersectional analysis to define important parallels and distinctions between the concepts of body labor and emotional labor. First, Hochschild's definition of emotional labor focuses on a particular form that "requires one to induce or suppress feeling in order to sustain the outward countenance that produces the proper state of mind in others - in this case, the sense of being cared for in a convivial and safe place" (1983, 7). While Hochschild develops this definition in reference to the specific case of flight attendants and the feeling rules that govern their work, this kind of caring, attentive service has become a

156

widely generalized definition, rather than being regarded as one particular form of emotional labor performed by mostly White, middle-class women largely for the benefit of White, middle- and upper-class men. Korean-owned nail salons thus serve as a contrasting site to explore other forms of emotional labor that emerge in work sites that are differently gendered, differently racialized, and differently classed. The patterns of emotional labor described in this study can illuminate similar sites in which emotional labor involves women serving women (as opposed to mainly women serving men), and is not necessarily governed by the social feeling rules of White, middle-class America.

By investigating the understudied area of body-related service occupations through an intersectional race, gender and class analysis, this study of body labor reformulates the concept of emotional labor to dramatize how the feeling rules governing its exchange are shaped by interlocking oppressions that operate at the macro-level (Collins 1991) and then emerge as different styles of emotional service at the micro-level.

Research and Design Methods
This study situates itself within feminist methodology and epistemology by beginning from the "standpoint" of women to investigate the "relations of ruling" in contemporary capitalist society (Smith 1987:46). At the same time, it does not privilege gender as the only or the most important framework for defining and investigating differences, and aims instead for an understanding of race, gender and class as cross-cutting forces (Chow 1994; Collins 1991; Glenn 1992; Hooks 1981; Hurtado 1989; Zinn 1989). By examining contrasting patterns of body labor between women of different racial and class backgrounds, this study reconstructs theories of emotional labor by addressing its embodied dimensions and the simultaneous influence of gender, race and class on its performance. In doing so, it follows the extended case method of making critical interventions in existing theory by explaining anomalies between similar phenomena, rather than seeking generalizations toward the discovery of new theory, as in the contrasting approach of

grounded theory. According to Burawoy, the primary architect of the extended case method, "The importance of the single case lies in what it tells us about society as a whole rather than about the population of similar cases" (1991:281) Thus, this study examines cases of specific nail salons not to formulate generalizations about all similar nail salons but instead to explain how social forces influence variation in the service interactions at these sites.

The data collection for this project involved fourteen months of fieldwork in New York City nail salons. The research design included in-depth interviews (N=62) and participant observation at three sites: 1) "Uptown Nails" - located in a predominantly White, middle- and upper-class commercial area; 2) "Downtown Nails" located in a predominantly Black (African American and Caribbean) working- and lower-middle class commercial neighborhood; 3) "Crosstown Nails" - located in a racially mixed lower-middle and middle-class residential and commercial area. I spent at least 50 hours at each salon over the course of several months. In the case of Crosstown Nails, which was located near my home, visits were shorter (2-3 hours) and more frequent (several times a week). The other two salons required long commutes so I usually visited once a week for 6-7 hours.

In addition to hundreds of unstructured conversational interviews conducted as a participant observer, the research included in-depth structured interviews with 10 Korean nail salon owners, 10 Korean nail salon workers, 15 Black customers, and 15 White customers. The customers interviewed at each salon are as follows. Uptown Nails included a lawyer, professor, pharmacist, flight attendant, secretary, personal trainer, accessories importer, homemaker (formerly computer programmer), fashion designer, and real estate broker. Customers interviewed at Downtown Nails included a package clerk, student/waitress, student/mother, grocery cashier, ambulatory service driver, county government administrative assistant, laboratory technician, nanny, therapist and elementary school principal. At Crosstown Nails, I interviewed 10 customers (five White, five Black). The White customers included a bartender, high school teacher, hairdresser, homemaker and retired insurance bookkeeper. The Black customers included a clinical researcher, theater technician/musician, management consultant, homemaker and student.

In-depth interviews averaged 45 minutes for customers and two hours for owners and workers. Customers were interviewed in English at the salon while they were having their manicures, and when necessary, a follow-up meeting or telephone interview was arranged. Owners and workers were interviewed in both Korean and English, depending on their preference and level of fluency. Bi-lingual research assistants helped with translation, transcription and follow-up interviews. I tape-recorded interviews in which consent was given, but in cases where respondents refused, I took extensive hand-written notes that I typed immediately afterwards. Both customers and service providers are referred to by pseudonyms that approximate the names they use in the salons. This convention captures the naturalistic setting where even co-workers commonly refer to each other by the "American name" that they employ at work. I have added a surname to citations and descriptions of owners and workers to differentiate customers from service providers.

Finally, I conducted key respondent interviews with two officials of the Korean Nail Salon Association of New York, two Korean ethnic press journalists, one New York State licensing official, and a representative of a Korean-operated nail school. I interviewed two Vietnamese nail salon owners and one Chinese and one Russian manicurist to provide preliminary comparisons to other ethnically-owned nail salon. To provide comparisons to other Korean-owned small businesses, I engaged in limited participant observation in a Korean-owned grocery store and interviewed the owner and manager.

Findings

<u>The Contours of Body Labor</u>

Body labor involves the exchange of body-related services for a wage and the performance of physical and emotional labor in this exchange. This study's findings illustrate three dimensions of body labor: 1) the *physical labor* of attending to the bodily appearance and pleasure of customers; 2) the *emotional labor* of managing feelings in order to display certain feeling states and to create and respond to customers' feelings regarding the servicing of their bodies; and 3) variation in the performance of body labor as explained through the intersection of gender with race and class. These dimensions vary across different research sites and emerge as three distinct patterns of body labor provision: 1) "high service body labor" involving physical pampering and emotional attentiveness serving mostly middle- and upper-class White female customers; 2) "expressive body labor" involving artistry in technical skills and communication of respect and fairness when serving mostly working- and lower-middle class African American and Caribbean female customers; and 3) "routinized body labor" involving efficient, competent physical labor and courteous but minimal emotional labor when serving mostly lower-middle and middle-class racially mixed female customers. The data presentation admittedly flattens some of the variation <u>within</u> each site in order to clarify distinctions <u>between</u> them, but this typology highlights the dominant physical and emotional style of service at each salon.

<u>Uptown Nails - High Service Body Labor</u>

A seasoned Korean manicurist who has worked at Uptown Nails for nearly ten years, Esther Lee is in high demand for her relaxing and invigorating hand massages. She energetically kneads, strokes and pushes pressure points, finishing off the massage by holding each of the customer's hands between her own and alternately rubbing, slapping and gently pounding them with the flare that has wooed many a customer into a regular nail salon habit. Margie, a White single woman in her mid-thirties who works for an accounting firm, smiles appreciatively and squeezes Esther's hand, "I swear, I couldn't stay in my job without this!" Esther reciprocates a warm, somewhat shy smile.

Uptown Nails boasts leafy green plants, glossy framed pictures of White fashion models showing off well-manicured hands, recent fashion magazine subscriptions stacked neatly on a coffee table, and classical CDs on the stereo system. The salon has been in operation for thirteen years, and three of the six employees have worked there over ten years. The customers sit quietly sipping their cappuccinos, updating their appointment books, or at times politely conversing with each other about the weather or the color of the nail polish they are wearing. Located in a prosperous business district of Manhattan, an Uptown Nail's manicuring experience involves not only the filing and polishing of nails but attention to the customer's physical and emotional comfort. From the gentle removal of undernail dirt, to the careful trimming of cuticles and buffing of calluses, to the massaging of hands and feet, Korean manicurists literally rub up against their customers, who are mostly White middle- and upper-class women. The owner, one of the earliest pioneers in the nail salon industry, currently operates six very profitable salons in prime Manhattan locations and only visits this salon once a week to take care of paperwork. The owner, manager and employees are all middle-aged Korean women with fluent English language ability, reflecting the greater expectations for communications with customers. The physical dimensions of body labor in Uptown Nails, including hot cotton towels, bowls of warm soaking solution, sanitized utensils, and calming background music, all indicate considerable attention to creating a pleasurable sensory experience for the customer. Particular attention is given to avoiding nicks and cuts, and sterilizing and apologizing profusely when they occur.

In addition to this extensive physical pampering, Uptown Nails prioritizes the emotional needs of customers regarding the servicing of their bodies. The mostly White middle-class customers at this salon place great importance on emotional attentiveness as a crucial component of the service interaction. Kathy, a personal trainer, elaborates:

> Having them done is a pleasure, a luxury. Doing them myself is tedious, having them done is a treat. It's the whole idea of going and having something nice done for myself. If I do them myself, it's just routine upkeep of my body - like washing your hair or keeping your clothes clean.... Of course it makes it more enjoyable if they are friendly and can talk to you. If they can't remember my name that's okay, but I think they should recognize me. (Kathy)

The proper performance of body labor thus transforms a hygienic process, otherwise equated with washing hair or clothes, into a richly rewarding physical and emotional experience. The satisfaction Kathy experiences from the manicure derives not only from the <u>appearance</u> of the nails but the <u>feeling</u> of being special that accompanies attentive body servicing. In order to generate this feeling, customers expect the manicurist to display a caring demeanor and engage in pleasant one-on-one conversation with them.

Service providers recognize customers' high expectations with regard to both the physical and emotional dimensions of body labor, and respond accordingly. Judy Cha, age 34 who immigrated in 1993, describes the emotional and physical stressors that accompany high service body labor, particularly giving massages to earn tips and engaging in conversation.

> Three years ago we didn't give a lot of massages but now customers ask more and more. It makes me weak and really tired.... I guess because I don't have the right training to do it in a way that doesn't tire my body. Some manicurists give massage all the time to get tips, but sometimes I don't even ask them if I'm tired. Owners keep

asking you to ask them, but on days I'm not feeling well, I don't ask.... One of my biggest fears working in the salon is, what if I don't understand what the customer is saying? They don't really talk in detail, just say, "how is the weather." But in order to have a deeper relationship, I need to get past that and to improve my English. It makes it very stressful. (Judy Cha)

Thus, manicurists work hard to conform to the high service expectations of middle-class, White women, but while the performance of caring, attentive emotional labor is noticeably higher than that afforded in the other research sites, it often does not meet customers' expectations. In particular, many Uptown Nails customers disapprove of the use of Korean language by the manicurists as a violation of proper attentiveness in beauty service transactions and suspect that they are being talked about (see Kang 1997).

Cathy Hong, a 32-year old manicurist who immigrated in 1999, sums up the assumptions many of the Uptown Nails customers have regarding access to a regular manicure delivered with high service body labor "These women get their nails done regularly because it has become a habit to them, they take if for granted. Just as we wash our face daily, American women get their nails done."

Downtown Nails - Expressive Body Labor
Entering another borough, the scene inside Downtown Nails differs as radically as the neighborhoods in which these two salons are located. Squeezed between a Caribbean bakery and a discount clothing store, a worn-out signboard displays the single word "NAILS" and a painting of a graceful, well-manicured hand holding a long-stemmed rose and pointing to a staircase leading to the second story entrance. Upon being buzzed in through the locked door, the customer is greeted with a display of hundreds of brightly-colored airbrushed nail tips lining an

entire wall. The noise level in the salon is high, as various electronic nail sculpting tools create a constant buzz to match the flow of the lively conversations among the mostly Black customers. On a weekend afternoon, Downtown Nails is filled to capacity and the wait for a preferred "nail artist" can be over an hour. Mostly Caribbean and African American women, the customers engage in animated conversations while sharing coco buns and currant rolls from the downstairs bakery. The banter ranges from vivid accounts of a recent mugging near the salon to news about the pay freeze in the nearby hospital where many of the women work as nurses or technicians.

A far cry from the spa-like pampering experience of Uptown Nails, a nail job at Downtown Nails is closer to a stint on a factory assembly line – highly mechanized and potentially toxic. Absent are the elaborate sanitizing machines and solutions, let alone the soft pampering touches. Despite these appearances, body labor at Downtown Nails involves a complex mix of physical and emotional labor that accommodates customers' desires to express a unique sense of self through their nail designs and their expectations that service providers demonstrate both individual respect and appreciation to the community.

The manicurists, or nail artists, provide less of the traditional, attentive style of emotional labor but focus their emotional management on communicating a sense of respect and fairness. These women tend to be more recent immigrants from more working class backgrounds with less English language fluency and are more likely to be working without legal immigration status or licenses. The owners, Mr. and Mrs. Lee are a married couple, both formerly school teachers, who immigrated in 1981 to pursue better educational opportunities for their children. Two years after their arrival, they opened a salon in this location because the rent was affordable, the customer base was strong, and they reside in a nearby neighborhood. The customers at Downtown Nails span a broad range in socioeconomic status, but most are working- to lower-middle class.

The importance of the physical appearance of the nails themselves as opposed to the pampering experience of receiving these services is dramatized by customers' concern with the design of the nails versus the massage and other services that customers at Uptown Nails regard as integral and Downtown Nails customers view as extraneous. Jamilla, a 26-year old African American part-time student and waitress proudly displays her inch-and-a-half long nails, each one adorned with the skyline of New York City in bold black, framed by an orange and yellow sunset. A regular patron of Downtown Nails for six years, she explains why she is willing to spend "$50-60 every two weeks" for elaborate hand-painted designs:

> Because I don't like looking like anyone else. My nails say 'me.' They're the first thing people notice about me. I have big hands for a female. I never had those long, thin ladylike fingers. My father used to say my hands were bigger than his. I want long nails because they make my hands look more feminine. (Jamilla)

Indicating a preference for nails that reflect very different norms of femininity than the demure, pastel tones prevalent at Uptown Nails, Jamilla elaborates further on her nail aesthetics. "It all depends on my mood. Like this design makes me feel like I'm on top of the city, like it can't bring me down (laughing).... No one's gonna mess with you when you got nails like these." Jamilla's pride in having originally designed nails that no one else can reproduce suggests the importance of her nails as an expression of her individuality that also communicate a sense of self-efficacy and protection as indicated in her comments that no one would "mess" with a woman with nails like hers. In order to meet the expectations of customers like Jamilla, body labor at Downtown Nails calls for development of expertise in sculpting and painting original nail designs rather than in the soothing, pampering services offered at Uptown Nails. Thus, the physical demands of body labor are not less, but simply of a different type.

165

Similarly, the emotional dimensions of body labor at Downtown Nails are not different in degree so much as kind. The customer's race and class location intersect to produce much lower expectations among working-class Black customers for emotional attentiveness than the White middle-class women at Uptown Nails. While it is clearly less attentive, Serena, an African American grocery store cashier, assesses the emotional labor at Downtown Nails positively.

> It's very good, I'm satisfied with it. They really just do the nails, no massages. That's fine with me. I just go in with my Walkman and listen to some good music and maybe just have a little basic conversation. (Serena)

Customers at Downtown Nails rarely are on a first name basis with the service providers and their preference for a particular manicurist is based much more on her technical skills than her emotional attentiveness. Serena elaborates:

> There are a few people I like and I go to whoever's open, but I'll stay away from certain people. I know they're not good cause I hear other people complain - I see someone come back and say that their nail cracked the next day, or I see someone get nicked with a filer.... No, it's not because they're rude or anything, it's because I know they don't do a good job.... Just like some people just can't do hair, some people just can't do nails.... (*Regarding relations with her current manicurist*) I feel comfortable with her, but it's more that she does an excellent job. If a wrap cracks or looks funny or I lose a nail, I'm not going back to her no matter how nice she is. (Serena)

While many working-class Black customers like Serena give little importance to a caring, attentive emotional display, they demand another style of emotional labor.

Emotional labor at Downtown Nails calls less for sensitivity to pampering of individual customers but demonstration of values of respect and fairness that recognize the complex dynamics of Korean businesses operating in Black neighborhoods. This includes efforts such as sponsoring a Christmas party to thank customers for their patronage, participating in community events, displaying Afro-centric designs and playing R&B (rhythm and blues) and rap music. Mrs. Lee, the co-owner of the salon, allows regulars to run an informal tab when they are short of money, and keeps a change jar that customers dip into for bus fare, telephone calls or other incidentals. It is not uncommon for customers to drop by even when they are not getting their nails done to use the bathroom or leave shopping bags behind the front desk while they complete errands. These efforts at "giving back to the community" entail a distinct form of emotional labor that conforms not to White, middle-class women's feeling rules of privilege and pampering, but to Black working-class women's concerns about being treated with respect and fairness.

Jamilla describes the importance of a sense of fairness and respect to Black customers and how this demands a particular form of emotional labor from Korean manicurists.

> It's kind of a Catch-22. Some customers feel like they're getting disrespected if you don't refer back to them or if you're having a side conversation. Then the Koreans get upset and think African Americans have an attitude, which then makes them talk more about us. You see, in the African American community, you can't outright say anything you want to say because we always have our guard up. We get it all the time, from the cops or whoever. I've seen it in the Hispanic community too - this thing about

honor and respect. "Don't disrespect me just because I'm Black or Hispanic. What I say does count." (Jamilla)

Thus, while the caring, pampering style of service is virtually absent at Downtown Nails, another form of emotional labor is necessary to negotiate and avoid conflicts with customers that can quickly become racialized into heated confrontations (Lee 2002). Serena describes a scene at another salon that illustrates how the failure to perform appropriately respectful emotional labor can quickly erupt into shouting matches that take on racialized and anti-immigrant overtones. "I've seen some customers really go off on them, 'You're not in your country, speak English.'" Her comments underscore how the race and class of the neighborhood complicate the processes of emotional management inside the salons.

Although disagreements between customers and workers do arise, at times resulting in heated exchanges, nonetheless, the relations in the salon are overall congenial, as the expressive style of emotional labor enables customers and service providers to voice and for the most part "work out" their differences. Mrs. Lee, explains that she prefers serving Black customers for this reason, and actually moved back to working in a low-income Black neighborhood after working for a period in Long Island.

> Working in the White neighborhood didn't match my personality. I don't deal well with picky customers.... In the Black neighborhood, it's more relaxed. They don't leave tips but they don't expect so much service either... (In Long Island) they want you to go slow and spend time with them. Here I just concentrate on doing a good job and working quickly. (Mrs. Lee)

Service providers invest less energy in displaying and creating convivial feeling states, which in some cases allows for a genuine affinity with Black customers and less of a sense of burnout from the effort involved in the manufacture of falsely convivial feelings.

"Expressive body labor" thus prioritizes both the meanings of the nails as a form of self-expression to working-class Black customers and the expression of symbolic but tangible efforts to respond to the feeling rules of respect and fairness governing Korean immigrant service providers in predominantly Black working-class neighborhoods.

Crosstown Nails - Routinized Body Labor
Located on the second floor above a fashionable boutique, Crosstown Nails is clean but sparse and utilitarian. In many ways, this salon is representative of the most prevalent style of service offered in Korean-owned nail salons - fast, cheap basic manicures and pedicures with no frills. The McDonald's of the nail salon industry, Crosstown Nails offers a manicure that is standardized and predictable in both its physical and emotional aspects.

This salon often has customers waiting, but even when it is busy, the line moves quickly as each customer is whisked in and out of the manicuring seat with crisp efficiency. The customer chooses her nail color, presents it to the manicurists who asks her to specify the desired shape of the nail, then soaks her nails briefly in a softening solution. Depending on her preference, her nails are either trimmed or pushed back. The manicurist offers to give a massage, but it is perfunctory and lasts usually not more than a minute. After carefully layering on two coats of polish and a quick-drying topcoat, the customer moves to a heated hand dryer where she converses with other customers, or more often "zones out."

Many customers come from the neighboring hospital during lunch hour or after work. Situated on the edge of a fashionable, high-rent, racially diverse residential district and a lower-income but also racially mixed neighborhood, Crosstown Nails captures the broad range of customer interactions which many Korean service providers negotiate in a given day. In large, high immigrant-receiving cities such as New York, service interactions often involve multiracial rather than binary interactions between Korean and Blacks or Koreans and Whites.

Susan Lee, age 39, founded Crosstown Nails in 1989 and is the sole owner. Divorced with one son, age 10, she immigrated in 1982 from Seoul with her husband, a graduate student. She graduated college with a degree in tourism and worked as a travel agent in Korea. In NYC, she first worked in a retail store in Manhattan, then began to work in a nail salon in Brooklyn to support her husband while he studied. After their marriage ended, she brought her mother from Korea in 1988 and with her help opened a convenience store, which failed shortly thereafter. She then opened Crosstown Nails a year later, and the business has thrived.

The secret of Crosstown Nail's success is its ability to appeal to customers who lack excess disposable income and normally would not indulge in a professional manicure, but are attracted by the convenience and price. Julia, a White bartender, comments:

> I'm kind of a ragamuffin, so it kind of surprises
> me that I get them done as often as I do, which is
> still much less than most people in the city. It's
> just so easy to do here, and cheap. (Julia)

Julia's description of herself as a "ragamuffin" suggests that she does not adhere to strict codes of femininity in her dress or other beauty routines, as indicated by her casual peasant skirt and no make-up. Nonetheless, easy and cheap access draws her into purchasing regular manicures. Many customers at Crosstown Nails seek manicures not as a pampering experience or as creative expression but as a utilitarian measure to enhance their self-presentation at work. Merna, an Afro-Caribbean clinical researcher, explains:

I only get them done about every two months. I don't want to get attached to it. For some women it's such a ritual, it becomes a job - maintaining the tips and stuff. I'm presenting my hands all day long so it's worth it to me to spend some time and money to make sure they look good. (Merna)

Merna regards manicured nails as a professional asset more than a core aspect of a gendered self. Thus, the style of her nails and the meaning she gives to them is more similar to the White middle-class customers at Crosstown Nails than to the Black working-class customers at Downtown Nails.

In general, middle-class Black customers like Merna mostly exhibited similar nail aesthetics to those of White middle-class women, suggesting the greater importance of class over race in influencing nail styles and expectations of body labor, particularly in routinized settings such as Crosstown Nails.

Discussion

The concept of emotional labor addresses how service providers present and manipulate their feelings in order to communicate a sense of caring and attentiveness to customers, or in Hochschild's words, where "the emotional style of offering service is part of the service itself" (1983, 6). This study of interactions in Korean-owned nail salons enriches the literature on emotional labor by expanding it to include embodied dimensions, or body labor. The embodied aspects of emotional labor not only heighten the intensity of commercialized feeling exchanges, but they point out variation in these exchanges beyond the White, middle-class settings explored by most researchers. Nail salon services, and body labor more generally, are gendered work processes, but they are enacted in different forms according to the influences of race and class.

In what ways is nail salon work gendered? In what ways are these gendered work processes remolded by race and class? Understanding the influence of race and class on the gendered performance of body labor in Korean-owned nail salons illuminates how gendered work processes reflect and reproduce racial and class inequalities at the level of social structures. Nail salon work is gendered in four major dimensions: 1) it involves mostly female actors, as both service providers and customers; 2) it focuses on the construction of beauty according to feminine norms; 3) it is situated in feminized, semi-private spaces; and 4) it involves the gendered performance of emotional labor.

In describing each of these dimensions, I do not emphasize how socialized gender roles are acted out in these establishments, but rather how gender operates as a social institution that lays the groundwork for the very existence of these businesses and frames the interactions that occur within them. Thus, I conceptualize these small businesses as constructed from the ground up through gendered ideologies, relations and practices that sustain systematic gender inequality at the micro-level of sex differences, at the meso-level of group conflict and the macro-levels of power, social control and the division of labor (Ferree and Hall 1996). At the same time, I argue that as gendered institutions, they cannot be separated from forces of racial and class inequality.

If as Paul Gilroy asserts, "gender is the modality in which race is lived" (1993, 85), then race, and I argue class as well, are lived in these nail salons, and other body-service sites, as differences in gendered styles of body labor. Interactions in Korean female immigrant-owned nail salons illustrate how the gendered practices of body labor become the locus of expressing and negotiating race and class hierarchies between White, Black and Asian women. "High service" body labor, as performed at Uptown Nails, is similar to the style of caring, attentive emotional labor practiced by Hochschild's flight attendants and conforms to the feeling rules of White, middle-class women. "Expressive" body labor focuses on the physical appearance and artistry of the nails and the communication of respect and fairness in serving mostly working- and lower-middle class African American and Caribbean female customers at

Downtown Nails. "Routinized" body labor stresses efficiency, predictability, affordability and competency in physical labor and a courteous but no-frills style of emotional labor geared toward mostly lower-middle and middle-class racially mixed female customers at Crosstown Nails.

These patterns of body labor conform to the racial and class positions of the customers and the associated feeling rules that define their service expectations. At Uptown Nails, race, gender and class intersect to produce an emotionally and physically pampering form of body labor that conforms to the expectations of White, professional women for caring and attentive service. These women have high expectations regarding massages, cleanliness, sensitive touch, and friendly conversation while Black, working-class women at Downtown Nails expect minimal pampering and focus on the appearance, originality and durability of the nails themselves. At Crosstown Nails, class prevails over race as both Black and White women of middle socio-economic status view the nails instrumentally as a no-nonsense professional asset, rather than conforming to traditional notions of pampered femininity. Thus, they trade-off the physical pleasure and emotional attentiveness of high service treatment for the convenience and price of routinized body labor.

Black middle-class women at Crosstown Nails share this instrumental view of nails and a preference for a routinized, hassle-free manicure. The style of nails and the meaning given to them by Black middle-class women radically differ from the working class Black women at Downtown Nails, who value nail art as a form of self-expression and demand emotional labor that communicates respect and fairness. This contrast between the Black middle-class and working-class women at Crosstown and Downtown Nails again suggests the greater salience of class over race in determining the type of body labor.

What structural factors explain the differences in the provision of body labor in these three sites? These body labor types, while enacted at the micro-level, reflect the social conditions of the neighborhoods in which the salons are located and the clientele they serve. Because of the reliance on tips in White, middle-class neighborhoods, service providers have greater incentive to cater to the emotional needs of customers like those at Uptown Nails in order to increase their earnings. In the Black, working-class neighborhoods where tipping is not a widespread practice, nail salon workers guarantee their economic livelihood by establishing a base of regular customers who seek them out for their technical and artistic abilities more than their emotional or physical attentiveness. In routinized body labor settings serving lower middle-class women of mixed races, service providers maximize their earnings by generating a high turnover of customers who receive satisfactory but not special emotional and physical treatment.

These patterns of body labor service reflect and reproduce racial and class inequalities between women. Korean service providers learn to respond to White, middle- and upper-class customers emotional pampering and physical pleasure, thereby reinforcing the invisible sense of privilege claimed by these customers. The expressive practices of creating artful nails and troubleshooting potential problems with Black working-class customers, while helping to smooth relations, can also serve to emphasize racial meanings in these interactions and enforce a sense of difference. The routinized style of body labor reflects the generic social position of women whose bodies are neither privileged nor pathologized, but simply treated with routine efficiency.

Conclusions

The exchange of manicuring services set up complex emotional and embodied interactions between diverse women. In introducing and exploring the dimensions of body labor, this article challenges the scholarship on emotional labor to take more seriously the growth in body-related service jobs, and to address the differences in these service interactions not simply in terms of gendered processes but through the lens of race, gender and class intersections. Thus, not only does the concept of body labor add embodied dimensions to emotional labor but it makes it more applicable to low-wage service work performed by immigrant women.

This study situates the practice of body labor in Korean-owned nail salons within the restructuring of the global economy and the transplantation of the practices of enhancing bodily appearance from private households into new forms of public urban space. A manicure is no longer something a woman gives herself, her daughter or a girlfriend in the quiet of her own bathroom, but it is something which she increasingly purchases in a nail salon. In purchasing these services, she not only expands the boundaries of the service economy to include formerly private regimens of personal hygiene, but she encounters the "other," often an immigrant woman of different racial and class background through physical contact that can generate highly charged feelings on both sides. These feelings manifest and are worked out differently in distinct styles of body labor that emerge through the intersection of gendered work processes with customers' racial and class positions and their associated service expectations.

Although so far I have drawn parallels between this process of exchanging body services for a wage with the commercialization of feelings in emotional labor, another parallel can be drawn to the encroachment of the capitalist system into the area of social reproduction. Glenn (1992) and others have illuminated how the performance of household work such as cleaning, cooking and caring for children and the elderly has become increasingly part of the capitalist market, and these low-paying, unprotected jobs (nanny, elderly caregiver, nurses aide) are most often filled by immigrant women of color. Similar to these dynamics of commodifying reproductive labor and farming it out at low-wages to less privileged women, this study has illustrated how body services and the emotional labor accompanying it, what I have conceptualized as body labor, have become increasingly commercialized and designated as racialized immigrant women's work.

Additional dimensions of body labor that I will explore in further studies include the impact of this form of work on the women who perform it and the ways they conform or resist its pressures, the role of managers in supervising body labor, the variation between body labor in non-essential beauty services such as nail salon work versus the work of social reproduction, and as previously mentioned, the ethnic-specific dimensions of Korean-Black and Korean-White relations. While this article has concentrated on the case study of nail salons, the concept of body labor can be applied to many other occupations, especially female-dominated service professions in which service providers and customers are of different race and class, including hairdressers, masseuses, nannies, nurses, doctors, personal trainers and prostitutes.

Finally, in mapping out the racial, gendered and classed complexity of body labor, this article highlights a kernel of social change that lies in negotiating service interactions between women of different classes, racial and ethnic backgrounds and immigrant statuses. While these interactions often mimic structures of power and privilege, they also create opportunities to contest these structures. The Korean salon owner of Downtown Nails learns to respect and show appreciation for Black working-class patrons. Korean manicurists at Uptown Nails assert their knowledge and expertise over their White middle-class customers. Routinized service at Crosstown Nails equalizes treatment of women across race and class.

From the customer's side, a weekly trip to the local nail salon can become a lesson in relating to a woman of a radically different social position whom she would rarely encounter in her own milieu. As these emotional and embodied interactions reflect larger systems of status and power, by re-writing the unspoken feeling rules of these interactions, women can take small but important steps in the creation of more equal relations with other women. Evelyn Nakano Glenn (2002) writes that "contesting race and gender hierarchies may involve challenging

176

everyday assumptions and practices, take forms that do not involve direct confrontation, and occur in locations not considered political" (p. 16-17). Exchanges involving body labor in Korean-owned nail salons are one such location where these everyday assumptions and practices can be recognized and possibly re-negotiated.

References

Amott, Teresa and Julie Matthaei. 1991. *Race, Gender and Work: A Multicultural Economic History of Women in the United States.* Boston: South End Press.

Banks, Ingrid. 2000. *Hair Matters: Beauty, Power, and Black Women's Consciousness.* New York: New York University Press.

Anderson, Margaret, and Patricia Hill Collins. 2001. *Race, Class, and Gender: An Anthology.* Belmont, CA: Wadsworth.

Banks, Ingrid. 2000. *Hair Matters: Beauty, Power, and Black Women's Consciousness.* New York: New York University Press.

Banner, Lois. 1983. *American Beauty.* New York: Alfred A. Knopf.

Bordo, Susan. 1993. *Unbearable Weight: Feminism, Western Culture and the Body.* Berkeley: University of California Press.

Burawoy, Michael (Ed.). 1991. *Ethnography Unbound.* Berkeley: University of California Press.

Chapkis, Wendy. 1986. *Beauty Secrets.* Boston: South End Press.

Cheng, Lucie, and Edna Bonacich. 1984. *Labor Immigration Under Capitalism: Asian Workers in the United States Before World War 2.* Berkeley: University of California Press.

Chow, Esther Ngan-Ling. 1994. "Asian American Women at Work." in *Women of Color in U.S. Society,* edited by Maxine Baca Zinn and Bonnie Dill Thornton. Philadelphia: Temple University Press.

Collins, Patricia Hill. 1991. *Black Feminist Thought: Knowledge, Consciousness, and the Politics of Empowerment*. New York: Routledge Press.

Ferree, Myra Marx, and Elaine J. Hall. 1996. "Rethinking Stratification From a Feminist Perspective: Gender, Race, and Class in Mainstream Textbooks." *American Sociological Review* 61:929-950.

Frank, Arthur W. 1990. "Bringing Bodies Back In: A Decade Review." *Theory, Culture, and Society* 7:131-62.

Furman, Frida Kerner. 1997. *Facing the Mirror: Older Women and the Beauty Shop Culture*. New York: Routledge.

Gimlan, Debra. 1996. "Pamela's Place: Power and Negotiation in the Hair Salon." *Gender and Society* 10:505-526.

Glenn, Evelyn Nakano. 1992. "From Servitude to Service Work: Historical Continuities in the Racial Division of Paid Reproductive Labor." *Signs* 18:1-43.

Hall, Elaine J. 1993. "Waitering/Waitressing: Engendering the Work of Table Servers." *Gender and Society* 7:329-346.

Hooks, Bell. 1981. *Ain't I A Woman: Black Women and Feminism*. Boston: South End Press.

—. 1990. *Black Looks: Race and Representation*. Boston: South End Press.

Hu-DeHart, Evelyn. 1999. *Across the Pacific: Asian Americans and Globalization*. Philadelphia: Temple University Press.

Hurtado, Aida. 1989. "Relating to Privilege: Seduction and Rejection in the Subordination of White Women and Women of Color." *Signs* 14:833-855.

Kang, Miliann. 1997. "Manicuring Race, Gender, and Class: Service Interactions in New York City Korean Nail Salons." *Race, Gender, and Class* 4:143-164.

Leidner, Robin. 1993. *Fast Food, Fast Talk: Service Work and the Routinization of Everyday Life*. Berkeley: University of California Press.

—. 1999. "Emotional Labor in Service Work." *AAPSS Annals* 561:81-95.

Lively, Kathryn. 2000. "Reciprocal Emotion Management: Working Together to Maintain Stratification in Private Law Firms." *Work and Occupations* 27:32-63.

Ong, Aihwa. 1987. *Spirits of Resistance and Capitalist Discipline: Factory Women in Malaysia*. Albany: State University of New York Press.

Pierce, Jennifer L. 1995. *Gender Trials: Emotional Lives in Contemporary Law Firms*. Berkeley: University of California Press.

Rooks, Noliwe. 1996. *Hair Rising: Beauty, Culture, and African American Women*. New Brunswick: Rutgers University Press.

Smith, Dorothy. 1987. *The Everyday World as Problematic: A Feminist Sociology*. Boston: Northeastern University Press.

Steinberg, Ronnie, and Deborah Figart. 1997. "Emotional Labor Since 'The Managed Heart'." *Annals AAPSS* 561:8-26.

Wharton, Amy. 1999. "The Psychological Consequences of Emotional Labor." *AAPSS Annals* 561:158-177.

Zinn, Maxine Baca. 1989. "Family, Race, and Poverty in the Eighties." *Signs* 14:856-874.

---

[1] I will examine the ethnic specific dimensions of customer interactions in the historical context of Korean-Black relations more fully in a separate article.

7. Korean Adoptees' Role in the United States

Eleana Kim

Korean adoptees in the United States number well over 100,000. Over half of these adoptees are adults, and they have begun, in recent years, to collectively publicize their unique identity as Koreans and as Americans. Following a brief history of Korean adoption, this paper examines Korean adoptees' relationship to Korea and asks how the overseas adopted Korean community movement might help us rethink what it means to be Korean in the diaspora. I end with some provisional thoughts about what the future role of Korean adoptees might be with respect to Korean unification.

A Brief History of Korean Adoption

The history of adoption from South Korea spans five decades, which makes South Korea's the longest continuous foreign adoption program in the world. Harry Holt, an evangelical Christian and logging magnate from Oregon, became a legendary figure in Korean adoptee history when he and his wife, Bertha, adopted eight GI babies in 1955. Largely through their efforts, both the Korean and the United States governments hastily passed legislation to facilitate the rescue of these children (Sarri et al. 1998). The Holts soon established Holt Adoption Agency (now Holt International Children's Services), which continues to be the leading agency for transnational adoption today.

Following the first wave of bi-racial children came full-blooded Korean "orphans," relinquished in large part to extreme poverty, a lack of social service options, and a staunchly patrilineal, "Confucian" society which places primal importance on consanguineous relations, especially on the status that comes with bearing sons. According to Alstein and Simon (1991), South Korea allowed "almost unrestricted adoption" of orphaned and abandoned children from the 1950s through the 1970s. Coinciding with the legalization of abortion and the political censure of transracial black-white adoptions in the U.S., adoption agencies in the 1970s expanded their international programs, and an increasing number of Korean children were adopted into Caucasian middle class homes. Children relinquished by their parents in Korea became legal "orphans" and were sent overseas to families who were motivated primarily by the desire to achieve the ideal nuclear family, rather than by the largely humanitarian goals of the previous generation (Alstein and Simon 1991).

Whereas the women who relinquished their children in the 1960s and 70s tended to be poor factory workers, by the 1980s, as South Korea's economic boom took off, unmarried college-age women were giving up their babies. Today, a trend in teen pregnancies has supported the supply of adoptable babies. No doubt, factors such as South Korea's rapid industrialization, unstable economic development, patriarchal attitudes about women's sexuality, residual gender ideologies in contradiction with liberal sexual practices, and the recent IMF crisis serve to perpetuate the social conditions which contribute to the abandonment or relinquishment of children in South Korea.

Between 1955 and 1998, over 197,000 South Korean children were adopted in South Korea and abroad, with around 150,000 sent overseas. Approximately 100,000 of those adopted were sent to American families, and the remainder were adopted into European families. In the United States, South Korean adoption accounted for over half of the total international adoptions during the 1980s and early 1990s. At its peak in the 1980s, over 8,000 South Korean children were sent for overseas adoption annually. In 1989, with most countries sending less than 1/10 of one percent of live births abroad, South Korea was sending one percent of live births (Kane 1993, 336), a rate that earned it the reputation of being "the world's leading exporter of children."

North Korea had already criticized the South Korean government for its liberal adoption policies in the late 1970s, and the government subsequently took steps to reduce the numbers of foreign adoptions by instituting the Five Year Plan for Adoption and Foster Care (1976-1981) that included measures to promote domestic adoption (Sarri et al. 1998). Then, when South Korea achieved international recognition and honor as the host of the 1988 Summer Olympics in Seoul, it also received negative scrutiny from the American press for exporting its "greatest natural resource," its children. Reportedly bringing in $15 to 20 million per year, adoption in South Korea had become a business and a cost-effective way of dealing with social welfare problems (Herrmann & Kasper 1992; Rothschild 1988; Sarri et al. 1998).

Due to growing ignominy in the eyes of the international community, the government soon announced a plan to gradually phase out adoption, implementing a quota system to reduce the number of children sent abroad by three to five percent a year. In addition, state policies in the early 1990s encouraged domestic adoptions through tax incentives and family benefits and gave preference to foreign couples willing to adopt bi-racial, or "special needs" children. An eleven-year decline in transnational South Korean adoption was reversed with the sudden economic crisis of 1998, which caused a concomitant crisis of overflowing orphanages. In 1996, approximately 5,000 children were placed in state care, and that figure was projected to double in 1998, leading the Ministry of Health and Welfare to announce that it "has no choice but to make changes to recent policy which sought to restrict the number of children adopted overseas." (Kim 1999)

Adoption from South Korea has proven to be extremely sensitive to economic fluctuations and concerns over the nation's international reputation. The most recent proposal to suspend foreign adoptions came in July 2002 following the successful co-hosting of the 2002 World Cup Games, when the government announced a plan to further bolster the nation's image through measures that would publicize South Korean products and technology, and that would address human rights issues that have been sources of censure, including adoption. These measures, drafted by the "committee for the improvement of the national image," address among other things, the human rights of migrant workers and the social welfare of disabled people, and call for another phasing out of overseas adoption (Shim 2002). It is too soon to determine whether this new plan will indeed lead to the end of international adoptions from South Korea, or whether it, too, will be reversed due to future economic pressures, as has been the case with other such plans over the past four decades.

What is certain, however, is that greater resources must be developed and funds allocated for the welfare of Korean women and children. With the lowest social welfare spending of any OECD country (Kim 2000, 260), South Korea's aspirations for advanced nation status may require the abolition of foreign adoption, yet the economic and material realities suggests that these plans may be short-sighted unless adequate reform of the welfare system is seriously undertaken. Other problematic hurdles to the curtailment of adoption are related to the deeply embedded patriarchal ideologies of South Korea--the social stigma associated with single parenthood, the low status of women, and the "Confucian" rejection of non-agnate adoption-- and they render the choice of single motherhood in Korea a hazardous or wholly unfeasible one for most women.

Domestic adoptions have been on a slow yet steady increase since 1995, with 1,726 adoptions by South Koreans in 1999, yet South Korean adopters can only partially alleviate the problem of 7,000 children in need of welfare intervention each year (Jang 2000). Public education campaigns encouraging greater receptiveness to domestic adoption have been instituted by adoption agencies in South Korea, and greater openness among parents of adopted children have helped to reduce some of the stigma of adoption in South Korea. Foreign adoptions from South Korea have dropped to around 2,000 per year, yet South Korea continues to rank third in the world—after Russia and China—in the number of children adopted by Americans annually. This international movement of 2,000 South Korean children is now matched by a reverse movement of 2,000 or more Korean adult adoptees who return to South Korea every year.

A Growing Korean Adoptee Transnational Movement

With generations of adopted Korean children having come of age since the 1950s, elaborations of a distinctive "Korean adoptee" identity have begun to emerge over the past few years. Many are now excavating their own pasts and critiquing assimilationist models to ask questions about kinship, social relations, biological ties and "family" ideology. Against the dominant discourses provided by Korean, American, and Korean-American communities, they are actively exercising a Korean adoptee "voice" in the process of naming and constituting what one Korean-American adoptee has dubbed a "fourth culture" (Stock 1999). Their experiences as "pioneers" of transnational adoption have made them valuable resources for rethinking adoption policy and practice. Some individuals and groups are participating in the current and future practice of Korean and transnational adoption as advisors and consultants to agencies and parents, or as mentors for younger adoptees. And adoptees are now increasingly adopting children from South Korea themselves, thus building multi-generational Korean adoptive families.

As adoption from China becomes increasingly prevalent and visible in cities such as New York and San Francisco, as well as in small towns throughout the United States, it would appear that transnational adoption from Asia is becoming almost faddish. Korean adoptees, therefore, play an important role in educating the next generation of Asian adoptees and their parents in the challenges of being a multiracial adoptive family in the United States.

The ability for overseas adopted Koreans to imagine themselves as part of a transnational community of adoptees, and as "Koreans" has only recently been made possible through global flows of communication and media, and also through the direct intervention of the South Korean State, which has begun to publicly acknowledge adoptees as part of the modern "global family" of Korea. Transnational flows and circulations have created more opportunities for adoptees and biological families to find and meet each other, with electronic registries and the Internet providing faster and more efficient means of tracking and disseminating information.

In addition, over the past decade, the Internet has facilitated growing numbers of organized groups of adult Korean adoptees around the world. They are beginning to elaborate a revisionist history to the official narrative of adoption produced by the South Korean State. Since the early 1990s, at least a dozen adult adoptee organizations and support groups have emerged worldwide – in Europe, Australia, the U.S. and South Korea. Along with numerous listserves, Web sites, newsletters, magazines, films, and literary anthologies, these "sites of collective articulation" provide spaces for the voicing and exploration of shared historical origins and common experiences with assimilation, racism, identity, and dual kinship. Adoptees of Korean descent are producing and managing a growing sense of collectivity from the available cultural and ethnic categories. They are performing their own form of cultural work, on the borderlands "beyond culture" (Gupta & Ferguson 1992), and asserting their position in a global "ethnoscape" (Appadurai 1996) constructed out of discourses of Korean diaspora and transnationality.

The "fourth culture" of Korean adoptees is one based on a common core experience of being adopted and Korean. Yet the balance of these two categories of identity varies among individuals, and at adoptee events, other vectors of identity such as regional commonalities seem more relevant than being either Korean or adopted. Nevertheless, the potent pull of "roots" has drawn a significant number of Korean adoptees to sites of collective articulation to begin to explore questions of kinship, ethnicity, and identity. This coming of age of transnational Korean adoptees is a distinctive articulation of an emergent Asian-American history and collective subjectivity.

Developing out of a common history and a growing globalized consciousness, this "imagined community" (Anderson 1991) negotiates and brings to light a complicated and troubled relationship to "Korea" as nation-state, culture and place. Common feelings of disorientation and alienation from Korean culture are expressed by adoptees who go back to Korea. Desires for "authentic" personhood (Yngvesson & Mahoney 2000) are frequently expressed in adoptee activities of self-narration. These narratives suggest that the ideal of building bridges, of being "flexible citizens" (Ong 1999) or post-colonial hybrid subjects may be more compelling in theory than it is in lived practice (cf. Maira 1999).

Transnational Korean adoptees have historical, biological, and ethnic connections to their country of birth, yet, for many of them, those connections are abstracted from their everyday lives, having been raised in majority white cultures in American and European Caucasian homes. A concern with identity and loss is central to much adoptee artwork, in which expressive practice enacts a recuperative (re)production or (re)creation of a memory of Korea that has been severed or forgotten (Kim 2001).

The Korean adoptee "movement" has been both a community-building project and a political one, exhibiting concerns with both cultural struggle and social policy. The first Korean adoptee group was formed in 1987 in Sweden, and a small group of adoptees started Minnesota Adopted Koreans in 1991. By 1994, there were other adoptee groups in Western Europe, in the Netherlands, Belgium, Denmark, France and Germany. And by 1998, Korean adoptees in America had organized regionally in New York, Washington D.C., Colorado, Washington State, and California. Global Korean Network, a Korean American organization in California, hosted an adoptee forum in 1997 which brought together 30 adoptees from all over the world, but it wasn't until 1999 that broad international interest became apparent. Three major international conferences took place that year: the Korean American, Adoptee and Adoptive parent Network (KAAN) Conference, the Global Overseas Adoptees'

Link (GOA'L) Conference and, The Gathering of the First Generation of Korean Adoptees.

Scholars of Asian America (Chan 1991; Eng 2001; Lowe 1996; Okihiro 1994; Palumbo-Liu 1999; Takaki 1994, 1995; Zia 2000) and those focusing on Korean diasporic communities (Kim 1996; Min 1998; Park 1997), have documented generations of Asians in the Americas, and analyzed immigrants' relationship to mainstream American culture and society. Yet the "quiet migration" (Weil 1984) of adoptions from Asia has not generally entered into their purview. Transracial, transcultural adoptees exist on the borderlands of "culture" and "ethnicity," and they present a different kind of diasporic subject from those offered by categories such as "immigrant," "exile," or "refugee," having migrated as infants or young children, and with little or no legal, political or personal agency.

Social science research on Korean adoptees has been overwhelmingly dominated by social work and psychology outcome studies that focus on the development of adoptees' racial and ethnic identity, given the fact that the great majority of them have been raised in Caucasian homes (Silverman 1993; Haugaard et al. 1997; Alstein and Simon 2000; Kim 1978), and also in light of the censure of domestic transracial Black-White adoptions as "cultural genocide" by the National Association of Black Social Workers (NABSW) in 1972. A few recent studies have taken samples from the adult Korean adoptee community, generally in Minnesota, which has the largest concentration of Korean adoptees in the U.S. (Meier 1998; Mullen 1996; Westhues and Cohen 1998; Evan B. Donaldson Institute 1999). Most of these studies find that Korean adoptees have adjusted well to their adoptive situations, though many, as youngsters and adolescents, expressed negative self-perceptions around physical appearance. A recent survey found that over 40 percent of respondents identified as "Caucasian" when they were adolescents, which suggests that ethnic identity is a major source of conflict for that generation of adoptees. Most, however, came to identify as Asian-American or as Korean when they matured, often when they moved on to college and were exposed to greater numbers of Asians or Asian-Americans, often encountering Korean and/or Korean-American students and colleagues for the first time.

An obvious comparison to the Korean adoptee experience is that of second- and 1.5- generation Korean-Americans, yet no studies (as of yet) have been published that attempt to draw these connections. Adoptees' anecdotal accounts suggest that the surface similarity between themselves and *chaemi gyop'o* (being raised as culturally assimilated Asian Americans in a dominant white society) does not account for the important difference in their private domestic life—that they were not raised by ethnic Koreans. Moreover, feelings of alienation and perceived discrimination from the Korean-American community have produced further discrepancy between themselves and their Korean-American counterparts.

Recently, however, there has been increasing interest on the part of the ethnic Korean media in the U.S. around adoptee issues, and greater inclusion of adoptees into Korean-American cultural and political activities. This is, in part, an achievement of adoptee activists' efforts to make their voices heard, as well as through important alliances with overseas Korean organizations such as the Korea Society. It also suggests that Korean-American communities are more receptive to adoptees and their families than in the past. The annual KAAN Conference has been instrumental in bringing together scholars and community leaders from the Korean-American community. Other local efforts by adoptive parents and adoptee groups also help to build bridges between Korean adoptee families and Korean-Americans.

Korean Adoptees Relationship to Korea
An increasing number of adopted Koreans have been returning to Korea since the 1980s through agency-facilitated "motherland tours," and also independently. They go there to travel, work, to search for their birth families, and to experience "Korea." Adoptees have an embodied and biological connection to Korea, but they often lack immediately available connections or cultural

competence. Their journeys to the "birth country" have become like a rite of passage for many adoptees as they unearth their pasts, recover embodied memory, and confront the "else-whereness" of their "authentic" identities.

For many adoptees who go to South Korea, the past weighs heavily, whether as something to actively explore through birth family searches, or as something to defer. Many confront their individual histories and understandings of cultural identity and belonging in ways that they may never have done before. This sense of belonging is, in some ways, connected to "Korea," as nation-state and ethnic-cultural paradigm, but it is also produced out of a disjuncture from "Korea."

Adult-adopted Koreans negotiate this complex relationship to "Korea" in a newly globalized economy that has made it possible for them to recognize their own ethnic identity in new ways, both individually and collectively. This identity is also being reformulated by the South Korean State in light of a broader political and social transformation that places Korean adoptees in an ambiguous position—being at once reminders of a difficult past and beacons of an ideal global future (cf. Hubinette 2002). This dialectical relationship raises questions about cultural citizenship and national belonging for a diaspora that is being newly (re)valued by the South Korean State.

The State is, in effect, rewriting adoptee status in Korean society, enrolling adoptees into a specific vision of "Korea" in the 21st century. Adoptees, once pitiable reminders of the social dislocation and poverty behind Korea's rapid modernization, are now being valued as cultural and economic bridges to the West. The liminality of their identity and status in Korea places them in a unique position with respect to the South Korean State, which—through policy reforms, official statements, sponsored "roots" tours, and public ceremonies—has been making efforts to control this liminality in the construction of a transnational Korean diaspora. "Official" nationalist discourse, in welcoming adoptees back to Korea, conjures an indigenous, primal relationship of "blood" that binds adoptees to the "motherland,"

and calls upon adoptees to play a mediating role in a new global economy in which they stand as representatives to the West (Kim 2001). In this way the nation's shameful past can be recompensed through the "success" of transnational adoptees, who are being positioned to contribute to the global reputation of Korea.

Transnational Korean adoptees have also been legally incorporated into the "global family" of South Korea as part of the cultural and economic "globalization" policy (*segyehwa*) inaugurated under former President Kim Young Sam and expanded under recent President Kim Dae Jung (see Kim 2000). OKF, established in 1997, is the prime government agency for incorporating overseas Koreans (*chaeoe tongp'o*) and has as its mission "to serve as the spokesperson on behalf of overseas Koreans worldwide. We recognize their immense contributions, which has provided a tremendous boost, not only to the Korean economy during the 1997 economic crisis, but also the morale of Koreans everywhere." (Overseas Koreans Foundation 2001) Overseas Koreans are welcomed back as part of a global economic consolidation project, as well to participate in Korea's global reputation. Recently gaining recognition as "overseas Koreans" in 1999, adoptees are now also eligible for F-4 visa status,[1] which allows them, as overseas Koreans, to stay in Korea for up to two years, with rights to work, make financial investments, buy real estate, and obtain medical insurance and pensions.

Based upon preliminary research, I argue that, when adoptees encounter "Korea," they negotiate notions of cultural authenticity and difference in the context of competing ideologies of nationalism and globalization (cf. Kim 2000, 262-63). Out of these complex relations and contradictions, I venture that adoptees are finding a space to inhabit and make claims to being "Korean," and, specifically, as Korean adoptees. These return trips to Korea challenge adoptees to reconsider their racial and cultural position in America and in relation to other Korean diasporas, expanding the imaginable bounds of citizenship both in Korean and in the Korean diaspora. My work, thus, explores the dynamic interplay of this inscription of "Koreanness" on adoptees' understandings of their cultural citizenship vis-à-vis Korea and America, and analyzes the ways that a newly constructed "Korean adopteeness" is being elaborated through social networks and emergent global formations.

In what follows, I discuss The Gathering, a seminal event in the emergence of the adult Korean adoptee community, to ethnographically explore the dynamic interplay of adoptee and government projections of "Korea" and their implications for adoptee identity and status.

The Gathering

In September 1999 over 400 Korean-born adoptees from 36 U.S. States and several Western European countries congregated for three days in Washington, D.C. [2] Heralded as the "first significant and deliberate opportunity for the first generation of Korean adult adoptees to come together," "The Gathering of the First Generation of Korean Adoptees," or "The Gathering," as it was called by participants, did not purport a specific political or ideological agenda, but rather was described as "a time for us to celebrate that which we all share. . . ." (Gathering 1999; ellipsis in original). Restricted to adoptees over the age of twenty-one and their spouses or partners, with some spaces reserved for "adoption researchers" and adoption agency "observers," The Gathering was one of three major international public events of 1999 that, together, represent a growing Korean adoptee presence, and a self-conscious production of what Fraser (1992) calls a "counterpublic."[3]

The Gathering was touted as the first conference organized by and exclusively for adult Korean adoptees. For many there, it symbolized an important moment of self-determination in which they asserted their autonomy from parents, agencies, and governments—institutions, which, since their relinquishment, had decided their fates and mediated their realities. The framing of adoption as an accomplishment was continually emphasized in the opening remarks of the conference, often with a sense of wonder, pride, or gratitude. No doubt, these dominant

191

representations exclude the negative experiences that many adoptees have endured due to their cultural displacement, anti-Asian racism, and the social stigma that accompanies transracial adoption.

The title of the conference, "The Gathering," carries with it connotations of communalism, nonpartisanship, and quasi-religiosity, underscored by the Korean translation which accompanied it, "da hamgae" (*ta hamgge*). Translated as "all together," this phrase is suggestive of a collective voice, or chorus, singing in unison. As articulated by Susan Soon-Keum Cox, then vice president of public policy and external affairs for Holt International, conceiver and primary organizer of the conference, and bi-racial adoptee who was adopted in 1956, the intention of the conference was to "focus on us," i.e., the adoptees, for whom the "connection to the birth country is forever."

This connection to the birth country for individual adoptees, however, has been fraught with difficulty, and, as mentioned earlier, only recently acknowledged by the South Korean State. For some adoptees, their actual experiences in South Korea have been marked by perceived rejection, outright discrimination, and painful alienation. After returning to their birth country, "Korea," for many of them, becomes demystified as a place of nostalgia or "home," as they come to accept that they are, as one American adoptee put it, "genetically Korean, but culturally American." At The Gathering, "Korea," as nation-state, as "culture," and as memory, was diversely articulated by government officials, adoption agency professionals and adoptees. An essentialized Koreanness was being drawn upon by all of those constituencies, but in very different ways, bringing out conflicting interpretations of whether or not Korean adoptees are "Korean," and, if they are, how they are.

The Global Family of Korea
In tandem with this recent proliferation of adult adoptee activity, the Kim Dae Jung administration has demonstrated a remarkably open attitude toward adoptees through policy

192

reforms, public recognition of Korean adoptees in South Korea, and official statements such as at this conference. A symbolic break occurred in 1998, shortly after President Kim's inauguration, when he invited twenty-nine Korean adoptees to the Blue House, and offered them an unprecedented public apology. Along with the visa rights granted to adoptees, the opening of the "Adoption Center" in Seoul in 1999 indicates the government's interest in openly addressing the public stigma of adoption in South Korea.[4] This recent recognition of overseas adopted Koreans has been credited in part to the advocacy and encouragement of President Kim Dae Jung's wife, the First Lady Lee Hee-ho. First Lady Lee has given a video address at every major conference for adoptees and publicly meets and greets adoptees during foreign diplomatic tours. At The Gathering, her image projected a matronly face for the symbolic "motherland," embracing adoptees as a source of pride for adoptive parents, Korean culture, and the South Korean State.

Her video address emphasized the ethnic roots of Korean adoptees, exhorting them to "forget your difficult past and renew your relations with your native country in order to work together toward common goals based on the blood ties that cannot be severed." Lee emphasized the role of adoptees in the future of South Korea, which, as she stated, is "developing day by day to become a first-rated nation in the 21st century. It will be a warm and reliable support for all of you." Drawing upon a globalization ideology, coupled awkwardly with metaphors of nurturance, her message was embedded in an economic discourse in which the South Korean nation continues to aspire to first world status. In this narrative, South Korea, which may have been unable to take care of her own in the past, is now capable of incorporating and "supporting" her abandoned children.

South Korean Ambassador Lee Hong Koo echoed the First Lady's sentiments, adding that the role of Korean adoptees would be to build a bridge "between the country of birth and the present country of citizenship." These statements reveal a significant proactive shift on the part of the South Korean State in defining the ambiguous position of Korean adoptees with respect to "the country of birth and the present country of citizenship." The distinction between the two seems to posit an opposition between the birth country to which, as Susan Cox stated, "the connection... is forever," and the adoptive country in the West, which is the contingent, "present" one of citizenship, rather than of blood. The birth country thus stands as an "authentic" source of Koreanness, an inalienable tie that binds Korean adoptees to the nation and, more overtly now, the State.

The rhetoric of "success" that echoed throughout the opening plenary was undoubtedly influenced by the elevated class status of these adoptees, as indicated by their college educations and professional occupations.[5] Ambassador Lee in his speech noted, "You demonstrate the capacity to transform oneself from humble beginnings to success." In many ways, then, adoptees would seem to reflect the same progress and development model offered by the narrative of South Korea's miraculous and meteoric rise, out of a colonial past, through the devastation of war, to its ascendance as a newly industrialized "Asian Tiger," boasting the world's eleventh largest economy in 1996.

These expressions are tokens of a larger national project that seeks to interpolate and co-opt adoptees as overseas Koreans to be integrated into a modern, hierarchically-structured Korean "family" (cf. Park 1996), even as the State and adoption agencies oftentimes discourage or frustrate adoptee searches for their biological families. These adopted children, now adults, are framed as cultural and economic bridges to the West, as representatives of Korean culture, and as potential mediators of global capital. The position of the Korean adoptee vis-à-vis the State, thus, reveals the competing discourses of nationalism and globalization for a modern, industrialized nation dominated by U.S. economic and cultural imperialism.

What emerged during the conference, however, was a dis-identification between the rhetoric of the South Korean State and the lived experience of adoptees who feel disconnected, culturally foreign and ontologically displaced in South Korea. What constitutes their ties to South Korea is precisely those memories of the "difficult past" which Lee Hee-ho exhorted the adoptees to "forget." Unearthing those memories is part of the process of return, search, and reunion for many of these adoptees. As Lisa Lowe points out, "'political emancipation' through citizenship is never an operation confined to the negation of individual 'private' particulars; it requires the negation of a history of social relations" (1996, 26-7). The "forgetting" of personal and national trauma is encouraged not only in American multiculturalist ideologies, but also in the recent attempts by the South Korean government to produce a homogeneously "Korean," yet heterogeneously dispersed "family" based on shared ancestors, or "blood."

Against the narrative of "success" and "achievement" that characterized the opening plenary, the adoptee-centered workshops complicated the meanings of that "success," with attendees sharing intimate and painful memories of Korea, their childhoods in America, and the negative experiences of living in a white culture--with a "white" name and family,[6] but an Asian physiognomy.

The experiences of adoptees in South Korea, as expressed in a workshop I attended,[7] reflected a sense of disappointment in the failure of the fantasy of "home" to live up in reality. For some it was a very painful time, as they faced their past, confronted their feelings about being adopted and worked out complicated issues about race, ethnicity, and culture. Many expressed amazement at finally being in a place where they looked like everyone else, but also the difficulty of not "relating" to Koreans or Korean culture. Others had more positive experiences, with one attendee insisting that one or two trips would not be enough, but rather, having himself been back to Korea six times, that "you have to go several times to understand your relationship to [Korea]."

Overwhelmingly, across all workshop groups, adoptees expressed feelings of discrimination from Americans and feelings of rejection from both South Koreans and Korean-Americans. The perception of being "looked down upon" was linked by adoptees to interactions with South Koreans who treated them as objects of pity. Other adoptees mentioned meeting South Koreans who were surprised at how well they had grown up, for they had only heard sensationalizing stories about sexual abuse and slavery of adopted children by foreigners. The primacy of "blood" in Korean cultural understandings of individual disposition and national character is also rejected by many adoptees who cannot accept the essentializing and ethnocentric assumptions of Koreans who subscribe to a strong cultural nationalism.

A survey of participants at The Gathering found that forty percent of respondents, as adolescents, identified as Caucasian, and would perceive Asians as the "Other" (Evan B. Donaldson Adoption Institute 1999). For adoptees who grew up isolated from each other and who identified primarily as Americans, therefore, racial discrimination posed a particularly difficult form of double-consciousness. Even the most empathetic parents were perceived as unable to fully relate to the experience of racism, thereby intensifying feelings of alienation and racial difference. Some described it as a pendulum swinging back-and-forth between "Korean" and "American" sides. Many agreed with one attendee's sense that "Koreans reject the American side, Americans reject the Korean side," adding that "Koreans reject the adoption side. For them, I ha[ve] no family, no history."

Adoptees who were encouraged to make connections to their Korean "heritage" by their adoptive parents often rejected those attempts as adolescents, with some feeling that the culture pushed on them was "overdetermined," as if they were "the only ones with an ethnic identity." As one adoptee said, "kids just want to fit in and be normal," and many agreed that they felt most comfortable in "mainstream" white culture. Another adoptee described her identity as being "about culture, and your culture is not your face—but you're pinpointed for that all your life." But the recognition of a broad historical and cultural shift was clear—as one adoptee stated, an "international identity is emerging," and another informed his cohort, "Don't you know? Asian people are 'in' now."

Much of the cultural work emerging at sites such as The Gathering is centered on the articulation of double consciousness, as well as a double "Orientalizing" move, one based on reified understandings of "culture" and "nation." Adoptees, who may feel alienated from Korea, as well as from "traditional" Korean or Korean diaspora communities, often "Otherize" Korea at the same time that they attempt to understand what it means "to be Korean." So, while many adoptees used the metaphor of a pendulum to describe the experience of swinging between Korean and American "sides," there is also a tendency to speak of being "Korean" in ethnicized and essentializing ways. At the same time, however, the Korean State is invested in a self-"Orientalizing" project that is tied to tourist discourses and its own vision of itself as an "Asian Tiger" (see Ong 1999).

This double "Orientalizing" move complicates any easy interpretations of Korean adoptee articulations of identity as subaltern interventions, and instead calls for an investigation of the dialectical relation between these practices and the dominant notions of being Korean in the diaspora and in South Korea. Louie (2000) writes about the Chinese-American youth on "roots" tours to China, arguing that the tours raise "tensions…between historically rooted assumptions about Chinese-ness as a racial category and changing ways of being culturally, racially and politically Chinese (in China and the diaspora)." (655) Adoptees, occupying an ambiguous and troubled place in the Korean imaginary, raise similar tensions. As reminders and remainders of South Korea's Third World past, the "illicit" sexual practices of Korean women, and American cultural and economic imperialism, they are the specters of a repressed history, one on which the official narrative of South Korean modernity utterly depends.

197

Yet adult adoptees now occupy a peculiarly privileged position in the context of the global economy. Having been reared in predominantly middle- to upper- middle class white families, adoptees may lack cultural "authenticity," but this is seen as a necessary loss, in return for the benefits of material wealth, "success," and the opportunities afforded by the West. In this way, international adoptees may be considered literal embodiments of the contradictory processes of "globalization." The play of identity and difference that characterizes Korean transnational, transracial adoption is one in which "Koreanness" is a national, political and cultural discourse which seeks to interpolate adult Korean adoptees into a productive role in the global economy, and one which Korean adoptees face when they encounter other overseas Koreans, and especially when they return to South Korea.

Adoption from South Korea is central to understanding South Korean modernity, and continues to be a part of its "postcolonial" history that is at once repressed, yet crucial to understanding how the official narrative of South Korea's "economic miracle" and "struggle for democracy" erases the violence of the military regime and of the draconian development and misogynistic population policies that produced South Korea's "successful" capitalist transformation. As Chungmoo Choi (1997) writes, "assuming South Korea to be postcolonial eludes the political, social and economic realities of its people, which lie behind that celebrated sign 'post' of periodization, without considering the substantive specificity of Korean histories" (349). My work is also, therefore, concerned with the "substantive specificity of Korean histories," in particular, a history that has moved forward in the past several years with the unexpected and unprecedented return of over 2,000 adoptees to South Korea every year, a previously unimaginable scenario for adoption agencies and the government.

Adoptees and social activists in South Korea have criticized the State's continued reliance on international adoption as a social welfare policy solution (Sarri et al. 1998), and its complicity in the perpetuation of gendered inequalities. Birth mothers--often working class women, teen mothers, abandoned single mothers, sex workers, and victims of rape--represent the most subordinated groups in an entrenched patriarchy and misogynistic state welfare system, and are brought into the public gaze with the arrival of adoptees and their desire to locate their social and biological connections.

Adoption from Korea resulted from the initial crisis of orphans and bi-racial GI babies during the Korean War and continued as a product of rapid economic and structural transformation, and as a consequence of Cold War population and development policies intended to build national "stability." Adoption flourished as a profitable enterprise in the 1970s and 1980s, during a period of political repression and massive social unrest. As adult adoptees organize a political voice, their collective counter-memories--composed out of individual memories (and lack of memories) of Korea, oftentimes tragic and painful pre-adoption histories, and return trips to South Korea--are important articulations of personal and national history that demand further investigation.

Transnational Korean adoptees challenge dominant ideologies that conflate race, nation, culture and language in the definition of what it means to be "Korean" and this distinctive subject-position potentially disrupts facile culturalist and nativist assumptions about belonging and identity.[8] There are a number of competing claims to the adoptee's "Koreanness," from the State, from adoption agencies, adoptee groups and adoptee artists, wherein nostalgia, "authenticity," and "tradition" are mobilized in the production of Korean "culture" and "identity." These claims have important ramifications for other internationally adopted individuals and adoptive communities who are themselves negotiating the vexing question of cultural heritage.

As the cultural work of Korean adoptees shows, Korean adoption has as much to do with re-imagining kinship as it does with recasting diaspora. Transnational families are becoming commonplace in many areas of the world, and the deep ethical ambiguities of adoption are increasingly being publicly explored in transnational adoption communities, including that of Korean adult adoptees.[9] Korean adoptees who, with their adoptive families and their biological families are building "superextended" families (Roe 1994), are also building a sense of kinship among themselves. This community based on common experience is extending into one based on solidarity and shared experience. Recognized as Korean, they are making claims as Koreans, but with a difference.

National Divisions: Unification and Adoptees
What does all this mean for adoptees and the goals for Korean unification? With the legal and cultural incorporation of adult adoptees into the Korean overseas community, we can begin to speculate on the affective dimensions of their ties to South Korea. As the Korean-American community reaches out to adoptees, there is the potential for greater self-incorporation of adoptees as part of the Korean diaspora, and with that, perhaps greater identifications with Korean history and political futures. Adoptees are intimately tied to the national division historically and spectrally through the Korean War--the "roots" of adoption and thus of their own history. That connection contains deep ironies especially around the role of U.S. soldiers; they were instrumental in rescuing many of the children who eventually became transnational adoptees, and also sired many of the bi-racial children that launched the initial humanitarian push by Henry Holt.

I was a counselor for the Overseas Koreans Foundation (OKF) Summer Cultural Awareness Program for Overseas Adopted Koreans in 2001. Elsewhere I discuss, in detail, how the construction of adoptees as tourists became a source of conflict on the trip, because their own deep and personal connections to Korea went under-acknowledged, and the difficult emotional circumstances that many faced upon return to their country of birth were not adequately recognized. Indeed, very little of the program was centered on adoption issues, but rather on introducing adoptees to a folklorized vision of "traditional culture," and adoptees were actively discouraged from experiencing contemporary urban Korean life. Programs such as this beg the question of how the globally-conscious, politically-legislated citizenship granted to adoptees is at odds with cultural citizenship in a profoundly nationalist state; and, furthermore, of how the restricted social citizenship and agency of Korean women are addressed or ignored in this process.

On the OKF trip, one exception to this tourist construction of the "motherland" was a visit to the memorial park in Kwangju, commemorating the victims of the 1980 Kwangju Uprising. There, the adoptees learned of that tragic event in the nation's history and cultural imaginary. For many, it was a moving and enlightening experience, to learn about this history and there was a realization that the South Korea that they had left was a very different one than the one they were now returning to. I was further struck by the fact that many of them, being in their twenties and early thirties, were born or relinquished during the reign of Chun Doo Hwan, perhaps making the visit to the park even more poignant and powerful.

Tobias Hubinette, a Korean-Swedish adoptee, activist and academic made explicit connections between the adoptee experience and that of many of the seven million globally dispersed Koreans who have been victims of tragic proportions in Korea's modern history. It could be argued that adoptees are of the most highly privileged migrants, yet their shared experiences of displacement and loss resonate with these other suppressed or difficult histories, and this sentimental connection may be the grounds for deeper connections to issues of unification.

Korean-American adoptees are producing an imagined community and their own historical narratives. The kind of political and cultural ties this group makes to Korea in the long run have yet to be determined, but it seems that some form of "imagined community," or perhaps even "long distance nationalism" (Anderson 1981, 1996) may emerge in the future.

What is clear is that the bold cultural nationalism of the South Korean government often serves to further alienate adoptees from "Korea," and that their own personal connections and experiences of loss must be acknowledged before any claims can be made about how "Korean" they are or should be.

---

1 Unlike other overseas Koreans, however, adoptees must be able to prove that they were born in Korea, by providing documentation from their adoption agencies.

2 The large majority of the 400 participants were from the U.S., with around a dozen European adoptees. For this reason, the perspectives of adoptees in the U.S. tended to dominate the discussion. The Oslo Gathering in 2002 was primarily attended by European adoptees, mostly from Scandinavia.

3 Fraser writes, "Subaltern counterpublics have a dual character. On the one hand, they function as spaces of withdrawal and regroupment; on the other hand, they also function as bases and training grounds for agitational activities directed toward wider publics. It is precisely in the dialectic between these two functions that their emancipatory potential resides" (1992: 110).

4 Unfortunately, the Adoption Center has not proven to be the resource it was intended to be. My visit there in the summer of 2001 suggested that it was underutilized and under staffed, and the databases and services it advertises were not in place.

5 According to a survey of The Gathering participants, 70 percent had graduated college, 24 percent had graduate degrees and 15 percent were enrolled in university or postgraduate work.

6 It is important to note that while the great majority of adoptees at the conference were raised by white middle class families, there was a great deal of diversity with respect to color, racial identification, class and sexuality.

7 The adoptees were divided into six groups according to the years in which they were adopted, with a seventh comprised of adoptee spouses and partners. I sat in on one session with a group of over fifty adoptees who had arrived between the years of 1967 and 1970.

8 See Moon (2000) for a discussion of similar impacts being made by the increasing presence of foreign migrant workers in South Korea.

9 Strong (2001) articulates well the ambiguities of transracial, transnational adoption: "Adoption across political and cultural borders may simultaneously be an act of violence and an act of love, an excruciating rupture and a generous incorporation, an appropriation of valued resources and a constitution of personal ties" (471).

8. The Coming of Age of Korean Adoptees: Ethnic Identity Development and Psychological Adjustment

Richard M. Lee, Hyung Chol Yoo, and Sara Roberts

The international adoption of Korean children in the United States formally dates back to the armistice treaty that ended the Korean War in 1953. During this early period, American families, predominantly White, adopted hundreds of orphaned Korean children and bi-racial Korean children of American military. By the 1960s, however, the availability of children adoption of Korean children as an alternate means to start and expand their families. Today, American parents, still mostly White, continue to adopt children from South Korea with an average of about 2,000 adoptions per year (U.S. State Department, 2002).

It is estimated that over 110,000 children have been adopted from South Korea during this 50-year period (Evan B. Donaldson Adoption Institute, 2002). The peak adoption period was in the early to mid-1980s when over 6,000 children were adopted annually. These numbers dropped dramatically after the 1988 Seoul Olympics when the Korean government responded to negative media coverage over the perceived abundance of children available for adoption by imposing limits on the annual number of international adoptions. Today, international adoption from Korean to the United States ranges from 1,700 to 2,000 children annually. According to 2000 U.S. Census data and annual immigration data, Korean adoptees now constitute approximately 5-10% of the total Korean-American ethnic population. Moreover, the majority of these children are "coming of age," that is, they are entering late adolescence and adulthood.

Despite constituting a sizable portion of the Korean-American population, Korean adoptees have been a relatively silent voice in the Korean immigration discourse. For many decades, adoptees were viewed as a source of shame for Koreans and Korean-Americans and they were overlooked by communities and scholars. However, in recent years, Korean adoptees and their families have taken it upon themselves to voice their presence in the community and to claim their place in Korean immigration history (e.g., Bishoff & Rankin, 1997; Robinson, 2002; Trenka, 2003). The centennial celebration of Korean immigration history cannot be complete without an acknowledgement and recognition of the experiences and contributions of Korean adoptees to our collective ethnic consciousness in this country.

This chapter aims to situate the experiences of Korean adoptees within this larger Korean immigration history by addressing the "coming of age" of Korean adoptees from a psychological perspective. We specifically describe an empirical study that examined the relationship between ethnic identity development and psychological adjustment among transracial Korean adoptees who are now adults in American society (hereafter referred to as Korean adult adoptees). The study draws upon a convenience sample of Korean adult adoptees recruited from adoption conferences, adoption agencies, and through snowball sampling procedures facilitated by Korean adoptee and non-adoptee undergraduate and graduate students in psychology. The majority of the participants attended the Korean-American, Adoptee, Adoptive Family Network (KAAN) annual conferences held in Seattle (August, 2001) and Minneapolis (August, 2002).

Transracial Adoption Paradox
Like other children who are adopted internationally and are raised transracially in White families, Korean adoptees live an ethnic and racial paradox that is unique to transracial adoptees and not experienced by Korean children raised by their biological families (Lee, 2003a). Specifically, Korean adoptees must negotiate what it means to be ethnic and racial minorities

in society, but to be perceived and treated by others, including oftentimes themselves and their adoptive families, as ostensibly White. This set of contradictory experiences that is nevertheless true presents unique psychological and social challenges to Korean adoptees across the lifespan. These ethnic and racial challenges include ethnic identity development, coping with prejudice and discrimination, developing and maintaining friendships and romantic relationships, and acceptance within different ethnic and racial communities.

These challenges associated with transracial adoption paradox are perhaps most evident among Korean adoptees who are now adults. The majority of Korean adult adoptees were adopted at a time in society – 1960s and 1970s – when ethnic and racial differences tended to be ignored or minimized within families and communities (Lee, 2003a). Of course, there were some adoptive parents from this generation who provided age-appropriate cultural experiences to help their children successfully negotiate ethnic and racial challenges. But for the rest, the familial and societal practice of cultural assimilation was believed to be in the best interest of the child, and it was reinforced by the lack of ethnic diversity within local communities and the disconnection with Korean immigrant communities. Most adoption agencies also did not provide post-adoption services to assist adoptive families when they were confronted with ethnic and racial problems. Similarly, post-adoption organizations and activities, such as Korean culture camps and language schools, which were run largely by adoptive parents, were not widely available during this period of history.

Transracial adoption advocates and critics alike now recognize that an unfortunate consequence of cultural assimilation is the potential inadequate preparation of children for life as ethnic and racial minorities in society (Register, 1991; Steinberg & Hall, 2000). Specifically, adoptees do not learn as children what it means to identify positively as a member of an ethnic and racial group and to cope effectively with prejudice and discrimination.

Consequently, Korean adoptees who are confronted with these issues later in life as adolescents and adults must learn to resolve these developmental challenges on their own. Recent Korean adoption narratives (Bishoff & Rankin, 1997; Robinson, 2002 Trenka, 2003), for example, depict the lives of adult adoptees who struggled to understand the meaning of ethnicity and race in their lives, long after they left the insular home environments in which they were raised. For some, ethnic identity development began after experiences with discrimination and racism. For others, ethnic identity development began when they found themselves amidst other adoptees and non-adopted Korean-Americans in college. In many of these stories, adoptees recounted the emotional highs and lows as they struggled to make sense of their unique ethnic and racial experiences in their families, in the larger Korean community, and in society.

The transracial adoption paradox, however, is not necessarily a problem for all adoptees. Some adoptees raised in predominantly White communities may not have had an impetus to explore their ethnic roots as children because ethnic and racial differences were not made salient by family, neighbors, and classmates. As adults, these adoptees have developed racial attitudes that overlook ethnic and racial differences, including instances of discrimination and racism that may be more apparent to others, and have chosen to situate themselves in predominantly White communities to which they feel a sense of belonging and attachment. While some critics may argue that these individuals have internalized White privilege and notions of tokenism, there is no evidence to suggest that they are more likely to experience psychological distress over their life circumstances. Clearly, some Korean adoptees choose to live their lives without the need to ever resolve the transracial adoption paradox.

Ethnic Identity Development
It is believed that the manner in which transracial adoptees, including Koreans, negotiate the transracial adoption paradox is best evinced in their ethnic identity development and that adoptees with positive and strong ethnic identities will be

206

psychologically well adjusted (Lee, 2003a). Unfortunately, there is a paucity of quantitative research on the ethnic identity development of Korean adult adoptees to support this claim, although there are some qualitative studies on this subject (Friedlander, Larney, Skau, Hotaling, Cutting, & Schwam, 2000; Huh & Reid, 2000; Meier, 1999). Instead, what is mostly known from a review of the literature is that there is a great degree of variability in the ethnic identity development of transracial adoptees. For example, Hollingsworth (1997) found in a meta-analysis that transracial adoptees had weaker ethnic identities than same-race adoptees. Other research found that transracial adoptees tended to be highly acculturated to White mainstream society (Andujo, 1988; Kim, 1977; Vroegh, 1997). Westues and Cohen (1998) found that transracial, international adoptees raised in Canada were equally likely to identify ethnically as Canadians and as members of their birth culture. At the same time, the majority of transracial adoptees in their study identified as racial minorities (73-79%) and not as White (11-17%). Benson, Sharma, and Roehlkepartain (1994) found that more than one-fifth of transracial adoptees wished they were a different race or felt ashamed of their racial backgrounds. In a recent survey of 163 Korean adult adoptees who attended a national conference specifically for Korean adoptees, Freundlich and Lieberthal (2000) found that, while growing up, 36% described themselves as Caucasian and 42% described themselves as Korean/Asian. By contrast, as adults, only 11% described themselves as Caucasian and 78% described themselves as Korean/Asian. While these studies shed some light on the complexity of understanding the ethnic identity development of transracial adoptees, they failed to address the relationship between ethnic identity and psychological adjustment.

In the only published quantitative studies to examine the relationship between ethnic identity development and psychological adjustment among Korean transracial adoptees, Yoon (2001) and Cederblad, Hook, Irhammar, and Mercke (1999) found seemingly divergent findings. In the first study, Yoon found that Korean adolescent adoptees with more positive ethnic identities, as measured by pride in one's ethnic group, described their parents as having actively promoted their Korean heritage growing up. Moreover, Yoon found that a positive relationship between ethnic identity and psychological adjustment. In the second study, Cederblad et al. conducted an epidemiological study on predominantly Korean international adult adoptees living in Sweden. Contrary to Yoon's study, they found that ethnic experiences, as measured by perceived discrimination and interest in one's ethnicity, were related to behavioral problems, emotional distress, and lower self-esteem. In other words, the two studies found that ethnic identity was positive or negatively related to psychological adjustment. This set of discrepant findings may be due to the distinct cultural context of the two countries, but there is some indication that it may be related to the different measurements of ethnic identity.

We conceptualized and measured ethnic identity as a multidimensional construct as proposed by Phinney (1990, 1992) and Lee and Yoo (in press). Phinney (1990) originally identified three critical aspects of ethnic identity that included a sense of identity achievement, affirmation and belonging, and ethnic involvement and practices. In their psychometric evaluation of Phinney's (1992) Multigroup Ethnic Identity Measure, based on her earlier conceptualization, Lee and Yoo (in press) re-conceived these three aspects of ethnic identity as cognitive clarity (e.g., clear sense of one's ethnicity), affective pride (pride in ethnicity), and behavioral engagement (e.g., active in ethnic organizations). Moreover, they found initial support for differential effects ethnic identity on psychological adjustment. Specifically, ethnic identity clarity and pride appeared most strongly associated with positive adjustment, whereas, ethnic identity engagement was not associated with psychological adjustment. In fact, ethnic identity engagement was negatively associated with adjustment when the other two aspects of ethnic identity were statistically controlled.

The adoption of a multidimensional model of ethnic identity development might help to explain the discrepant findings between Yoon (2001) and Cederblad et al. (1999). Specifically, it is possible that Yoon found a positive relationship between ethnic identity and adjustment, because ethnic identity was measured as a sense of ethnic pride, which past research has found to be related to positive adjustment (Lee & Yoo, in press; Phinney, 1990). By contrast, it is possible that Cederblad et al. found a negative relationship between ethnic identity and adjustment, because ethnic identity was measured as a sense of interest and engagement, which Lee and Yoo found to be less related to positive adjustment. This latter finding may reflect the ongoing struggle with the transracial adoption paradox for Korean adult adoptees and, specifically, the stress associated with learning about one's ethnic heritage which has been long denied. It is understandable that Korean adult adoptees raised as ostensibly White but now interested in their ethnic heritage will experience positive and negative emotions associated with their ethnic identity development, depending upon which aspect of ethnic identity is made most salient. Altogether, these experiences reflect normative developmental processes associated with the search for and establishment of a positive ethnic identity (Phinney, 1990).

Study Purpose and Hypotheses

The purpose of this study was to examine the ethnic identity development of Korean adult adoptees and its relationship to psychological adjustment. If Korean adult adoptees did not have a chance to develop their ethnic identities at an earlier age, because of pressures to culturally assimilate into society, then it was expected that they would seek to negotiate the transracial adoption paradox and, specifically, to establish positive ethnic identities as adults. In support of this idea of a deferred developmental task, we compared the ethnic identity development of Korean adult adoptees with a sample of non-adopted Korean-American college students who were drawn from a previous study (Lee, 2003b). While we recognized that this Korean-American sample was not an ideal comparison group, we felt that it would sufficiently illustrate differences in ethnic identity development between these two groups and serve as a starting point for future research on the ethnic identity development of Korean adoptees. We specifically hypothesized that Korean adult adoptees would report lower levels of ethnic identity clarity and pride than non-adopted Korean-Americans, because of their ongoing struggle as adults to negotiate the transracial adoption paradox. At the same time, we hypothesized that Korean adult adoptees would report similar levels of ethnic identity engagement as non-adopted Korean-Americans, because adult adoptees, particularly as represented in our sample, were actively interested in their ethnic birth culture and sought to establish more positive ethnic identities.

We also were interested in the extent to which different aspects of ethnic identity contributed to the psychological adjustment of Korean adult adoptees. Specifically, we addressed the discrepant findings by Yoon (2000) and Cederblad et al. (1999) and hypothesized that, for Korean adult adoptees, ethnic identity clarity and pride would be related positively to adjustment, while ethnic identity engagement would be related negatively to adjustment. Psychological adjustment was assessed by life satisfaction and psychological distress. We also controlled for four variables at the individual level that were identified as relevant to ethnic identity and adoption experiences. First, one of the most consistent predictors of psychological adjustment among adoptees is age at adoption. Research strongly suggests children adopted at a later age demonstrate a higher risk for psychological and behavioral problems in later childhood and adulthood (Sharma, McGue, & Benson, 1996; Verhulst, Althaus, & Verluis-Den Bieman, 1990). Second, gender tends to be predictive of adjustment with boys exhibiting greater behavioral problems than girls (Sharma, McGue, & Benson, 1998). Third, individuals who are high in negative affectivity and low in positive affectivity tend to hold more negative self-views and to be more vulnerable to psychological distress (Watson & Clark, 1984). Finally, we elected to control for perceived discrimination, given theoretical support that suggests ethnic identity development is mediated by perceived discrimination (Phinney, 1990).

Method
Sample and Procedure
The Korean adult adoptee sample consisted of 67 adults (11 men, 55 women, 1 unidentified) with a mean age of 27.25 years (*SD* = 6.57) and an age range from 18 to 49 years old. The adoptees were recruited between July 2001 to August 2002 from national conferences for Korean adoptees and families and local adoption agencies and organizations in Minnesota and paid $5.00 for their participation. The majority of adoptees (52%) were from Minnesota, and the remaining sample was predominantly from states in the Midwest, West, and Northeast. The overwhelming majority (94%) had some college (33%), a college degree (42%), or a graduate degree (19%). Of the 58% of the sample who provided their marital status, 85% were single, 13% were married, and 3% were divorced. Nearly three-fourths (72%) had at least one adopted sibling. The average age at adoption was 21.97 months (*SD* = 29.46) with a median of 9 months and a range from 0 to 195 months with the next highest age at adoption of 84 months. Prior to adoption, the majority (60%) had only one pre-adoption placement (e.g., orphanage, foster family) with another 28% having two pre-adoption placements.

The non-adopted Korean-American sample was drawn from another study (Lee, 2003b) and used only to compare scores on a measure of ethnic identity in this study. A total of 84 Korean-American undergraduate students were recruited during Spring of 2000 from Asian-American courses and student organizations at a large, public, Southwestern university and paid $5.00 for their participation. The sample consisted of 43 men and 39 women (with two unidentified) with a mean age of 21.18 years (SD=1.56) and an age range between 18 to 28 years. Slightly more than half (55%) of the participants emigrated from Korea, while 43% were born in the United States (2 participants did not report generation status).

Instruments

Korean adult adoptee participants completed the Multigroup Ethnic Identity Measure (Phinney, 1992), Perceived Discrimination Scale (Finch, Kolody, and Vega, 2000), Positive Affect Negative Affect Schedule (Watson, Clark, & Tellegen, 1988), Satisfaction with Life Scale (Diener, Emmons, Larsen, & Griffin, 1985), and the Hopkins Symptom Checklist-21 (Green, Walkey, McCormick, & Taylor, 1988), as well as a demographic sheet. Only data on the Multigroup Ethnic Identity Measure was selected from the non-adopted Korean-American comparison sample.

Multigroup Ethnic Identity Measure (MEIM; Phinney, 1992).

The MEIM is a 14-item self-report measure of three aspects of ethnic identity – ethnic identity clarity (EI-Clarity), ethnic identity pride (EI-Pride), and ethnic identity engagement (EI-Engage) (Lee & Yoo, 2003). The scale items are rated on a 4-point scale from 1 (strongly disagree) to 4 (strongly agree) with a higher score reflecting a more positive ethnic identity. One item from the original MEIM ("strong attachment to group") was not included in the computation of scale scores based on previous factor analytic research (Lee & Yoo, 2003). For the Korean adult adoptee sample, the mean item score for the five-item EI-Clarity was 2.82 (SD = .64) with an internal reliability estimate of .72 (α). The mean item score for the three-item EI-Pride was 3.33 (SD = .57) with an internal reliability estimate of .74 (α). The mean item score for the five-item EI-Engage was 3.02 (SD = .70) with an internal reliability estimate of .78 (α).

Hopkins Symptom Checklist-21 (HSCL; Green et al., 1988).

The HSCL is a 21-item version of the Hopkins Symptom Checklist (Derogatis, Lipman, Rickels, Uhlenhuth, & Covi, 1974) and is a self-report measure of psychological distress and physical symptoms associated with general stress. The scale items are rated according to level of distress during the past seven days on a 4-point scale from 1 (not at all) to 4 (extremely) with a higher score reflecting greater distress. For this study, the mean item score was 1.64 (SD = .42) with an internal reliability estimate of .89 (α).

Satisfaction with Life Scale (SWLS; Deiner et al., 1985).
The SWLS is a 5-item self-report measure of subjective well-being. The scale items are rated on a 7-point scale from 1 (strongly disagree) to 7 (strongly agree) with a higher score reflecting greater life satisfaction. For this study, the SWLS was modified to assess satisfaction across three life domains (personal, family, and social) for a total of 15 items (5 items x 3 domains). The mean item score was 4.73 (SD = 1.23) with an internal reliability estimate of .94 (α).

Positive Affect Negative Affect Schedule (PANAS; Watson et al., 1988).
The two 10-item mood scales measure positive and negative affectivity (PA and NA, respectively). The scale items are rated according to level of agreement in general (i.e., how you feel on the average) on a 5-point scale from 1 (very slightly or not at all) to 5 (extremely) with higher scores reflecting greater positive affectivity. For this study, the mean item score for the PANAS total scale was 3.95 (SD = .47) with an internal reliability estimate of .86 (α).

Perceived Discrimination Scale (PDS; Finch et al., 2000).
The PDS is a brief 3-item measure of perceived personal ethnic discrimination that has been used in previous studies of Asian-Americans (Lee, 2003b). The three items are rated on a 4-point scale from 1 (strongly disagree) to 4 (strongly agree) with higher scores representing higher personal ethnic discrimination. For this study, the PDS mean item score was 1.67 (SD = .76) and the internal reliability estimate (α) was .79.

Results
To compare the ethnic identity development of Korean adult adoptees with non-adopted Korean-Americans, a MANCOVA was performed with the three measures of ethnic identity (EI-Clarity, EI-Pride, and EI-Engage) as the dependent variables. Participant age was entered as a covariate in the analysis because of the large mean age difference in the two samples. A multivariate main effect was found to be statistically significant (Wilkes Lambda' F (3, 135) = 5.40, p < .005, η^2 = .11). Tests of

between-subjects comparison found significant group differences on EI-Clarity (F (1, 137) = 14.62, p < .001, η^2 = .10) and EI-Pride (F (1, 137) = 5.65, p < .05, η^2 = .04). As hypothesized, Bonferroni pairwise comparisons of estimated marginal mean scores found that Korean adult adoptees had lower EI-Clarity (2.77 vs. 3.24) and EI-Pride (3.29 vs. 3.57) scores than non-adopted Korean-Americans. By contrast, there was no significant group difference on EI-Engage (2.96 vs. 3.12).

To assess the extent to which different aspects of ethnic identity contributed to the psychological adjustment of Korean adult adoptees, above and beyond confounding risk factors, two hierarchical multiple regression analyses were performed with psychological distress (HSCL) and life satisfaction (SWLS) as the separate dependent variables. For each regression equation, demographic variables (gender, age, age at adoption) were entered in Step 1; mood or positive affect (PANAS) was entered in Step 2; perceived discrimination (PDS) was entered in Step 3, and the three measures of ethnic identity (EI-Clarity, EI-Pride, EI-Engage) were entered in Step 4. Prior to the regression analyses, a Pearson product-moment correlation was calculated to examine the inter-correlations among scales (see Table 1).

For psychological distress, the overall multivariate effect of the regression was statistically significant (F (8, 52) = 3.08, $p < .01$; R^2 = .32). Contrary to hypothesis, no aspect of ethnic identity contributed uniquely to lower psychological distress (see Table 2). However, participant age was related negatively to psychological distress (β = -.39; sr^2 = .11), and age at adoption was related positively to psychological distress (β = .29; sr^2 = .06).

For life satisfaction, the overall multivariate effect of the regression was statistically significant (F (8, 52) = 4.01, $p < .001$; R^2 = .38). As hypothesized, aspects of ethnic identity contributed uniquely to greater life satisfaction (see Table 2). Specifically, EI-Engage was related negatively to life satisfaction (β = -.36; sr^2 = .07). The relationship between EI-Pride and life satisfaction was not statistically significant at the $p < .05$ level (β = .26; sr^2 = .04), but a closer examination of the magnitude of effect size (sr^2), which is unaffected by sample size, suggests that EI-Pride was related positively to life satisfaction. In addition, positive affect ($\beta = .29$; $sr^2 = .06$) and perceived discrimination ($\beta = -.27$; $sr^2 = .07$) were related to life satisfaction. Specifically, positive affect was related positively to life satisfaction, whereas, perceived discrimination was related negatively to life satisfaction.

Discussion

The transracial adoption paradox refers to the contradictory but true experiences that adoptees confront society as an ethnic and racial minority while ostensibly perceived and treated by others as White. For many Korean adoptees, these conflicted experiences oftentimes are left unexplored until they have "come of age" as adults. It is at this point in time that they are confronted with the challenge of establishing positive ethnic identities. This study, therefore, examined the ethnic identity development of Korean adult adoptees, in comparison with non-adopted Korean-Americans, and the extent to which different aspects of ethnic identity contributed to the psychological adjustment of Korean adult adoptees, above and beyond previously identified risk factors for international and transracial adoptees (i.e., gender, age, age at adoption, mood, and perceived discrimination).

This study represents the first documented comparison between adopted and non-adopted Korean-American adults in their ethnic identity development. A word of caution, however, is necessary before further interpretation of these findings. As stated earlier in the study purpose (and again later in the limitations of the study), we recognize that this non-adopted sample of Korean-American college students is not an ideal comparison group, especially because of the age difference, but the comparison nevertheless sufficiently illustrates group differences in ethnic identity development and serves as a starting point for future research. With this limitation in mind, we found that, as hypothesized, Korean adult adoptees had lower levels of ethnic identity clarity and pride than non-adopted Korean-Americans. This expected finding supports the likelihood that transracial Korean adult adoptees were given less cultural socialization opportunities to explore and establish positive and secure ethnic identities while growing up. It also is corroborated by personal narratives and anecdotal stories told by Korean adult adoptees who have expressed high degrees of ethnic identity confusion growing up in White families and communities with minimal contact with other Korean families (Freundlich & Lieberthal, 2000; Meier, 1999).

We also found that, as hypothesized, there was no significant difference in ethnic identity engagement between adopted and non-adopted Korean-Americans. This finding likely reflects the active negotiation to resolve the transracial adoption paradox and to establish positive ethnic identities by Korean adult adoptees seeking to learn more about their Korean heritage and culture. It also is less surprising given that this sample of Korean adult adoptees were recruited primarily from adoption conferences, organizations, and agencies. These Korean adult adoptees may not be necessarily representative of the general Korean adult adoptee population, such as those who would not attend Korean adoption-related events, but the similar levels of ethnic identity engagement suggest that some Korean adult adoptees are interested in their Korean culture and heritage as much as non-adopted Korean-American college students. Moreover, we found that ethnic identity engagement was correlated strongly with ethnic identity clarity and pride. As such, it represents an important developmental activity that is related to a more positive and secure ethnic identity. This interpretation is consistent with ethnic identity development theory (Phinney, 1990).

Using a multidimensional measure of ethnic identity, two aspects of ethnic identity were found to have differential effects on life satisfaction and psychological distress for Korean adult adoptees. Specifically, ethnic identity engagement was related to lower life satisfaction, whereas ethnic identity pride was related to higher life satisfaction. However, no aspect of ethnic identity was related to psychological distress. The effects of these aspects of ethnic identity on life satisfaction were relatively robust, even after taking into account adoption-related risk factors. In particular, we covaried the effects age, age at adoption, gender, mood and perceived discrimination and still found ethnic identity to have unique effects on life satisfaction.

The differential effects on life satisfaction help to clarify earlier discrepant findings on the relationship between ethnic identity and psychological adjustment by Cederblad et al. (1999) and Yoon (2000). The finding with ethnic identity engagement is consistent with earlier research by Cederblad et al. and suggests that adoptees may experience temporary, subjective feelings of confusion and lower life satisfaction when they actively engage in ethnic activities and explore what it means to be an ethnic minority in society. The finding with ethnic identity pride, by contrast, is consistent with earlier research by Yoon and suggests that feeling proud, good, and happy to be a member of an ethnic group helps to fulfill one's overall life satisfaction across multiple domains (e.g., personal, social, family). Taken altogether, the findings confirm that ethnic identity can be associated with either emotional highs or lows depending on which aspect of identity is made salient.

Aspects of ethnic identity, however, do not appear to be related to psychological distress, a finding that is not consistent with research by Cederblad et al. (1999). One possibility is the use of different identity and distress measures in the two studies. For example, we measured general psychological distress, whereas, Cederblad et al. measured behavioral problems. Another possibility is the different geographical contexts and age groups of the samples. It was interesting to note that adoption-related risk factors, particularly participant's age and age at adoption, were related to psychological distress. For example, older adoptees reported less distress. This finding is consistent with the notion that older adults tend to have more life stability and security and, therefore, have relatively fewer life stressors. Perhaps more interesting is the fact that age at adoption remains a significant predictor of maladjustment into adulthood. This finding extends past adoption research, which only had samples of children and adolescents (Sharma et al., 1996; Verhulst et al., 1990). Clearly, the persistent negative effect of age at adoption beyond childhood warrants further investigation.

This study has a number of methodological limitations that need to be addressed in future research. First, our sample of Korean adult adoptees is relatively small and based on convenience sampling, thereby limiting the generalizability of the results. We readily acknowledge the difficulties in collecting this type of community data, particularly when the sample is geographically dispersed and, like other minority communities, concerned about feeling objectified by researchers. Second, our comparison sample of non-adopted Korean-Americans was drawn from another data set (Lee, 2003b). We attempted to control for inherent differences in the samples (e.g., both data sets were collected around the same period of time and we covaried age in our analysis), but future studies need to better match samples. It also is simply not possible to compare Korean adult adoptees raised in White families with Korean adult adoptees raised in Korean- or Asian-American families (perhaps the ideal comparison sample), because there are so few same-race Korean adoptions taking place in the United States. Third, more theory-driven research is necessary to elucidate the differential effects of ethnic identity on psychological adjustment and other outcome variables. Risk and resilience theory (Luthar, Cicchetti, & Becker, 2000; Masten, 2001), for example, provides a framework to understand ethnic identity as a psychological resource that potentially mediates the negative effects of known risk factors, including pre-adoption risks (e.g., age at adoption) and post-adoption risks (e.g., prejudice and discrimination).

In summary, the life stories and experiences of Korean adoptees are a part of the Korean-American immigration history. By studying their experiences from a psychological perspective, we gain a greater understanding of the transracial adoption paradox and the ethnic identity development of Korean adult adoptees. As more Korean adoptees "come of age" and begin to negotiate the transracial adoption paradox for themselves, it remains important to acknowledge and to consider their unique experiences and challenges as they establish positive ethnic identities and situate themselves within the larger Korean-American community.

References

Benson, P.L., Sharma, A.R., & Roehlkepartain, E.C. (1994). *Growing Up Adopted: A Portrait of Adolescents and Their Families*. Minneapolis, MN: Search Institute.

Bishoff , T., & Rankin, J. (1997). *Seeds from a Silent Tree: An Anthology By Korean Adoptees*. San Diego: Pandal Press

Cederblad, M., Hook, B., Irhammar, M., & Mercke, A. (1999). Mental health in international adoptees as teenagers and young adults. An epidemiological study. *Journal of Child Psychology & Psychiatry & Allied Disciplines, 40*, 1239-1248.

Diener, E., Emmons, R. A., Larsen, R. J., & Griffin, S. (1985). The Satisfaction With Life Scale. *Journal of Personality Assessment, 49*, 71-75.

Derogatis, L.R., Lipman, R.S., Rickels, K., Uhlenhuth, E.H., & Covi, L. (1974). The Hopkins Symptom Checklist (HSCL): A self-report symptom inventory. *Behavioral Science, 19*, 1-15.

Evan B. Donaldson Adoption Institute (2002). *International Adoption Facts*. Retrieved October 16, 2002, from http://www.adoptioninstitute.org/FactOverview/inter national.html.

Finch, B.K, Kolody, B., & Vega, W.A. (2000). Perceived discrimination and depression among Mexican-origin adults in California. *Journal of Health and Social Behaviors, 41*, 295-313.

Freundlich, M., & Lieberthal, J.K. (2000). *The Gathering of the First Generation of Adult Korean Adoptees: Adoptees' Perceptions of International Adoption*. Retrieved October 16, 2002, from http://www.adoptioninstitute.org/.

Friedlander, M.L., Larney, L.C., Skau, M., Hotaling, M., Cutting, M.L., & Schwam, M. (2000). Bicultural identification: Experiences of internationally adopted children and their parents. *Journal of Counseling Psychology, 47*, 187-198.

Green, D.E., Walkey, F.H., McCormick, I.A., & Taylor, A.J.W. (1988). Development and evaluation of a 21-item version of the Hopkins Symptom Checklist with New Zealand and United States respondents. *Australian Journal of Psychology, 40*, 61-70.

Harrison, A.O., Wilson, M.N., Pine, C.J., Chan, S.Q., & Buriel, R. (1990). Family ecologies of ethnic minority children. *Child Development, 61*, 347-362.

Huh, N.S., & Reid, W.K. (2000). Intercountry, transracial adoption and ethnic identity. *International Social Work, 43*, 75-87.

Lee, R.M. (2003). *Transracial adoption paradox: History, research, and counseling implications of cultural socialization*. Manuscript in press in *The Counseling Psychologist*.

Lee, R.M., & Yoo, H.C. (2003). *Structure and measurement of ethnic identity for Asian American college students*. Manuscript in review.

Luthar, S. S., Cicchetti, D., & Becker, B. (2000). Research on resilience: Response to commentaries. *Child Development, 71*(3), 573-575.

Masten, A. S. (2001). Ordinary magic: Resilience processes in development. *American Psychologist, 56*(3), 227-238.

Meier, D. I. (1999). Cultural identity and place in adult Korean-American intercountry adoptees. *Adoption Quarterly, 3,* 15-48.

Phinney, J.S. (1990). Ethnic identity in adolescents and adults: Review of research. *Psychological Bulletin, 108,* 499-514.

Phinney, J.S. (1992). The multigroup ethnic identity measure: A new scale for use with diverse groups. *Journal of Adolescent Research, 7,* 156-176.

Register, C. (1991). *"Are Those Kids Yours?": American Families with Children Adopted from Other Countries.* New York: Free Press.

Robinson, K. (2002). *A Single Square Picture: A Korean Adoptee's Search for Her Roots.* New York: Berkley Books.

Rutter, M., Pickeles, A., Murray, R., & Eaves, L. (2001). Testing hypotheses on specific environmental causal effects on behavior. *Psychological Bulletin, 127,* 291-324.

Sharma, A. R., McGue, M. K., & Benson, P. L. (1996). The emotional and behavioral adjustment of United States adopted adolescents: Part II. Age at adoption. *Children & Youth Services Review, 18*(1-2), 101-114.

Sharma, A.R., McGue, M.K., & Benson, P.L. (1998). The psychological adjustment of United States adopted adolescents and their nonadopted siblings. *Child Development, 69,* 791-802.

Steinberg, G., & Hall, B. (2000). *Inside Transracial Adoption.* Indianapolis, IN: Perspectives Press.

Trenka, J.J. (2003). *The Language of Blood.* Minneapolis: Borealis Books.

U.S. Department of State. (2002). *Immigrant visas issued to orphans coming to the U.S, FY 1989-2001*. Retrieved October 16, 2002, from http://travel.state.gov/orphan_numbers.html.

Verhulst, F.C., Althaus, M., & Verluis-Den Bieman, H.J.M. (1990). Problem behavior in international adoptees: II. Age at placement. *Journal of American Academy of Child and Adolescent Psychiatry, 29*, 104-111.

Watson, D., Clark, L.A., & Tellegen, A. (1988). Development and validation of brief measures of positive and negative affect: The PANAS Scales. *Journal of Personality and Social Psychology, 54*, 1063-1070.

Watson, D., & Clark, L.A. (1984). Negative affectivity: The disposition to experience aversive emotional states. *Psychological Bulletin, 96*, 465-490.

Table 1.

Inter-correlations among measures of ethnic identity, mood, perceived discrimination, and psychological adjustment

	EI-Clarity	EI-Pride	EI-Engage	PANAS	PDS	HSCL	SWLS
EI-Clarity	--						
EI-Pride	.55	--					
EI-Engage	.62	.54	--				
PANAS	.03	.28	.01	--			
PDS	-.04	-.01	.10	-.15	--		
HSCL	-.02	-.14	.03	-.44	.16	--	
SWLS	.03	.24	-.15	.43	-.35	-.36	--

Note. N = 61 after listwise deletion. EI-Clarity = Ethnic identity clarity; EI-Pride = Ethnic identity pride; EI-Eng = Ethnic identity engagement; PANAS = Positive Affect Negative Affect Schedule; HSCL = Hopkins Symptom Checklist; SWLS = Satisfaction with Life Scale.

Table 2.

Hierarchical multiple regression analyses testing differential effects of ethnic identity on psychological adjustment

Dependent Variables	HSCL				SWLS			
Independent Variables	B	SE	β	sr^2	B	SE	β	sr^2
Age	-.03	01	-.39**	.11	.00	.03	.00	.00
Gender	-.19	.14	-.17	.02	.45	.37	.14	.02
Age at adoption	.00	.00	.29*	.06	-.00	.01	-.14	.01
Positive affect	-.23	.12	-.25	.05	.72	.32	.29*	.06
Perceived discrimination	.10	.07	.16	.02	-.46	.19	-.27*	.07
Ethnic identity clarity	-.06	.12	-.09	.00	.34	.31	.17	.01
Ethnic identity pride	-.02	.12	-.03	.00	.56	.31	.26	.04
Ethnic identity engagement	.12	.10	.19	.02	-.61	.26	-.36*	.07

Note: N = 61 after listwise deletion. * p < .05. ** p < .01. HSCL = Hopkins Symptom Checklist. SWLS = Satisfaction with Life Scale. For HSCL, Step 1 R^2 = .19; Step 2 $_\Delta R^2$ = .09; Step 3 $_\Delta R^2$ = .03; Step 4 $_\Delta R^2$ = .02. For SWLS, Step 1 R^2 = .05; Step 2 $_\Delta R^2$ = .17; Step 3 $_\Delta R^2$ = .08; Step 4 $_\Delta R^2$ = .09.

9. Independent and Interdependent Self-Construals of Koreans and Korean-Americans: the Effects of Gender and the Level of Acculturation

Yoon Joh

The study investigated self-construal of the 1.5 generation[1] Korean-American college students in relation to counseling and therapy. Self-construal is a critical concept for the 1.5 generation Korean-American college students who live in the United States and are raised by immigrant parents who impose traditional Korean culture on them. Multicultural counseling literature overlooks challenges encountered by this generation living in two conflicting cultures.

Using the variables of acculturation, gender, and generation, the current study investigated their effects on the self-construals of the 1.5 generation Korean-American college students and the combined group of the 1.5 and second generation Korean-American college students. The study also described characteristics of the independent versus interdependent self-construal groups among the 1.5 and second generations Korean-American college students.

---

[1] The term Korean-Americans refers to Korean immigrants in the United States. To avoid confusion in the text, the following distinction has been made among self-identified Korean and Korean-Americans. The term Korean immigrants has been applied to Korean immigrant parents, and their children, the 1.5 generation Korean-Americans who immigrated to the United States at a young age with their parents. American-born individuals are considered second generation. The 1.5 are Korean-born, and are normally classified as 1st generation in the literature (Suinn, Rickard-Figueroa, Lew & Vigil, 1987).

Data on independent and interdependent self-construals were obtained using the *Self-Construal Scale (SCS)*, which measures these two dimensions of the self. A total of 142 Korean-American undergraduate and graduate college students comprised the participants of the descriptive and inferential statistical investigation of the study. Data collection lasted approximately 2.5 months in the summer of 1997. The participants were recruited from five Korean churches in the New York City metropolitan area. Descriptive statistics examined group differences for independent and interdependent self-construals.

Multivariate analysis of variance (MANOVA) was used to investigate the effects of gender and acculturation on self-construal. Discriminant function analysis (DFA) provided information on the specific acculturation functions, as measured by the *Suinn-Lew Asian Self-Identity Acculturation (SL-ASIA)*. Generational differences were also investigated by MANOVA procedures.

Significant Findings and Conclusions

The findings of the study show that their self-construals are significantly influenced by the level of acculturation, English proficiency, and their generational position in the United States. and.

Descriptive Analysis

The mean score on the *SCS* in the present study for the independent group was 4.6973 (M = 4.6973), and 4.9954 for the interdependent group (M = 4.9954), with standard deviations of .6881 and .6389, respectively (SD = .6881, SD = .6389): The *SCS* is a Likert scale in which 1 indicates "strongly disagree" and 7 indicates "strongly agree." The mean scores of the present study are also similar to those of the study by Singelis and Sharkey (1995). In their study, Korean-American college students had a mean score of 4.67 on the independent subscale (M = 4.67) and 4.93 on the interdependent subscale (M = 4.93). In both the present study and that of Singelis and Sharkey (1995), Korean-Americans showed higher interdependence than independence.

One unexpected finding of the present study was that 68.20% of the respondents were identified as bicultural on the *SL-ASIA*, yet the mean score of the group was higher on interdependence ($\underline{M}$ = 74.24) than on independence ($\underline{M}$ = 71.01). The results may be due to the fact that Korean-Americans as a group have higher interdependence than independence, as evidenced by the study of Cross (1995).

The independent group consisted of 74.0% United States citizens, and the interdependent group consisted of 34.8% Korean citizens. Also, 88% of the study participants who responded that their English was excellent showed higher independence than interdependence, and 39% of the participants who rated their English as good showed higher interdependence than independence. Fifty percent of individuals who have lived in the United States for more than 10 years had higher independence, and 100% of the participants who have lived in the United States for less than 10 years had higher interdependence.

Acculturation and Gender

The main effects of acculturation on the self-construals of the 1.5 generation, and the combined group of 1.5 and second generations, also are consistent with the findings of Singelis and Sharkey (1995), whose study indicated that Asian-Americans were higher on interdependence ($\underline{F}$ = 12.89, $\underline{p}$ <.001), and lower on independence, than Euro-Americans ($\underline{F}$ = 15.94, $\underline{p}$ < .001). In the present study, the grand mean scores of the 1.5 generation Korean-American college students were higher on interdependence ($\underline{M}$ = 74.24) than on independence ($\underline{M}$ = 71.01) (see Table 1, Appendix). Thus, results of the present study indicate, as predicted, that more acculturated Korean-American college students have a higher level of independence than their less acculturated counterparts; and, also, that less acculturated Korean-American college students have a higher level of interdependence than more acculturated individuals ($\underline{F}$ [4, 270] = 15.954, $\underline{p}$ < .05) (see Table 2). In the present study the discriminant function equation for the level of acculturation was statistically significant, with a Chi square of 32.589 (p < .05) ([4, N = 91] = 32,589, p < .05) (see Table 3).

One notable finding is that the level of acculturation, as well as generational differences, had a significant effect on the independent subscale of the SCS, but not on the interdependent subscale (see Tables 4 and 2). This may be due to the fact that, as a group, Korean-American college students (1.5 and second generations) have higher interdependence than independence, thereby reducing statistical significance on the interdependent subscale.

In their study of ethno-cultural groups, Singelis and Sharkey (1995) found that, on the interdependence subscale of the SCS, Korean-Americans had a mean score of 4.93 with a standard deviation of .68 (M = 4.93, SD = .68). The Korean and Korean-American mean score of 4.93 was the highest among the groups which included Euro-American, Chinese-American, Filipino-American, and Japanese-American groups (Singelis & Sharkey, 1995). Again, the findings are similar to those of the present study, which had a mean score of 4.99 with a standard deviation of .6389 (M = 4.99, SD = .6389) on the interdependent subscale of the SCS.

The results of the present study, regarding interaction effects of gender and acculturation on the SCS conflict with the findings by Kashima et al. (1995). In the present study, there was no interaction effect of gender by acculturation on independent and interdependent self-construals of Korean-American students. However, the study by Kashima et al. (1995), involving five cultures, showed that univariate F tests of a culture and gender interaction was significant for allocentrism, the individual-level construct that corresponds to collectivism at the cultural level. The effect of gender by acculturation on self-construal thus needs further investigation.

Nevertheless, in the current study, the main effect of gender was not statistically significant. The researcher initially anticipated females would score higher on interdependence than their male counterparts. One possible explanation for the lack of statistical significance in the current study is that although cultural and gender differences have little overlap (Miller, 1994), the variations between independent and interdependent self-construals may be due to a cultural dimension rather than a gender dimension. Similarly, Kashima et al. (1995) found gender effect was non-significant on collectivism, but was significant for emotional relatedness.

Furthermore, Kashima et al. (1995) found that individualistic, collective, and relational dimensions of self are empirically separable. The finding of no main effect for gender on independent and interdependent self-construals of Korean-American college students in the current study, therefore, may confirm that independent and interdependent self-construals are characterized by cultural rather than gender dimensions.

English Proficiency

MANOVA results of the present study indicated that a main effect for English proficiency was statistically significant (F [4, 276] = 4.077, p < .05) (see Table 5). A 3 x 2 design (English proficiency x self-construal) yielded anticipated results, as confidence in one's English has been found by Pak, Dion, and Dion (1985) to be positively related to perceived control over one's life for Chinese in Canada. Perceived control over one's life (internal control), as opposed to external control, is related to independence (Uba, 1994). Further, one type of acculturative stress comes from the difficulty learning English (Uba, 1994). Thus, Korean-American students who rated their English to be excellent perceive themselves to have higher independence than their counterparts with lower English proficiency.

Generation

In the present study, generational differences showed statistically significant effects on self-construals (F [2, 139] = 8.244, p < .05) (see Table 6). These results were consistent with Phinney's (1990) findings that second generation Chinese-Americans showed lower ethnic identity than first generation

Chinese-Americans. The generational differences appear to have a direct relationship to acculturation, thus affecting independent and interdependent self-construals.

Implications
The findings of the study were intended to help counselors better grasp the sense of self of the 1.5 generation Korean-American college students who were born in Korea, yet who have spent the majority of their developmental years in the United States (Yu, 1988). The purpose of the study was also to challenge the Western sense of self commonly accepted in counseling and therapy, which may not be appropriate for individuals such as the 1.5 generation Korean-Americans.

The study indicated that the 1.5 generation Korean-American college students' self-construals vary depending on their level of acculturation and English proficiency. More specifically, the 1.5 generation Korean-American college students have a higher degree of independence, which is emphasized in American culture, if they have a higher level of acculturation (Western identified), and are fluent in English. Differences also exist between the 1.5 and second generations in that the 1.5 generation is less acculturated, and has a higher level of interdependence than the second generation. Also, Korean-American students who have a lower level of acculturation (Asian identified), who are the 1.5 generation, and who are less fluent in English demonstrate higher interdependence.

One implication of these findings is that counseling approaches need to be modified for the 1.5 generation Korean-American students. First, their communication difficulties in English need to be recognized. Although they have spent the majority of their developmental years in the United States, they come from bilingual settings in which Korean may be the primary language spoken at home. Second, individual variation of acculturation must be addressed. As the findings of the current study indicate, an individual's level of acculturation has a significant impact on his or her thoughts, feelings, and actions concerning his or her relationship to others.

For the 1.5 generation Korean-American college students, counselors need to recognize features emphasized in interdependence. Hierarchical order in social relationships inevitably leads to proper conduct, and emotional harmony is essential in such relationships. Emphasis on proper conduct and emotional harmony leaves no room for open expression of feelings and self-actualization, often stressed in counseling and therapy. Thus, counselors working with the 1.5 generation Korean-Americans may not encourage direct expression of feelings and individuality, but understand the importance of maintaining emotional harmony with others. Furthermore, counselors need to be aware of conflicts this generation experiences living in two cultures.

Counselors may adopt the bicultural model that embraces both American and Korean cultures. Adopting this model requires a great amount of flexibility and open-mindedness by counselors. Appropriate graduate and professional training in multicultural counseling that emphasizes group differences in self-construal and a bicultural model would likely facilitate this kind of shift. Another implication of the study findings is multicultural counseling literature needs to recognize variations within the Korean-American population in terms of acculturation, gender, citizenship, duration of residence in the United States, generational differences, and English proficiency. Also focusing on descriptive information about Korean-Americans as a single group is to be avoided. Such singular approaches, although not intended, lead to stereotypes.

Recommendations for Future Study
The findings of the study lead to additional questions relevant for future research on this topic. The following recommendations are presented as avenues for further investigation regarding the self-construals of Korean-American college students.

1. Having identified in this study that acculturation level has a significant relationship to independent and interdependent self-construals of the 1.5 and second

generation Korean-American college students, additional factors of acculturation, such as family structure, should be examined in order to fully understand the range of variables of acculturation that affect self-construals of Korean-American students.

2. Further research should also determine who specifically constitutes the 1.5 generation. For example, future study requires that specific limits of the 1.5 generation be established in terms of the age at which they immigrated to the United States, because the age variable is likely to affect an individual's acculturation level.

3. Additional research is needed to examine the relationship of independent and interdependent self-construals of Korean-American college students to other variables; for example, management of stress and perception of counseling.

4. Due to conflicting findings in the research literature and the present study, future research should further examine gender in relation to independent and interdependent self-construals in different cultural groups.

5. In-depth research is needed to examine the relationship between parenting style of Korean-Americans and its effect on independent and interdependent self-construals of their children. A qualitative research approach would be especially helpful in observing and identifying Korean-American parenting style in fostering self-construal in children.

6. Future research needs to investigate the variable of religion in relation to self-construals. Because the sample in the present study was drawn from Korean churches in the Korean community, it may not reflect other religions in the Korean community.

7. The impact of Christianity on independent and interdependent self-construals of Korean-Americans, likewise, needs to be further investigated.

8. In the current study, generation in the United States and citizenship of the study participants were self-identified.

Future research is thus needed regarding definition and documentation of factors associated with "generation" and "citizenship."

9. The results of this study have been based on responses from a limited number of Korean churches in a geographic area with a high Korean population (i.e., New York City). Additional studies that examine self-construals of Korean-American students, with no religious affiliation in different regions of the country, could add to the knowledge base and expand the generalizability of the present findings.

References

Abe, J. S. & Zane, N. W. (1990). Psychological maladjustment among Asian and White American college students: Controlling for compounds. Journal of Counseling Psychology, 37, 437-444.

Arrendono, P., Psalti, A., & Cella, K. (1993). The woman factor in multicultural counseling, Counseling and Human Development, 25, 57-62.

Ary, D., Jacobs, L., & Razavieh, A. (1996). Introduction to Educational Research (5th Ed.), New York: Harcourt Brace.

Atkinson, D. & Thompson, C. (1992). Racial, ethnic, and cultural variables in counseling. (1992). In S. D. Brown & R. W. Lent (Eds.), Handbook of Counseling Psychology (2nd Ed. pp. 349-382). New York: John Wiley & Sons, Inc.

Birman, D. (1994a). Acculturation and human diversity in a multicultural society. In J. Trickett, R. J. Watts, & D. Birman (Eds.), Human diversity: Perspectives on people in context (pp. 261-284). San Francisco: Jossey-Bass.

Birman, D. (1994b). Biculturalism and ethnic identity: An integrated model. Focus, 8(1), 9-11.

Cross, S. (1995). Self-construals, coping, and stress in cross-cultural adaptation. Journal of Cross-Cultural Psychology, 26(6), 673-697.

Helms, J. E. (1995). The conceptualization of racial identity and other "racial" construct. In J. Trickett, R. Watts & D. Birman (Eds.), Human diversity: Perspectives on people in context (pp. 285-309). San Francisco: Jossey-Bass.

Kashima, Y., Kim, U., Gelfend, M., Yamaguchi, S., Choi, S., & Yuki, M. (1995). Culture, gender, and self: A perspective from individualism-collectivism research. Journal of Personality and Social Psychology, 69(5), 925-937.

Kerwin, C. & Ponterotto, J. G. (1996). Biracial identity development: Theory and research. In J. G. Ponterotto, J. M. Casas, L. A. Suzuki, & C. M. Alexander (Eds.), Handbook of multicultural counseling (pp. 199-217). Thousand Oaks, CA: Sage Publications, Inc.

Markus, H. & Kitayama, S. (1994). The cultural construction of self and emotion: Implications for social behavior. In S. Kitayama & H. Markus (Eds.), Culture, self, and emotion (pp. 89-130). Washington, DC: American Psychological Association.

Miller, J. (1994). Cultural diversity in the morality of caring: Individually-oriented versus duty-based interpersonal moral codes. Cross-cultural Research, 28, 3-39.

Pak, A., Dion, K., & Dion, K. (1985). Correlates of self-confidence with English among Chinese students in Toronto. Canadian Journal of Behavioral Science, 17(4), 369-378.

Remirez, M. (1994). Psychotherapy and counseling with minorities: A cognitive approach to individual and cultural differences. Needham Heights, MA: Allyn & Bacon.

Singelis, T. (1994). The measurement of independent and interdependent self-construals. Personality and social psychology bulletin, 20(5), 580-591.

Singelis, T. & Brown, W. (1995). Culture, self, and collectivist communication. Human communication Research, 21(3), 354-389.

Singelis, T., & Sharkey, W. H. (1995). Culture, self-construal, and embarrassability. Journal of Cross-cultural Psychology, 26(6), 622-644.

Singelis, T., Triandis, H., Bhawuk, D., & Gelfend, M. (1995). Horizontal and vertical dimensions of individualism and collectivism: A theoretical and measurement refinement. Cross cultural Research: The Journal of Comparative Social Science, 29(3), 240-275.

Sue, D. & Sundberg, N. D. (1996). Research and research hypotheses about effectiveness about in intercultural counseling. In P. Pederson, J. Draguns, W. Lonner, & J. Trimble (Eds.), Counseling across cultures (4th ed. pp. 323-352). Thousands Oaks, CA: Sage Publications, Inc.

Suinn, R., Ahuna, C., & Khoo, G. (1992). The Suinn-Lew Asian self-identity acculturation scale: Concurrent and factorial validation. Educational and Psychological Measurement, 52, 1041-1046.

Suinn, R., Rickard-Figueroa, K., Lew, S., & Vigil, P. (1987). The Suinn-Lew Asian self-identity acculturation scale: An initial report. Educational and Psychological Measurement, 47, 401-407.

Triandis, H. (1993). Collectivism and individualism as cultural syndromes. Cross-cultural Research - the Journal of Comparative Social Science, 27(3-4), 155-180.

Uba, L. (1994). <u>Asian Americans</u>: <u>Personality patterns, identity, and mental health</u>. New York: Guilford Press.

Yu, E. Y. (1988). Population characteristics of Koreans in America and their settlement patterns. In J. R. Kim (Ed.), <u>The Korean community in America</u> (pp. 12-25). New York, NY: The Korean Association of New York.

Yu, K. & Kim, L. (1983). The growth and development of Korean-American children. In G. Powell (Ed.), <u>The psychosocial development of minority group children</u> (pp. 147-158). New York: Brunner/Mazel.

Appendix

Table 1
<u>Grand Mean Scores of the 1.5 Generation on SCS (N = 91)</u>

Source	M	SD	SEM
Independent self-construal	71.01	11.64	1.43
Interdependent self-construal	74.24	8.37	1.15

Table 2
<u>Multivariate Analysis of Variance Summary for Acculturation by Gender</u> (N = 142)

	Multivariate ANOVA				Univariate ANOVA	
Source	df	F	df		(1)	(2)
A	(4, 270)	15.954 *	(2, 136)	F	12.801 *	4.175
G	(2, 135)	1.198	(1, 136)	F	.064	2.011
A x G	(4, 272)	1.445	(2, 136)	F	.735	2.287

Note: Univariate analyses are on (1) Independent self-construal and (2) Interdependent self-construal.

Table 3

Discriminant Function Analysis Summary for the 1.5 Generation (N = 91)

Eigen-value	% Var.	Canonical Correl.	Wilk's Lambda	Chi sq.	df	F-Prob
.488	99.5	.556	.689	32.589 *	4	.000

Note. *p < .05

Table 4

Multivariate Analysis of Variance Summary for Acculturation by Gender for the 1.5 Generation (N = 91)

	Multivariate ANOVA			Univariate ANOVA	
Source	df	F	df	(1)	(2)
A	(4, 168)	8.535 *	(2,85)	F 5.447 *	2.381
G	(2, 84)	.568	(1,85)	F 1.057	.750
A x G	(4, 168)	.469	(2,85)	F .694	.828

Note: Univariate analyses are on (1) Independent self-construal, and (2) Interdependent self-construal.

Table 5

Multivariate Analysis of Variance Summary for English proficiency for the 1.5 and Second Generations (N = 142)

	Multivariate ANOVA			Univariate ANOVA	
Source	df	F	df	(1)	(2)
English Proficiency	(4, 276)	4.077 *	(2, 139)	F 3.276 *	1.786

Note: Univariate analyses are on (1) Independent self-construal and (2) Interdependent self-construal. *p < .05.

Table 6

Multivariate Analysis of Variance Summary for Generation (N = 142)

Multivariate ANOVA			Univariate ANOVA		
Source	df	F	df	(1)	(2)

Generation (2, 139) 8.244 * (1,140) F 5.318 *   4.376 *

Note: Univariate analyses are on (1) Independent self-construal and (2) Interdependent self-construal. *p < .05

238

10. The Role of Korean Churches in Formation and Incorporation of the Korean Community in the Washington, D.C. Area[1]

Okyun Kwon

I. The Role of Korean Churches in Formation of the Korean Community

Church as a Community Center from the Beginning of Korean Immigration

The Washington, D.C. metropolitan area is home to 51,268 Koreans, according to the 2000 U.S. Census (D.C.: 1,095; three adjacent counties in VA: 30,935; two counties in MD: 19,238). According to a local Korean business directory (*han-in-rok*, 2002), the Korean community in the Washington, D.C. metropolitan area has 192 Protestant churches, 4 Catholic churches, and 9 Buddhist temples, 11 bureaus of Korean government, 4 Korean-American associations, 26 social service agencies, 14 socio-cultural organizations, 23 business associations, 42 athletic organizations, 15 hometown associations, 58 fellowship associations, 29 religious organizations (other than churches and temples), 8 Protestant seminaries, 74 Korean language schools, and 2,527 Korean-owned businesses.[2]

Although the Korean community in the Washington, D.C. area is the nation's third largest in its numerical size, according to the 2000 Census, next to the Los Angeles and New York, it is no doubt the nation's oldest. The official Korean immigration to the U.S. (Hawaii) began in 1903 with 102 contract laborers, but quite a few students, government officials, political refugees, U.S. government employees, and Protestant leaders sojourned or permanently resided in D.C. since the establishment of first diplomatic relationship between the two countries in May 1882. A year later, the Korean government sent 11 officials to

Washington, D.C. for its official state visit to the U.S. to strengthen its diplomatic relationship with the U.S. government. They were the first Koreans who officially landed in America, 20 years before the official Korean immigration to the U.S. began.

Largely due to its symbolic status as the U.S. capital, Washington, D.C. attracted quite a few Korean political elites, Protestant leaders and young students, who were very much concerned about independence and development of Korea, as soon as the Korean government established diplomatic relations with the U.S. These groups first formed the Korean community in D.C. while their home country was under the control of the international superpowers. For this reason, according to a local history book, the *Washington Korean History, 1883-1993*, the Korean community in D.C. has been very concerned about the political situation of Korea from its initiation in the late 19th century (Chae 1994).

Koreans' patriotic political movement was first organized in Washington, D.C. as soon as the Korean community took its rudimentary form. A series of political movements focused on the improvement of democracy in Korea were organized in this area until the first legitimate government was established in Korea in the late 1980s. These political movements would not have been successful without the institutionalized support of the Korean churches and the leadership role of the leading Christian political elites in this area.

Despite its central role in the Korean independence movement in the U.S., however, the D.C. Korean community had not developed into an identifiable ethnic community until the early 1950s when a substantial number of Koreans resumed moving in. Before Korea's independence in 1945, the Korean population in D.C. was composed mostly of political exiles and students, but most of them returned to Korea upon her independence. No Korean churches had been organized yet. However, the influence of Christianity was dominant in the D.C. Korean community. This tradition did not fade out, but it rather continuously reinforced with the successive waves of Korean immigration in the 1960s and the 1970s.

The D.C. Korean community began to flourish again when an official diplomatic relationship between the U.S. and Korea resumed in 1949, and when the Korean War broke out in 1950. Although it is based on unofficial estimates of community leaders, the number of Koreans in the D.C. area has increased from approximately 50 in 1950, to 400 in 1960, 3,000 in 1970, 35,000 in 1980, 80,000 in 1990, and 100,000 in 2000 (Chae 1994: 31).[3] The number of Korean Protestant churches and Korean-owned businesses has grown proportionately much greater than that of Korean immigrants in this area. Especially, the number of Korean churches has grown exponentially from 2 in 1960 to 5 in 1970, 50 in 1980, 113 in 1990, and 192 in 2000. According to the *2001 Korean Church Directory of America*, published by the Christian Press, about 9 percent of 3,402 Korean Protestant churches in the U.S. are concentrated in the Washington, D.C. area next to the California (37%) and New York and New Jersey metropolitan areas (16%).

Considering that the majority of Koreans regularly attend religious services (Hurh and Kim 1990; Min 1992; Kwon 2003, 2004), Korean religious congregations form a spiritual backbone of the Korean community and played the role of community center in the Washington, D.C. area since the beginning of community formation.

The Early Korean Churches in D.C.
The early Korean community in D.C. took its form when the early voluntary ethnic organizations such as the Korean American Association of Washington, D.C. (1950) and Korean Student Association (1955) were organized. Korean churches in D.C. began to organize at the same time these voluntary ethnic organizations were formed. These ethnic organizations also became more specialized and diversified, as the community has grown larger. With the growth of the Korean community in D.C., the number of Korean churches has also grown by leaps and bounds each year, and their denominational affiliation has

become diversified.   These voluntary organizations, including churches, framed the early Korean community in D.C.

Regardless of religious traditions, organization of Korean churches in D.C. coincided with the presence of religious leaders, as with the cases of Korean communities in other metropolitan areas.   This was an important reason why Korean Buddhist temples and Catholic churches had been organized much later than their Protestant counterparts. Korean Buddhist temples and Catholic churches were organized in D.C. when a few Korean leaders of these religious traditions began to immigrate with fellow Korean believers in the early 1970s.

The early Korean immigrants shared a consensus of building an ethnic church although not every Korean immigrant at that time was Christian.   Koreans' marginal immigrant status and their homeland's international pariah status helped them form the consensus and encouraged them to initiate religious gatherings for prayer, supplication, and psychological comfort. Largely due to frequent fluctuations in numbers of Korean residents in D.C., however, the first Korean church was organized relatively later than other major metropolitan areas in the U.S.[4]

According to a description by an early Korean church member, Koreans' feeling of estrangement from American churches, feeling of belonging with the same ethnic members, and common patriotic sentiment, motivated them to organize an independent ethnic church. The editor of the history of the first Korean church of the D.C. area explained why the early Korean immigrants were eager to build their own ethnic church and to participate in the service with their own ethnic members:

> Most early Koreans felt a deep responsibility for the well-being of Korea which was in a brutal civil war. When they met fellow Koreans on the street, whether they were believers or not, they would exchange a strong wish for the well-being of Korea. So they said to each other, 'let us pray for our home

country.' Before our church was organized, many Koreans attended American churches. But due to language barrier and cultural differences, Koreans realized that they had difficulties in maintaining a vital Christian *Koinonia* with American members. Furthermore, Koreans realized that Americans were not concerned about the well-being of Korea as much as they were. (Chang 1988: 21)[5]

Early historical records also show that, from the beginning of Korean immigration to the U.S., church building has become an unwavering tradition of Korean immigrants, and churches have performed an important role in formation of the Korean community in the U.S. in the absence of effective community service organizations (Choy 1979; Kim 1981). Individual church histories repeatedly point out that Koreans' church-building efforts were very closely associated with formation of the larger ethnic community. One old timer (Dr. Jae Chang Choi), who was an active member of the first D.C. Korean church, recalled that approximately 80 percent of all Koreans of this area attended the church in 1960 (Chae 1994: 122). The editor of the history book of the first Korean Church in D.C. also recalled:

> Since almost all members of the early Korean community associations in D.C. were also our church members, most church events were held in collaboration with the Korean community associations. Official meetings of the Korean community associations were held after the church's annual picnic or any other church-wide social events. Our church played an important role of the Korean community association. (Chang 1988: 26)[6]

A close relationship between the Korean church and community changed in the late 1970s, when the role of Korean community associations became more diverse and many ethnic voluntary organizations were organized (Chae 1994: 70). Although rudimentary, this relationship still remains in the D.C. Korean community today. An example is the collaboration between the local Korean church council and the Korean associations over important community issues, such as construction of the Korean youth center.

The majority of leaders and members of the Korean community organizations and Korean NGOs are also active church members, and they work cooperatively with their churches over community-wide issues, such as the human rights problem in North Korea, reunification of Korea, North Korean famine assistance program, inter-group conflicts in D.C., and issues of illegal immigrants. These members of Korean community organizations have brought the community issues to the forefront of their churches. In this sense, Korean churches of the Washington, D.C. area are not only religious centers but also important community centers.

Geographical Distribution and Denominational Affiliation of Korean Congregations

The ten oldest churches listed in Table 1 had been organized in the Washington, D.C. area before a massive number of Koreans began to enter the U.S. in the early 1970s. Unlike most Korean churches organized after the 1970s, the first three churches had located their worship places in the inner city area. Yet similar to those organized after the 1970s, the first ten churches were affiliated with the three major denominations (Presbyterian, Methodist, and Baptist) (see Table 1 and Table 2). One of them also merged into the other Korean church of the same denomination (Southern Baptist Convention). The first three oldest churches, however, all moved out to suburban areas (Fairfax, VA and Montgomery, MD) later as more Koreans settled in suburbia in the 1980s and 1990s. Currently no Korean churches are located within D.C., except for one that serves mostly African-American homeless people and their families, while more than 1,500 Korean-owned businesses are located in D.C.

Korean churches' suburban concentration and affiliation with the major denominations continues today. And the early Korean churches also show that religious leaders were the major players in organizing churches. Out of the ten oldest Korean churches, only two were initiated by lay members.

Korean churches in the Washington, D.C. area are located wherever Koreans live. The number of Korean churches is almost proportionate to the number of Koreans throughout the Washington, D.C. metropolitan area. Among 207 Korean congregations of all religious traditions listed in the 2002 Korean business directory (*han-in-rok*), the majority (71%) are concentrated in five counties adjacent to Washington, D.C.: Montgomery and Prince George's in Maryland, and Fairfax, Arlington, and Alexandria in Virginia. Over 60% of the congregations in these five counties are concentrated in the three counties of Northern Virginia (Arlington, Alexandria, and Fairfax) (see Table 2). A little fewer than half (40%) are located in the two counties of Maryland (Montgomery and Prince George's). Between the two counties of Maryland, however, the majority of Korean churches (30% of all five counties and 75% of the two counties) are concentrated in Montgomery County, while the rest (10% of all five counties and 25% of the two counties) are located in Prince George's County. This indicates that the distribution pattern of Korean churches in the Washington, D.C. area is almost identical with that of the area's Korean population (see Table 2), except for the inner D.C. area, where none of the Korean churches serve Koreans any longer.

These summary tables reveal several interesting facts. First, the increased rates of Korean Protestant churches in the major Korean concentration areas (Fairfax in Virginia; Montgomery and Baltimore in Maryland) have almost doubled while those of the Korean population have grown 1.5 times at most during the last two decades. Second, the number of Korean congregations of other religious traditions has not only grown very slowly but also started much later. Currently only four Korean Catholic churches

Table 1. Location and Denominational Affiliation of the Early Ten Korean Churches (1951-1974)

Denominational Affiliation	Location (County) (then/now)	Year Organized	Church Name
United Methodist Church	D.C./McLean, (Fairfax) VA	1951	Korean United Methodist Church of Washington
Southern Baptist Convention	D.C./Silver Spring, (Montgomery) MD	1955	Korean Baptist Church of Washington
Presbyterian Church of America	D.C./Burke, (Fairfax) VA	1965	Korean Presbyterian Church of Washington
Presbyterian Church, U.S.A.	Bethesda, (Montgomery) MD	1969	United Korean Presbyterian Church
Southern Baptist Convention	Bethesda, (Montgomery) MD / Merged with KBCW, 1971)	1969	Bethesda Korean Baptist Church
Southern Baptist Convention	Fairfax Station, (Fairfax) VA/ same place	1972	Virginia Korean Baptist Church
Presbyterian Church, U.S.A.	Lanham, (Prince George's) MD/ same place	1972	Maryland Korean Presbyterian Church
Presbyterian Church, U.S.A.	Riverdale, (Prince George's) MD/ same place	1973	First Korean Presbyterian Church of Maryland
Presbyterian Church of America	Vienna, (Fairfax) VA/ same place	1973	Korean Central Presbyterian Church
Southern Baptist Convention	Silver Spring, (Montgomery) MD/ same area	1974	Global Mission Church of Washington (former First Korean Baptist Church)

Source: Adapted from Young Chang Chae (ed.), 1994. *Washington Korean History, 1883-1993*. Seoul, Korea: Paek-San Printing Company. pp. 106-129.

Table 2. Geographical Distribution of Koreans and Korean Congregations in the D.C. area (2000)[7]

Religious Traditions & No. of Koreans	Virginia Fairfax, Arlington, Alexandria No. of Congregations	Maryland Montgomery County No. of Congregations	Maryland Prince George's County No. of Congregations	Total
Protestants	116 (60%)	57 (30%)	19 (10%)	192
Catholics	1	2 (1 in Baltimore)	0	4
Buddhists	4	3 (2 in Baltimore)	0	9
Other	0	0 (1 Jeng-San-Kyo in D.C.)	1 (Chun-Do-Kyo)	2
No. of Koreans	30,935 (60%)	15,380 (30%) (1,095 in D.C., 2%)	3,858 (8%)	51,268

Table 3. Change in Distribution of Korean Congregations in the D.C. area (1985, 1990, 2000)[8]

Religious Traditions	Virginia (Fairfax, Arl., Alex.) 1985	1990	2000	Maryland Montgomery 1985	1990	2000	Prince George's 1985	1990	2000	D.C. 1985	1990	2000	Other D.C. Areas Baltimore 1985	1990	2000
Protestant		61	116		29	57		18	19		2	1		30	70
Catholic	1	1	1	0	0	2	1	1	0	0	0	0	1	1	1
Buddhist		1	4		2	3	0	0	0	0	0	0		1	2
Other						1		1	1			1			1

Table 4. Denominational Affiliations of Korean Churches in the D.C. Area (1960-2000)*

Year	2000	1990	1980	1970	1960
Presbyterian	82 (42%)	43 (38%)	-	2 (40%)	-
Baptist	58 (30%)	31 (28%)	-	2 (40%)	1 (50%)
Methodist	15 (7%)	10 (9%)	-	1 (20%)	1 (50%)
Catholic	4 (2%)	3 (2%)	2	-	-
Other**	37 (19%)	26 (23%)	-	-	-

* Korean Churches in the Baltimore area are not included in this table, except for Catholic.

** "Other" category includes the Full Gospel (Korean version of the Assembly of God), the Holiness, the Seventh Adventist, the Nazarene, C&MA, and Independent (or Inter-denominational).

- Either none or unidentified.

including Baltimore. According to our survey for the "Religion and the New Immigrants" project, hosted by the Life Cycle Institute of the Catholic University of America during the period 2000-2003, the four Korean Catholic churches serve 4,105 Korean Catholics, while another four Buddhist temples I surveyed serve 200 Korean Buddhists regularly. But the number of registered Buddhist members of these four temples is much larger (about 8 to 10 times larger than the number of regular attendees). Following their pre-migration practice style, few Buddhists regularly attend religious services after immigration. The core members of Korean Buddhist temples, however, still hold a strong Buddhist identity. Nonetheless, Buddhists and Catholics began to form their ethnic congregations much later than their Protestant counterparts. The first Korean Catholic church in the D.C. metropolitan area (Holy Korean Martyrs Catholic Church, Baltimore, MD) began to serve Korean Catholics in 1972, and the second Korean Catholic church (St. Andrew Kim Korean Catholic Church, College Park, MD) in 1974. The first Korean Buddhist temple (Korea Temple, Germantown, MD) was initiated by a Korean Buddhist leader (Ko Sung sunim) as a form of zen (Korean: sun) center with American practitioners, but it began to serve Korean immigrant practitioners in 1976. The second (Bub Ju Sa, Burtonsville, MD) and the third Korean Buddhist temples (Bo Rim Sa, Fairfax, VA) were organized in 1982 and 1984 respectively. Third, only the Protestant churches affiliated with the two major denominations, Presbyterian and Baptist, have grown substantially for the last three decades. Fourth, as in the other metropolitan areas, Buddhists become an absolute numerical minority despite their equal or majority status in Korea, and Catholics maintain more or less the same numerical status before and after immigration.

Characteristics and Issues of Korean Congregations
Old vs. New and Growing vs. Stagnant
Histories of individual churches and interviews of the church leaders reveal that successful churches have experienced a so-called take-off period in a certain stage of growth. The take-off period is described as a specific growth state through which

successful churches transform from a small and unstable state to a large and self-sustaining one. It generally shows three distinctive characteristics: first, a clear demarcation between social-club-style gatherings and pious religious ones; second, a resource mobilization with effective church organization; and third, an active engagement in missionary activities, either domestic or overseas, while still maintaining a theological conservatism or orthodoxy.

For instance, the pastor of the oldest Korean church in the Washington, D.C. area, Rev. Young Jin Cho, who has served the church for 24 years, states:

> The old timers, who played an important role in initiating our church, were unique in their religious orientations. The majority of them hold professional occupations and consider themselves as upper-middle class before and after immigration. Reflecting their occupational status and educational level, their religious orientation was very reason-centered. But I realized that this reason-centered style of practice did not help their spiritual growth. When I began to serve the church I tried to maintain a more balanced pastoral emphasis; I mean, between faith and reason. As the new wave of massive immigration began in the early 1970s, the old timers suddenly became a numerical minority in both our church and the Korean community. Their style of practice was also challenged by the new immigrant members. Compared to the old timers' religious orientation, the newcomers' orientation was a little too much spiritualistic and supplication oriented. It took us long time to narrow the gap between the two groups' style of practice. As a means for narrowing the gap, I began to focus on Bible studies and missionary activities. With resistance to my new pastoral emphasis, two streams of the

old timers left our church and formed new churches. For me, it was one of the biggest challenges in serving immigrant church. Our church, however, has grown steadily since we successfully narrowed the gaps between the two groups.

Rev. Cho also mentioned that one of the major reasons that the early Korean church became a social-club-style church was because of the members' lack of liturgical training. It was true that the majority of the early Korean immigrants began to attend religious services after immigration. The Protestant group in Korea only recently became a numerical majority in Korea. Koreans' religious participation is more salient among immigrants. Korean Christians' convert history was also relatively short. As with the case of early Korean immigrants, the majority of Korean immigrants began to join their ethnic churches after immigration for social reasons, for example, loneliness, hardship, and feeling of belonging. Believers' lack of religious training, short history of conversion, and immigration experience were the major reasons why the early Korean churches ran like a social-club style of gathering.

A Presbyterian pastor of one of the ten oldest Korean churches, Rev. Paul T. Kim, who has served the church for more than 25 years, also recalls:

When I began to serve the church, I had a hard time to transform the social-club-like church to a church-like one. I remember that every time our church members had a worship service, most of them gathered at a member's home afterward. Many of them enjoyed drinking and smoking there. It was very hard for me to stop their bad habits because I empathetically understood their difficulties of immigration lives. But soon I began to educate them that churches should differ from social-clubs. It took me quite a long to straighten up our church. If I had failed to correct their bad habits and ideas about church, our church would have been disappeared long time ago. Our church has grown steadily once it became a church-like one. From that time on, I had focused more on Bible studies, prayer meetings, and missionary activities, which held the members tighter.

A lay leader of one of the largest Korean Baptist churches in Maryland, Deacon Sung Hee Yun, who has served the church for more than 25 years, states:

> Our church has experienced three distinctive growth stages. In the first stage, which I call it a 'launching stage,' the pastor's sacrificial service was the most important factor for growth. The pastor did everything he could to take care of all the needs of immigrant members, from pick-ups at airports to job and housing searches. The pastor's sacrificial services formed a centrifugal point for the members' congregational gathering. In the second stage, which I call it a 'lifting-off stage,' the pastor's clear and noble vision and lay members' organized support for the vision were the key. We needed visions, strategies, resources, and actions to make our church grow. In the third stage, which I call it a 'growing stage,' efficient resource mobilization, effective church organization, mission strategy, and social engagement became most important keys for our church growth. I believe that as a missionary organization church should concern about social needs as much as it grows. In the case of our church, missionary activities serve as an overarching goal for church growth.

As the leaders of these three large churches pointed out, religious leader's devotional services and clear vision, lay members' organized support for the church leadership, well-designed mission strategies and social participation, and well-operating church management are important keys for the transformation and growth of Korean churches. All these churches also have experienced a taking-off period that demarcates between social gathering and religious one.

But the majority of Korean churches in the D.C. area have begun with small-group gatherings without sufficient resources and institutionalized support from denominational authorities. They all look like a small grass-root organizations, having their central concern with the Korean community. This also suggests that immigrants' social needs, e.g., assistance with their initial adjustment, emotional sharing, and sense of belonging, have become an important motivation for organization of their ethnic church. With a relatively short immigration history, the majority of Korean churches in the Washington, D.C. area are still in the pre-taking-off stage, in which leaders' sacrificial services play a key role in church growth. Unlike the early period of Korean immigration, however, the Washington, D.C. Korean community has a few mega churches now, which are able to provide numerous community service programs. Although most small churches are not operated like social-clubs any longer, they experience double difficulties in church growth. Religious leaders' sacrificial services cannot be as effective as they used to be two or three decades ago, as a few mega churches now provide various social services much more effectively. As a result, the mega-churches grow larger while the small churches become smaller.

Small and Single Ethnic
As Table 3 and Table 4 show, the majority of Korean churches in the Washington, D.C. area have been organized recently. The growing number of Korean churches and the decreasing number of new immigrants in recent years also foreshadow the fates of small churches. As a result, the majority of them are small and struggle for growth as they are lacking in resources, vision, and missionary or social outreach activity participation.

According to a survey of 125 Korean congregations (out of a total of 183) in the Washington, D.C. area in 2000 for the Catholic University's Pew-funded research project, "Religion and the New Immigrants," only five congregations (four percent, including two Catholic churches) of this area have more than 1,000 members. Ten percent of them have members between 300 and 500. The remaining 86 percent have 299 or fewer, with 36 percent having fewer than 50. The average number of registered members of D.C. area Korean churches is 162. Sixty-four percent also rent or share their worship facility. Korean congregations also tend to be single ethnic; 59 percent have Korean members only, while another 34 percent are 90 percent or more Korean members. Only seven percent have more than 20 percent of non-Korean members.

Growing Second-Generation Congregations

Although the majority of Korean churches are single ethnic, our survey results also show that the majority of them (69 percent) use both Korean and English languages for services and Sunday school classes. This also indicates that a majority of Korean churches in this area have a significant number of English-speaking second-generation members.

Church members' generation (first- vs. later-generations) and migration (old timers vs. newcomers) transitions have been the most important factors that determine Korean churches' programs, services, and worship styles. As the aforementioned interviewees agreed, Korean Protestant church programs have changed since the massive influx of new immigrants since the early 1970s. According to them, most Korean churches had only a Sunday service before the new wave of immigrants came. The new immigrants brought their styles and forms of practice from Korea, such as daily dawn prayer meetings, Wednesday evening services, Friday prayer meetings, intercessory prayer meetings, revival rallies, retreats, cell-group meetings, and special prayer meetings. Almost all Korean Protestant churches in the Washington, D.C. area adopted these service forms as early as 1970s when a massive number of Korean immigrants began to enter, and now they practice them on a regular basis.

Second-generation members' style of practice is also very different from their first-generation counterparts' style. Not only do second-generation members use English, but they also perform rock-music style contemporary gospel songs in services. They do not participate in all the service meetings with their parents, but they organize their own with different meeting schedules in more Americanized forms and styles of service.

Second-Generation Congregation Models
With the rapid growth of second-generation members, most of whom prefer to speak English at home and church, a majority of first-generation churches are now rushing to provide services and programs that meet the linguistic and cultural needs of the second-generation members. Only a few large churches have begun to establish an English Ministry department within their churches. There are, however, divergent views about the operation of English Ministry among the ethnic church leaders. In terms of the English-speaking congregation's degree of dependence (both managerial and liturgical) on its Korean-speaking counterpart, it has developed into three styles: dependent, independent, and interdependent congregations.

Largely due to the short history of immigration, a full-fledged experiment of each model of the second-generation congregation has not yet been carried out. As first-generation churches grow larger, however, most second-generation congregations experience a gradual transformation from dependent to independent ones. But quite a few (first-generation) pastors, who maintain the interdependent congregational model, express the usefulness in resource mobilization for their church communities and the possibility of longer duration. Most Korean pastors I interviewed while working on the "Religion and the New Immigrants" project advocated the interdependent model for its possible effectiveness in resource mobilization from both congregations sheltered under the same roof.

However, regardless of the congregational formatio
whether the second-generation Korean congregations are g
to develop into a multi-ethnic and a multi-racial congregation is
still a cause for speculation, as with only one second-generation
Korean organized multi-ethnic congregation in the Washington,
D.C. area so far. Two cases of first-generation Korean churches'
merge with American congregations (one Lutheran and one
PCUSA) were found in the Washington, D.C. area as of August
2002. But these two merged congregations hold separate
linguistic worship services with different service schedules.

II. The Role of Protestant Churches in Incorporation into U.S. Society

As the majority of Korean immigrants participate in religious
activities after immigration, Protestant churches have performed
a critical role in both formation of the Korean community and its
incorporation into the larger community from the beginning of
immigration, which is also critical for the survival of immigrants
and the host society. As with Korean churches elsewhere, Korean
Protestant churches in the Washington, D.C. area have performed
multiple roles of pseudo-social service organization in
development of the Korean community and its incorporation into
the larger society. For example, they have been a religious
organization that provides a sense of purpose for living for many
Korean immigrants, and at the same time they have been a
primal social and ethnic organization that provides the members
with a sense of community and togetherness and connects them
to the larger world. In the Korean community in the U.S. non-
Protestant Korean congregations also have almost inevitably
played the same role for their respective religious groups (Kwon
2003). In regard to the role of ethnic churches in assisting
members' incorporation into the larger U.S. society, however,
there has been both progress and resistance. In other words, the
religious congregations have simply not played a strong enough
role toward incorporation of Korean immigrants into U.S. society.

They rather have looked to be a self-segregated religio-social organization in most cases.

Among the recent immigrant communities in the U.S., according to the immigration and religion research project that I have been involved in, the Korean community is one of the most well-organized communities in many respects. Unlike other multi-ethnic and multi-lingual Asian nationalities, e.g., Asian Indians, Filipinos, and Chinese, Koreans maintain a single ethnic and monolingual tendency, which makes them much easier to keep ethnic solidarity after immigration. Koreans' heavy concentration in Protestantism and self-employed business after immigration also helped them organize their community structure relatively easily.

The most common types of community organization found in the Korean community are self-help political organizations, religious organizations, business organizations, and various voluntary social organizations. The self-help political organization is commonly called Korean Associations (Korean: *han-in-hoe*) and is divided by regional representative bodies. The religious organization is dominated by Protestant groups and is also divided by denominational groups and regional representative groups. The business organization is commonly called *sang-jo-hoe* and is also divided by regional and sub-regional representative bodies. Most voluntary social organizations resemble grass-root-type gatherings in accordance with members' social and economic interests. A few voluntary organizations form regional or nationwide representative bodies, but most of them do not do so. The types of voluntary social organization found in the Korean community vary, but the most popular types include social service organizations (or NGOs), professional occupation groups, surname groups, alumni groups, sport activity groups, hometown groups, and other special interest groups.

rean communities in the New York and Washington, D.C. olitan areas show that among these four general types of organizations, religious organizations are the most active and steady in maintaining their regular activities and community incorporations. It is thus worth describing how the Korean Protestant community constructs their organizational structure and maintain it in conjunction with the larger ethnic community organizations in and out of the Korean community. The Korean community in the Washington, D.C. area might be considered itself as a voluntary ethnic organization in the larger U.S. society. But within the Korean community these four types of social organizations connect individual Korean immigrants to the Korean community and U.S. society.

Organizational Structure of the Korean Protestant Community
The Council of Korean Churches in the Greater Washington, D.C. Area
As with Korean Protestant communities in other metropolitan areas in the U.S., the Korean Protestant community in the Washington, D.C. area formed an umbrella organization, called the *Council of Korean Churches in Greater Washington,* as early as a rudimentary form of ethnic community had organized. As soon as it was organized in 1975, it performed various religio-social activities in and out of the Korean community in this area, focusing on community liaison activities and a consolidation of religio-social energy of individual Korean congregations.

The council is an exclusively ethnic interdenominational network organization. However, it excludes Catholic churches, non-Christian groups, and other unconventional Protestant sects that are considered heretical by the mainline Protestant groups. Individual congregations' membership affiliation is voluntary, but the majority of Korean churches in this area are members of the council. Payment of membership dues is also voluntary. Their voluntary participation, however, makes the council quite weak financially and organizationally, but it is still the most powerful religious organization that draws Korean community's concerns and issues.

The council elects the board members and leaders every year, but their rights and duties remain at a nominal level. Although the majority of Korean Protestant churches maintain a double or triple membership with either the American Protestant denominations or the Korean ethnic Protestant denominations, many of them also maintain membership within this ethnic church council.

The usefulness of the Korean church council mostly lies in the reinforcement of the solidarity of Korean churches and thus of the Korean community. It also forms the inter-regional networks in the U.S. One of the major roles of the council is to publish a directory and to support sub-councils' evangelical and social service activities. But its religio-social activity participation is limited largely because of its lack of financial resources and authority. The scope and sphere of the activities of the council are neither as broad nor as deep as the name implies. Roughly, half of Korean Protestant churches in the Washington, D.C. area participate in the meeting. The number of participant churches has recently been increasing.

Ten sub-councils are in charge of specific tasks, e.g., theology, proselytization, education, juveniles, public relations, music, social service, women, mission, and ethics. Each sub-council has it own action plan under the elected leader's guidance. Sub-council activities are not as active and influential as lay people expect. All activities of the general and sub-councils are quite limited and sometimes superficial mainly due to its limitation in financial resources and authority.

Korean Pastors' Association of the Washington, D.C. Area
The Korean Pastor's Association formed four years earlier (1971) than the Korean Church Council of the Washington, D.C. area. This organization is independent of the Korean Church Council in its activities and organizational structure. But the memberships within these two ethnic religious organizations greatly overlap. It is interdenominational as well. While the unit of membership in the ethnic church council is the individual church, that of the Korean Pastors' Association is the individual pastor.

While the Korean Church Council was organized to facilitate Korean church networking, the Pastors' Association was mainly organized to take care of members' needs, such as fellowships, condolences, cooperation, and development of educational programs for the members. Except for fellowship and condolences, the scope of its activities somewhat overlaps with that of the church council. Although all the organizational procedures of the Korean pastors' association are similar to those of the Korean Church Council, the association runs quite informally, like many other non-religious fellowship organizations. The Korean Pastors' Association members also maintain personal relationships with each other.

Apart from this larger pastors' association, there are quite a few pastors' fellowship organizations in the Korean Protestant community in the Washington, D.C. area. They keep their own goals in accordance with members' denominational affiliations, but their activities are more or less similar to those of the larger pastors' association.

Other Small-Group Religious Organizations
There are twenty other Korean small-group religious organizations that maintain a close relationship with the Korean Church Council and the Pastors' Association. They support the various activities of the Korean Church Council or the Korean Pastors' Association in accordance with their missions. Their leaders also maintain membership within one or more of the larger organizations. In this respect, they are virtually sub-organizations of the larger Korean church organizations.

The *2003 Korean Church Directory*, compiled by the Korean Church Council, listed twenty small-group organizations that actively participate in service activities in the Korean community.[9] They are by and large gender and profession specific. A few of them have nation-wide or global networks although most of them are region-based. All members and leaders of these small-group associations also hold membership with an individual church in this area. When they launch specific projects, they draw their churches' attention and assistance. They also maintain collaborative relationships with local non-governmental activist groups.

Korean Theological Schools
In addition to these small-group religious associations, there are nine Korean Protestant Theological Schools listed in the *2003 Korean Church Directory of the Washington, D.C. Area.*[10] Some of these ethnic theological seminaries confer their own diplomas, while some award certificates only. The numerous Korean seminaries in this area indirectly demonstrate Koreans' high level of religious participation. As the Korean Protestant community increasingly produces its own ethnic religious leaders through these ethnic institutes, a greater number of Korean churches are organized to meet the demand of ethnic clergy members. This in turn contributes to the increase of church membership. This is a major reason why the Korean Protestant community grows larger. From the beginning of Korean immigration to the U.S., the number of Korean Protestant clergy has been disproportionately larger than that of other religious communities (Kwon 2003).

NGOs, Churches, and the Korean Community
Besides religious organizations and voluntary associations, about twelve Korean NGOs actively engage in their missions in the Washington, D.C. area. In terms of their religious affiliation, they form two groups; the religiously oriented groups and the religiously neutral ones. Six of them are religiously oriented, and all of these religiously oriented groups are Protestant affiliates. All Korean NGOs in this area are organized by relatively young first-generation Koreans, except for the Korean American Coalition (KAC). KAC was organized by the 1.5 and 2nd generation Koreans in the aftermath of the 1992 L.A. incident for protecting socio-economic interests of the Korean community for themselves.

Regardless of their religious affiliations, however, their activities are mostly focused on community-wide issues. Two of them focus on the inter-racial or inter-ethnic community issues, while three are pan-ethnic issues, specifically focused to the reunification movement and the North Korean refugee problem. One group focuses on the Asian comfort women issues. KAC activities are mostly focused on the protection of the Korean community and maintenance of a good inter-community relationship with other racial and ethnic groups.

Both leaders and members of all these NGOs are members of local Korean churches. Many of them also hold leadership positions in their churches. As with leaders and members of the small-group religious associations, Korean NGO members also bring their current activity issues into their local churches. Whenever it is necessary, they draw support from their churches by mobilizing church resources. In this way, local churches and the larger Korean community meet over important community issues. The same is true with a few local Korean community service centers.

In addition to their social service agency role, Korean churches have also performed a crucial role in organizing specialized community service centers from the early stage of community formation, in the absence of effective ethnic social service organization. Many Korean Protestant church members and pastors therefore believe that the Korean church is in fact the community center, although a large number of Koreans and non-Protestants do not believe so. A Presbyterian pastor, H.J. Cho, who has served a Korean congregation for 22 years reports:

> The early Korean churches in D.C. area played a very important role in organizing and forming the larger Korean community. Because of the language barrier and cultural unfamiliarity, most Korean immigrants encountered difficulties in communication with local and federal government authorities. Korean church leaders played a role of mediator or facilitator in solving the problems the newcomers encountered. As an example,

currently the two most important Korean community service organizations were initiated by two Korean church leaders with assistance of a few professional church members. The Korean Community Service Center of Greater Washington, which is the largest ethnic social service organization in the Korean community, was originally initiated by a pastor of the United Korean Presbyterian Church in the early 1980s. Another Korean social service organization, the Korean-American Service Center, located in Silver Spring, was also originally initiated by a pastor (Rev. Ham) of a Korean Church in Montgomery County in need of the community members' social service organization. The Korean churches were the only social service organization that was able to take care of the problems of the early Korean immigrants. Church was the core of the community since the beginning of Korean immigration to the U.S.

Linkage between Korean Churches and the Larger Community
Because individual Korean churches differ in their social outreach programs, it is difficult to summarize the pattern of the Korean churches' linkage to the larger community. A few large churches are more focused on evangelical outreach or mission programs, while the majority of Korean churches in this area are more focused on church growth. In general, however, church size and leaders' philosophy about social participation seem to be the major factors that determine individual churches' level of social engagement.

In general, the larger the congregation, the more frequent its participation in social outreach programs, regardless of the ethnic and racial backgrounds of the target communities. However, the majority of Korean churches in this area are small in size and strive for numerical growth. Despite this unfavorable condition for social incorporation, many capable churches have shown four distinctive types of incorporation into the larger community.

Their efforts, however, still remain amateurish and small in scale largely because of their lack of resources.

Type I: Church-Wide Participation in Either Missionary Activity or Social Service Program

While many small Korean churches have formed their own methods for connecting their churches to the larger community, some large churches directly participate in social outreach programs either by organizing their own social service programs or by directly dispatching their members as missionaries to the target communities in the U.S. and overseas communities. All four congregations I have observed engage in religio-social participation activities by performing either one of these two.

Type II: Subgroups' Participation in Social Service Activities

Regardless of church size, some subgroup members of Korean churches, such as Men's and Women's evangelical groups, participate in social outreach activities either by contributing money to the needy and to social service activist groups or by engaging in proselytization activities by themselves. Most Korean churches form these subgroups at the initial stage of their church organizations. The members of these subgroups make every effort to attract newcomers and plan various social outreach programs as soon as they grow large enough.

Type III: Professional Members' Engagement in Social Activism

Another form of linkage between individual churches and the larger community relies on the professional members' engagement in specialized social outreach activities. If a church has a substantial number of professionals, such as physicians, nurses, social workers, bilingual teachers, college professors, lawyers, musicians, and accountants, the church usually develops specialized social service programs by mobilizing these human resources. For instance, since the famine problem of North Korea caught media attention in the early 1990s, quite a few professionals of large Korean churches have launched numerous food assistance programs for the North Korean famine victims. Their activities have drawn collaboration from numerous specialized NGOs, including the United Nations. Collecting medicines donated by various pharmaceutical companies, a few doctors and nurses of these churches also regularly send them with other voluntary medical professionals to South American countries, mostly to Mexico and Peru. This kind of social outreach, however, is possible only when a church has a substantial number of professionals and has grown large enough to draw human resources effectively. Currently only about ten of the largest Korean churches in this area are able to engage in this type of social outreach program.

Type IV: Monetary Donations to the Local Church Council
Quite a few small Korean churches, which are not able to launch their own social outreach programs, indirectly participate in social outreach by providing monetary contributions to the local Korean Church Council. The church council launches a few professional social outreach programs for both the Korean community and the larger community. The sub-councils of the local church council launch local social outreach services through the funds sent from the individual churches. Thus the local church council becomes a mediator that links individual churches to both the Korean community and the larger community.

Not all Korean churches contribute to the ethnic church council. According to my observation of the annual church council meeting, fewer than half of Korean churches offer monetary contributions to the local church council. The amount of contributions of the member church also varies in accordance with its financial situation and membership size. It ranges from $50 to $500. The size of the church is the major determinant of its contribution.

Throughout these four types of social engagement, therefore, individual churches' financial capability and human resources are the most consistent factors for their participation in social outreach activities. Church size is directly associated with these two factors.

Resistance in Civic Incorporation
Lack of Leadership and Resources

Many Korean Protestant leaders are also aware that Korean church leaders' lack of consciousness about their role in social and civic incorporation is the most significant problem as an ethnic congregation. For the majority of Korean churches, social participation is still an unresolved endeavor largely due to their lack of resources and leadership. A few Korean Protestant leaders view themselves as a self-segregated religious group. Two close-to-1.5 generation Baptist pastors (Rev. J. Khim and Rev. S. K. Chang) point out the problems of church leaders in Korean churches' social incorporation. Rev. J. Khim, who has served a Korean church in Springfield, VA, for more than 15 years, said:

> I definitely think that the problem of the Korean Protestant community is its lack of leadership. There are so many pastors in the Korean community, but they are mostly lacking in their leadership capability largely due to their limited linguistic ability and shortcomings in understanding of American society. They are making self-segregated ethnic churches. Pastoral activities of the majority of the first-generation Korean pastors are focused on numerical growth of their self-segregated churches. Because of their lack of leadership, resource, knowledge, and ability of participation, most of them do not have room to concern themselves with the larger community. Their biggest concern is how to make a self-standing ethnic church by purchasing or building sanctuaries for their ethnic members. Their cultural experience of desiring for owning their own land and house also exacerbates their incorporation effort, by focusing their energy on only owning their own sanctuaries—an exclusive place for worship. Worshiping only with their own ethnic members, they reinforce their exclusive tendency after immigration. I personally think it

does not sound like a real Christian way of believing.

Rev. S.K. Chang, who serves a Korean Baptist church in Falls Church, VA, also said:

> In my opinion, the most important issue related to Korean church members' incorporation into U.S. society is Korean churches' lack of both human and material resources. They also lack leaders who are able to maximize these resources. For example, only few of them speak English well, know about the U.S. society, and intend to incorporate into U.S. society. For the pastors and lay leaders who are eager to incorporate into U.S. society, linguistic ability becomes the biggest barrier.

Self-Help vs. Self-Segregation
Rev. Chang's social participation effort is motivated by his religious and ethnic identity. But criticizing typical first-generation leader's lack of leadership, he suggests that the leaders should do whatever they can do with their capability to promote their members' social incorporation. He shares his experience:

> Unfavorable inter-group relationship with other ethno-racial groups is another problem. I personally think that these problems are not surmountable easily. I decided to begin with a project that I am able to manage. I have been helping some Koreans who are in need. I actively participate in two NGO groups that are concerned with Koreans and their future: one is KASM (Korean American Sharing Movement); and the other is FK (Future of Korea). Both groups are working toward reunification of Korea and the social well-being of the underprivileged Koreans. I have become involved in these NGO groups for

266

two main reasons: one is that as a religious leader I am obliged to help underprivileged people; and the other is that as a Korean descendent I am also obliged to help the fellow Koreans first. I have been observing numerous conflicts between African-Americans and white Americans, suburban and urban residents, Koreans and non-Koreans. As long as I identify myself as a Korean-American, I think it is better for me to work for the well-being of our ethnic members first. And without helping others my Christian identity becomes meaningless. Once our fellow Korean immigrants become well off, I am sure they are going to turn their evangelical eyes and hands to the larger community. Korean churches even have had difficulties getting generation conflicts, let alone their willingness to incorporate into the larger community.

Lack of Consciousness

Korean religious leaders' lack of consciousness about social incorporation is also closely associated with their asocial viewpoints about the society. A 1.5 generation Presbyterian pastor observes that many religious leaders do not have a sound philosophy for their social involvement. According to him, many Korean church leaders still hold the idea that church should stay in a sacred place by separating from the secular world. In his view, this is one of the most important reasons why so few Korean churches are willing to advocate their social incorporation. He (Rev. S. Choi) shares his idea:

> I strongly believe that the church, including the immigrant churches, has to actively engage in social participation to make the society a better place. As a church minister, I cannot even imagine the reasons for the existence of church if it separates from the society. I think church should stand firmly in the society, and it should show the society a good and healthy direction. This could be

a sense of purpose, values, orientation, and morality. They are already in the Bible. I believe that church would not be a church anymore if it would not concern about problems of society.

While describing the impact of the Korean Protestant communities on the larger ethnic community, a first-generation Methodist pastor, I.N. Jung, also revealed his viewpoint about the importance of the role of church in society. He strongly argued that church and society should maintain a strong tie and bond. He said that the ideal relationship between church and society should be like a unified entity:

> They are two entities in a same body. They should not be separated. They have to work together all the time. Church exists for the well-being of society, and society builds the church to get a better sense of direction and purpose. In this sense they are the same entity.

Role of Reception Desk Only
He continued to state his opinions about the current relationship between Korean churches and the larger community:

> The immigrant churches, especially Korean churches are peculiar in many respects. They have played a role of reception desk only, not a role of active social participation agency. Our immigrant churches should overcome this limitation and go beyond. If a church plays the typical, traditional church roles only, I mean the role of sacred temple, it would not be a church any longer. The biggest deficiency of our immigrant church is the church leaders' lack of participation in the larger society. Their lack of understanding of the larger society directly causes the problem. They know only about their ethnic community. Only a few of them are familiar with American society, I mean its economic and political systems. In both

theoretical and practical levels, if they are separated from the systems of the mainstream society, they are not able to take care of their congregation members effectively. This is the problem that our Korean churches encounter now.

Notes

[1] The Washington, D.C. area included for the study was six adjacent counties of the District of Columbia, Virginia, and Maryland. They are the District of Columbia, Alexandria (VA), Arlington (VA), Fairfax (VA), Montgomery (MD), and Prince George's County (MD).

[2] Park, Wha Gyu. 2002. *The Korean Directory of the Great Washington, D.C. Area (han-in-rok)*. Fairfax, VA: Giant Publishing Company.

[3] As author mentioned, these figures are based on unofficial estimates of the leaders of the Korean community.

[4] The first Korean church in Hawaii was organized in 1903, the very same year the first group of Korean immigrants entered to the U.S.; Los Angeles, in 1904; New York, in 1921; and Chicago, in 1923 (Chang 1988: 27). Most of these early Korean churches were organized with help of the U.S. Methodist Church. The Methodists were more open to minority churchgoers than other major denominations (Chang 1988: 27; Chae 1994: 110). Ironically, the Presbyterians, who had most actively engaged in missionary activities in Korea since late 19th century (1885), maintained a one language policy in the U.S. until 1959 (Chae 1994: 110).

[5] Interpretation by author.

[6] Interpretation by author.

[7] The Number of Protestant churches is from *The Korean Church Directory of Washington Area, 2001*, compiled by the Council of Korean Church of Washington. The Number of Koreans is from the 2000 U.S. Census. The number of Catholic, Buddhist, and other religious congregations is from the *Korean Directory of the Greater Washington, D.C. Area (Han-In-Rok 2002)*, published by Giant Publishing Company.

[8] The data are drawn from the *Korean Business Directory (1985-2002)* published by the Korea Times/Korea Advertising Agency and from the *Korean Church Directory of the Washington, D.C. Area (2001)* published by the Korean Church Council of Greater Washington, D.C.

9 They include "Senior Pastors' Association of the Greater Washington Area," "Ministry Development Association of the Greater Washington Area," "To-the-Ends-of-the-Earth Missionary Association," "Siloam Missionary Association," "Women's Evangelical Association of the Greater Washington Area," "Wheat ('Milal' in Korean) Missionary Association in America," "Noah Missionary Association in the Greater Washington Area," "Washington Christian Gospel Broadcasting Service (WCRS)," "Washington Praise Voice Broadcasting Service (WDCT Radio)," "The Korea Gospel Weekly," "The Korean Gospel Association," "Washington Gospel Missionary Broadcasting Service," "Water Fountain of the Noon," "Korean Occupational Missionary Association of America," "Korean Occupational Missionary Association of the Greater Washington Area," "Korean Christian Martial Arts Association of America," "Korean Christian Businessmen's Association," "One Media Mission Association," "Washington Women's Torch Light Association," "Washington Pastors' Spirituality Development Association," and "Christian Mission of Hope in Washington."

10 They are the Korean Branch of the Southern Baptist Theological Seminary, the Bethesda Korean Theological Seminary, the Baltimore Bible Theological Seminary, the Washington Reformed Presbyterian Theological Seminary, the Washington Theological Seminary, the Washington Baptist Theological Seminary, the Washington Korean Bible Seminary, the Washington All-Inclusive Korean Seminary, and the Union-PSCE Theological Seminary.

PART III.

THE FUTURE

11. Confucian Ideals and American Values

Brian Lee

To most Korean-Americans, Confucius may seem like a mythical figure whose teachings are now antiquated and irrelevant. To us, he is another Plato or Aristotle – someone who made important contributions to civilization, but not necessarily to modern society. But as I came to learn more about the teachings of Confucius, I realized how much his teachings still influence second generation Korean-Americans. He wrote primarily about the importance of family, the value of education, and the need for conformity and social order. As Korean-Americans, we can see the remnants of this philosophy in our everyday lives. We see it in the way we interact with our parents, the way we view education, the way we perceive ourselves. Thus far, the Korean emphasis on education, self-discipline and families has served second-generation Korean-Americans well. It is because of this mindset that so many Korean immigrant families produce doctors, lawyers and bankers.

However, there remain some Confucian ideals that are inherently incompatible with American values, such as individualism, egalitarianism and diversity. These opposing principles put Korean-Americans in a unique position. It allows us the opportunity to pick and choose which ideals we live by. Some abide strictly to Korean Confucian ideals; others stick to American principles. But if Korean-Americans want to make a visible impact on the United States, we must strike a delicate balance between the two. This means abiding by American values, but retaining the Confucian ideals that have served us well.

One of the primary tenets of Confucianism is the importance of family and the hierarchy within it. According to its teachings, there must be a strict hierarchy within the family so children dutifully respect their parents. Although Korean society has changed rapidly in the past few decades, this divide between child and parent is still very evident. For Korean-Americans, this has created a fundamental difference in how we view the parent-child relationship. It is quite rare to find a Korean parent who is genuinely friends with his child. Many of my non-Korean friends joke and laugh with their parents; they share intimate details of their personal lives with their parents; they watch movies and go to concerts together. But amongst my Korean friends, it is rare to find such personal connections between parent and child.

This is due to a combination of factors. First, there is obviously a generational divide between the Korean parents and the Korean-American children, which makes communication more difficult. Our parents are products of South Korea during the 1960s, 1970s and 1980s. The country was developing, it was ruled by a series of dictatorships, and the citizens were xenophobic. In marked contrast, most of us Korean-Americans grew up in relatively affluent homes with the privileges of education and other first-world amenities. These differences often impose somewhat of a cultural barrier between Korean parents and their children.

The second reason for this less personal parent-child relationship is filial piety, the idea that children must respect their parents. This leads to the perception that the parents' primary role is to provide for their children, while the children's primary role is to serve and respect their parents. This can sometimes lead to a rather distant relationship between parent and child.

The notion of filial piety also extends to the general adult-child relationship. Confucianism has created a strict societal hierarchy, which remains firmly in place in modern Korean and Japanese societies. The idea that children must respect their elders is apparent in so many aspects of Korean and Japanese cultures, from speech levels to table manners. This has made it increasingly difficult for second-generation Korean-Americans to develop sincere relationships with adults. As children, we look to adults as people who should respect and serve, not people with whom we should joke or become friends.

Confucius' emphasis on family and filial piety has obvious advantages for Korean immigrants. These ideals have prevented broken homes and encouraged family cohesion, something that is critical for immigrant families. The prominence of filial piety has also aided in making Korean society more orderly. However, filial piety can also have some drawbacks for Korean-Americans. To succeed in America, it is imperative for people to relate and connect to people of all ages. As a Korean-American who was conditioned to only respect elders, I have often found it difficult to become friendly with those older than me. Such perceptions of elders can have a deterrent effect on ambitious Korean-Americans striving for success.

Another critical tenet of Confucianism is education. Distinguishing between one's "outer" and "inner" beings, Confucius characterized education as a means of self-improvement, a way to cultivate conscience and character. Becoming a more knowledgeable person will allow one to do good for society. But amongst Korean-American families, it appears as though this philosophy has been lost.

Instead, education for the second-generation is seen as a status symbol, as the emphasis is placed on name recognition and GPAs, not on knowledge and self-improvement. Most Korean parents sacrifice significant time and money for their children's education – something for which 2nd generation Korean-Americans should undoubtedly be grateful. However, parents pursue such drastic means because they are obsessed with the names of colleges, the pristine chimes of "Harvard, Yale, Princeton." Many parents are interested in education for the brand names, for the bragging rights, for the Kodak moment when they can emblazon their cars with names of prestigious Ivy League schools.

Regardless of the motives, this emphasis on education has served the Korean-American population extremely well. This is evident in the relatively high number of Korean students enrolled at America's top universities. In turn, the academic excellence of Asian students has led to a rather favorable perception of Asian immigrants in America. Asians are often coined the "model minority" or the "new Jews." This may give the impression that Koreans' approach to education is correct and beneficial, but this is not necessarily the case.

Most Korean parents simply view education as a means to a lucrative end. (Their logic is that a degree from a brand name college will lead to a stable profession and a substantial salary. This, in turn, will benefit their children when they are looking for potential spouses. In the end, Korean parents imagine their children with high-paying jobs, perfect spouses and a stable family. This social conditioning has been great for getting Korean-Americans into high-brow professions, such as law, medicine and business. However, the problem with this "ideal vision" is its limited scope. Korean parents rarely encourage their children to pursue dreams other than one of a stable job and good family. Korean parents often discourage jobs in government service, music, sports, the arts, etc. As a result, second-generation Korean-Americans tend to take fewer risks and often choose the safe path.

This approach to education is at odds with the American ideal of entrepreneurship. Korean-Americans must be more ambitious and more willing to take risks if they are to make a dent in American politics, entertainment, sports or arts. Nearly every celebrity or politician or artist took a major risk to get where they are. Korean-Americans must combine this mindset with the Confucian ideals of self-discipline and self-improvement.

Currently, Korean-Americans occupy a respectable place in the United States. But we are also at a unique crossroads because we are the first generation of Koreans to grow up in the United States.

We know this country and its ways. Now it is up to us to combine our American ideals with our Confucian roots.

12. Acculturation Without Assimilation: The Korean-American Dream

Jane Euna Kim

Asian immigration to the United States of America began in the second half of the nineteenth century. Since then, many individuals have come to sow their hopes and dreams in this Land of Opportunity, and Koreans have been no exception. The first Koreans ever to arrive on U.S. soil paved the way for future immigrants. They were the dreamers and the survivors that have enabled the Korean-American community to grow into its second generation. Today, Korean-Americans are present in nearly all avenues of American life, ranging from television broadcasting to medicine and research. However, the road has not been easy.

Asian-Americans have been traditionally viewed through four different "lenses." Before the 1960s, minorities were depicted in history books as "deviant" or "deficient." The consensus was that the minority groups had to shed their own cultures and assimilate into an Anglo-American one. During the time of Martin Luther King, Jr., however, the cultural contributions of various ethnic groups were emphasized, praised, and encouraged. But the main problem with this type of celebratory view is that it "often fails to question why different components of America's multiethnic mosaic have not been treated equally" (Chan xiii). Once this passionate wave of ethnic pride slowly quieted down, a new perspective was adopted. Asian-Americans were soon portrayed as the unfortunate victims of racism, prejudice, and violence. The exploitation of immigrants and their families became the focal point, rather than their triumphs and successes. Clearly, not one of the previous perspectives has done justice to the Asian-American communities. But gradually, a new perspective on Asian-Americans is being adopted.

According to Sucheng Chan, a professor of Asian-American Studies Program at the University of California, Santa Barbara and author of *Asian-Americans: An Interpretive Story*, the history books, as well as the Euro-Americans of the United States, have finally begun to give the Asian-American community its due. At last, Asian-Americans are seen as what Sucheng Chan labels "agents of history," individuals who make their own choices and who ultimately shape their own future and way of life. It is clear that this perspective best explains Asian-Americans as they really are: independent, self-sufficient, and motivated. But even with this recent breakthrough, there is still a problem. One pressing question still remains: Why has it taken so long?

Change is, indeed, slow, and a true revolution of thought and way of life takes an even longer period of time. But why *this* long?

Without intending to, Korean-Americans have prevented the speedier growth, improvement, and development of its own community. Instead of pouring our hearts and passions into improving the welfare of our community, we have allowed ourselves to be pinned under by unnecessary details. We have allowed deep divisions and gaps to form among the 1st, 1.5, and 2nd generations. We are all Korean-Americans, yet we choose to categorize ourselves into smaller and more exclusive groups, making it difficult for all Korean-Americans to unite as one.

Furthermore, we have yet to fully view ourselves as the "agents of history" that we so want to be regarded as by the Euro-Americans. Our community praises the members of the younger generation who go into medicine or law, but discourages those who want to write, paint, or create music. The accumulation of wealth and prestige that usually accompanies careers in medicine and law have become synonymous with being truly accepted by Euro-Americans, but this is just not so. Being agents of history means choosing one's own life path, not following the latest career trends. If we, as the Korean-American society, do not view ourselves as independent, self-sufficient, and motivated agents of our own history and our own lives, how can we expect others to?

But the mistakes of our past should not discourage us, nor should they dampen our spirits. Instead, the Korean-American community should learn from such missteps and move forward with a renewed sense of purpose and direction. There is still time for change and for progress.

Acculturation without assimilation is the means through which such advancement can be achieved. The difference between the two methods of adaptation is subtle, but important nonetheless. Assimilation occurs when one allows him- or her-self to be completely absorbed into the culture and identity of another group. Such a loss of one's true identity and history is quite threatening to the older generations, and understandably so. The elders of the Korean-American community fear that the rich culture they came from will be forgotten by the younger generations who choose to assimilate into American culture. By contrast, acculturation implies a "merging" of cultures, a type of harmony in which individuals create their own unique identities that include favorable characteristics of all the cultures of which they are a part. Not only does acculturation better fit the needs of the individual, but it also indicates willingness to move forward while still holding on to the vital aspects of one's cultures. So how is one to achieve acculturation? How is one to become an active agent of history?

The answer lies within a community project that incorporates all the generations of Korean-Americans and the other unique communities in the United States. My goal is to document the life histories of those courageous Korean-Americans who successfully acculturated themselves to become members of both the Korean and American communities. I want to meet the individuals who sought to create their own identities, those who refused to follow career trends and instead chose to branch out. I want to give them a chance to speak out about their experiences. After conducting the interviews, I plan to compose a book and create a documentary filled with testimonies of how Korean-Americans became exactly that: both Korean and American. The testimonies would then be shared with others, as all types of history should be, with each individual reading his or her own story. But the most important aspect of such a community outreach event is that all types of people attend, not just the 1st, 1.5, or 2nd generations of Korean-Americans, but also other Asian-Americans, Euro-Americans, and all others who call the United States home.

Such a gathering would accomplish so much for the Korean-American community. It would embody the type of progress for which we have been yearning. Non-Asians would get a glimpse of the rich Korean culture that we are all so proud of. They would finally be able to hear firsthand how Koreans have struggled, endured, and survived. Non-Koreans would be able to compare and contrast their own cultures with ours and realize that we have both had similar experiences. Out of such recognition would come empathy and compassion, and perhaps help us realize that there really is no need for division among Asians. And lastly, Korean-Americans themselves would gain a wealth of understanding and perspective from such an event. The older Korean-American generations would finally be able to tell their diverse life stories to a larger audience, thereby sharing their wisdom and proving that acculturation without assimilation is, indeed, possible. And younger generations would gain an appreciation of the struggles of those who came before us, and harbor renewed hope of the possibility of being active, contributing members of *two* cultures. Very often, youths rebel when their families' histories, cultures, and customs are forced upon them. But at such an event where the purpose is to share, and not patronize, the youths would be more than willing to learn about their families' pasts, and to recognize the diverse opportunities that have been made available to them thanks to the previous generations.

Most importantly, however, such a project would bring the 1st, 1.5, and 2nd generation-Korean-Americans together, an occasion that has, unfortunately, become too rare. It would celebrate those who have dared to take chances, who have courageously become the active agents of history that the Korean-American society needs. "There has never been just one way to be Korean, American, or Korean-American." (Kim 358) Korean-American writers, painters, and musicians have contributed immeasurably to the Korean-American community. However, their creative gifts have too often been overlooked. In addition, not many of the Korean-American youth are encouraged to follow in the footsteps of such artists. Even creative doors must be allowed open for our youth, not just those leading to fields in medicine, business, and law.

Once such progress is achieved, then we will be one step closer to true acculturation without assimilation: the Korean-American dream. And once Korean-Americans, as a people *and* a culture, accept ourselves as active agents of history, just imagine the contributions in medicine, business, law, *and* art that we could make to both the United States and Korea.

Works Consulted

Chan, Sucheng. *Asian-Americans: An Interpretive History*. New York: Twayne Publishers, 1991.

Kibria, Nazli. Becoming *Asian-American: Second Generation Chinese and Korean-American Identities*. Baltimore: Johns Hopkins University Press, 2002.

Kim, Elaine H. & Eui-Young Yu. East to America: Korean-American Life Stories. New York: The New Press, 1996.

13. Collegevoter.org

Sean Oh

Despite the significant progress of Koreans in America, there is still one area in which we have had little impact - that of politics. Though Koreans have achieved prominence in business, science, technology, medicine, and all other sorts of fields, politics remains one that has yet to be penetrated. While the lack of political participation is a particular problem with minorities, it is one which is not only confined to Koreans and other ethnic groups. In a nation where only about half of eligible voters care enough to elect their political leaders, efforts must be made to both increase civic participation as well as ensure that tomorrow's leaders are being engaged in politics and developing an interest in civil service. The community service project that I propose will have a profound impact on political participation and engagement of college students. It is a website entitled Collegevoter.org that provides the information necessary to make an informed vote for the 2004 Presidential elections as well as to provide a forum in which college students can build a foundation in political issues.

The Problem
The Korean community in particular, and the Asian community in general, have had little impact in the political field. This lack of participation is marked at two levels. The first is that of Korean political leadership. Though I can name prominent African-Americans like Condoleeza Rice, Colin Powell, and Clarence Thomas and prominent Jews like Henry Kissinger and Joe Lieberman, I cannot think of even one Korean politician, whether it be at the local or national level. In addition, there are no major political lobbyist or advocacy groups representing and defending the rights of the Korean people in Washington, D.C. Though African-Americans are represented by the NAACP and the Jewish people are represented and protected by AIPAC and the Anti-Defamation League, Asians, and Koreans in particular, have no

such prominent representation. Of the presidential primary debates that are scheduled, one was hosted by the Congressional Hispanic Caucus and another will be hosted by the Congressional Black Caucus. Why is there no such event sponsored by Asians or Koreans? The lack of Asian and Korean leadership is to blame for the political marginalization of our substantial ethnic group.

The second level in which the Korean community lacks political influence is that of grassroots and voter participation. In the 2000 general elections, the turnout rate for Asians and Pacific Islanders was 43 percent. This was significantly lower than the turnout rate for the general American population at 60 percent.[1] While this data may be troubling, an aspect of political participation that is even more disturbing is that of both American and Asian-American youth. In the 2000 elections, voters between the ages of 18-24 had a participation rate of only 18.5 percent.[2] Asian-American youth of the same age-group had an even lower participation rate of 15.9 percent.[3] These participation rates clearly signal a need for civic and political engagement of America's youth.

The Solution
Over the course of the summer, I have created a website to fight political apathy and to provide a means of providing political information for college students. Our mission statement is as follows:

> Collegevoter.org is a non-partisan, non-profit organization that is designed to help facilitate and enhance the democratic process by providing pertinent political information to college students

---

[1] *Registered Voter Turnout Improved in 2000 Presidential Election, Census Bureau Reports*, 2002, US Census Bureau, <http://www.census.gov/Press-Release/www/2002/cb02-31.html>
[2] *Voter Registration and Turnout by Age, Gender, and Race*, 1998, Federal Election Committee, <http://www.fec.gov/pages/98demog/98demog.htm>
[3] *Reported Voting and Registration by Race, Hispanic Origin, Sex, and Age for the United States: November 2000*, 2002, US Census Bureau, <http://www.census.gov/population/socdemo/voting/p20-542/tab02.pdf>

over the Internet. Collegevoter.org seeks to engage young voters with easy to access and easy to read information on American and International politics, with an emphasis on the subjects that interest and affect college students the most. This is a website that is by college students and for college students, with the purpose of providing a starting point for the young adults of America to make informed votes and to engage in political issues.

In essence, Collegevoter.org will:

- Provide neutral, easy to read **information** on political candidates
- Raise **awareness** of contemporary political issues
- Show the **connection** between politics and the individual student's life
- Allow for **coordination** with other organizations and movements
- Provide a forum for public political **debate**

About Collegevoter.org
Website Arrangements and Format
Collegevoter.org will, for the time being, be solely an Internet based organization. As of now, the website will feature the following:

- Coverage of Candidates
- Coverage of Major Issues
- Online Discussions
- Bulletin Board
- Weekly Political News
- Voter Registration Information
- Quickvote
- Links

Coverage of Candidates

Researchers at Collegevoter.org seek to capture the essence of the Presidential candidates in a few paragraphs. Instead of focusing on where he/she stands on each individual issue - information that can be found on numerous other sites - Collegevoter.org shows how each candidate is distinct in his or her own way. Who is the candidate appealing to? What separates him or her from the rest of the pack? What are areas of interest and what are areas of concern?

Collegevoter.org will be in contact with each of the candidates' campaigns to get exclusive information on what each candidate has to say specifically to college students. This may include information on affirmative action, education, jobs, and social security.

Coverage of Major Issues

Brief outlines of major, contemporary issues would include:

- Historical overview
- Pro/Con
- Overview of actors
- Links to relevant websites
- How and why the particular issue pertains to young voters.

Topics include:

- Abortion
- Affirmative Action
- Civil Liberties since 9/11
- The Death Penalty
- The Economy
- Education
- The Environment
- Gay Rights

- HIV/AIDS
- Homeland Security
- Iraq
- Israel/Palestine
- Military and Defense
- North Korea
- Terrorism

Online Discussions

An area where visitors can post their thoughts on the above topics and candidates and have an online forum for political debate.

With the increasing popularity of online messaging and *weblog* (or *blog*), young adults are becoming more and more accustomed to discussions over the Internet. Collegevoter.org seeks to capitalize on this trend by providing a forum for political debate and reflection. Visitors will be able to post messages regarding the various Presidential candidates, issues, and current events.

In addition, Collegevoter.org will show the personal connection between political issues using *blog* technology. Collegevoter.org will seek out young adults to post their experiences and thoughts in various areas. Possible topics include:

- Life on the Frontline (Iraq, Afghanistan)
- Life in Israel
- Life as a Palestinian Refugee Worker
- Life working on a Candidate's Campaign

Bulletin Board

Colleges, activist groups, and other political organizations can post their activities and upcoming events.

Weekly Political News

A synopsis of the week's major political events. Links to *CNN, Washington Post, Roll Call*, etc. can be accessed for the full story.

Voter Registration Information

A complete guide on the voter registration process. Specific information for college students would be highlighted. This would include absentee voting, registering in a new state, and possible effects of a change of address on financial aid.

Quickvote

An unofficial survey for any visitor who chooses to participate. It will feature a weekly question on the hottest topics.

Links

Links would include major government sites such as:

- Whitehouse.gov
- Senate.gov
- House.gov
- Democrats.org
- Republicans.org

In addition, there would be links to related sites and sponsors such as:

- Rockthevote.com
- Youthvote.org
- Vote-smart.org

How This Affects the Korean Community

Up until I heard about the KAC scholarship, I did not think about ways of leveraging my experience and status as a Korean-American to make Collegevoter.org specifically address minorities. However, with the scholarship money that I will hopefully obtain, I can maximize this to the fullest extent.

Through my previous experience as President of the Dartmouth Asian Organization (DAO) and as a member of the Executive Board for the Korean-American Students Association (KASA), I have had the opportunity to meet many Korean and Asian people at various colleges. With the KAC scholarship, I can utilize these contacts and spread knowledge of the site by word of mouth. With an aggressive grassroots approach to publicize the site, combined with an emphasis on increasing the Korean vote, I will boost civic participation amongst Korean-American youth. In addition, I am sure that through this approach, I will meet people who are interested enough in the concept of Collegevoter.org that they would be willing to work with me in achieving our vision. I would, thus, be providing an opportunity for Korean-Americans to develop their interest in politics by allowing them to partake in this independent, student-run organization. In doing this, I would be addressing the two problems that I have outlined above. I would be increasing civic participation of Korean-American youth as well as providing opportunities to develop future Korean-American leaders.

Progress Thus Far

Throughout the summer, I have been working with over a dozen students in developing content for the website. We currently have write-ups completed for almost all of the Presidential candidates as well as for the major issues outlined above. Programming for the site is currently ongoing, but will be completed by the end of September.

I have received the endorsement of Dartmouth's political center, the Rockefeller Foundation (www.dartmouth.edu/~rocky). They have generously provided $2,500 in grant money for the creation of Collegevoter.org along with office space and invaluable academic assistance. I am currently in the process of contacting other foundations and organizations to establish more partnerships and to publicize the site before its launch. In addition, we are beginning to establish relations with members of the candidates' campaigns so that we will have in-depth knowledge of ongoing activities.

Conclusion

With the launch of the site aimed for the beginning of October, it is now time to publicize Collegevoter.org and to start generating enthusiasm for the 2004 Elections. The KAC Scholarship money will allow me to do this for the Korean-American college community. It will provide the funds for me to make phone calls and travel to different schools to promote the website as well as to help fund the daily costs of running the organization. I truly admire the goals of the KAC Foundation, and I sincerely hope that the vision and the means by which I seek to achieve my vision, are in accordance with that of the KAC Foundation. Now is the time to make the Korean voice count in the 2004 elections and to establish Korean leadership in the political arena.

14. Korean-American Youth: Almost There, Yet So Far Away

Howard Han

The other day I was eating with a group of my friends in the dining hall and I got up to get myself a drink. I happened to walk by two Korean-Americans speaking over dinner. I couldn't help but catch one part of their conversation: "We are the future leaders of Korean-Americans," as I returned back to my seat. This comment stuck with me for the rest of the night and I can vividly hear it resonating in my mind even today. I wasn't completely sure why it struck me as odd until I realized why it bothered me so much. Granted, I did know the context of their conversation, this snippet illustrated a major problem with Korean-American youth: Korean-Americans lack ambition and aim low.

Korean-Americans aim low and lack ambition? Initially you may disagree. In American society, Korean-Americans seem to be very successful, consistently channeling Korean educational values into Ivy League educations and professional degrees. But then why are there no Korean Senators? If you respond that a Korean Senator may be a bit much, then I ask why are there no Korean Congressmen? Or Mayors? Or even actors or actresses? For that matter, why can I only think of a few Korean-Americans on major nationwide television networks or even in the public sphere? This is because of the lack of ambition that I define as not the lack of academic or structural success but instead, the lack of ambition in visible, socially uplifting positions, such as politics and media which I believe translate to power. This lack of ambition is founded on lowered aspirations and the belief that Korean-Americans cannot make it in America because of racism.

If you say that America is racist, you may conclude that Korean-Americans can only go so far in America. Yes, America is racist and the institutions of power are mostly White but this does not mean that Korean-Americans cannot succeed. Racism is a part of America, and is a part of the world, if you cannot accept that fact, then you will never succeed in America or anywhere else. The way I see it, racism is another challenge that all of us must deal with, like any other uncontrollable force like your height or intelligence, and a force that can only be overcome and controlled by accepting it and attacking it from within. Thus, it is not racism that keeps Korean-Americans from infiltrating positions of power.

Then what does keep Korean-Americans from positions of power? First, Korean-Americans do not seem to be vying for these positions in mass numbers. Instead, like many other minorities, Korean-Americans look for the path that is not only most secure but also meritocratic. It is very rational to believe that if you study hard, attend an elite undergraduate institution, a top graduate school, and become a professional at a name-brand firm that will constitute success. In many ways, this is very true, clear, and straightforward. For the most part, this is also a sure avenue to success. Hard work is indeed rewarded in America; unfortunately hard work only gets you so far.

This leads me to my belief that the primary cause for the lack of ambition for public positions is that Korean-Americans think they are different enough that they can't make it. Though again, I recognize the societal pressures to feel this way, but like I said before they simply must be accepted and confronted. Therefore, essentially Korean-Americans are not acquiring these positions of power because of a self-inflicted wound, what I term "self-segregation."

I will break self-segregation into two categories, personal and social self-segregation. Personal self-segregation is the limitation of ones own abilities and manifestation of the belief that because you are not White, you cannot achieve certain successes in America. This is a strong motivating factor behind career choices and one of the two reasons why Korean-Americans do not infiltrate politics and media.

Social segregation is the segregation of oneself to Korean-American social groups. Of course it is important to socialize with people with common backgrounds and values, but since few Korean-Americans are in positions of power, socializing with other Korean-Americans will not help you acquire these positions of power. Simply put, it isn't because Korean-Americans are not qualified or because America is racist, it is because not enough people try because they think they won't succeed.

But why then, if they do try, do Korean-Americans still fail to acquire these positions of power? This leads me to my second major point that Korean-Americans do not have access to institutions of power and fail because they do not have access to social networks of power in America that are undeniably White. Political office, partnership in a firm, media positions, etc. All high power positions in America are linked by one commonality. They are positions achieved with hard work, doubtless, but, more importantly, they are connected by a social network which places someone over the top.

Thus, I have identified two major problems that keep Korean-Americans from succeeding in attaining positions of power in America: self-segregation and lack of access to institutions of power. What can we do as Korean-American youths to solve these problems?

First, keep doing what we're doing right. Education and academic success is a bare minimum in order to acquire these positions of power. As a minority you must be at top institutions in order to even view institutions of power. Education sets the foundation for raising yourself up.

Second, end personal and social self-segregation. Even if racism is a factor, act as if it were not. Harness all of your abilities and battle through every obstacle in order to realize your dream. Be bold and overly ambitious, if not for yourself, then for your people. Furthermore, do not isolate yourself to Korean-American friends. America is beautiful and incredibly successful because of its diversity. Embrace your American-ness by associating with all types of people. Do not discriminate, for you are only doing what you assume everyone does to you. Furthermore, forget not that every action you do in your self-interest can and will affect Korean-Americans. You never know when you will become an idol or a bad example.

Third, we must access social networks of power. In order to achieve positions of power that are based on social connections, we must access these social networks. This is again connected to Ivy League institutions but it also means what you do at school. Join extracurricular organizations and be social with a diverse group of people (again aiming at ending social self-segregation). Be involved with athletics and other civic organizations, aspiring to rise to leadership positions. The connections that you create within a social atmosphere directly connect to professional appointments and hiring. These are the institutions of power that can only be accessed through social networks.

Finally, as a group, young Korean-Americans must develop and cultivate a sense of civic duty. Korean-Americans do not vote and are rarely civically involved. This perpetuates a negative stereotype of the submissive Korean-American, assiduous yet quiet, and servile. We must attack these stereotypes by actively acting against such, involving ourselves in local government and state government, as well as actively petitioning and lobbying governmental organizations. Furthermore, we need to vote. Korean-Americans are currently not a voting block that has any power and will never be if we don't vote. Cubans are a great example of a minority group that is not very large yet very influential because they have managed to tap into their small numbers and create a sense of civic duty. In Miami, not only have they managed to acquire many positions of power, but they also have a sizable influence on the national political scene.

These political actions will help develop and ready the institutions of power for Korean-American leaders of the world.

Korean-Americans are assiduous, ambitious, and innovative individuals. They have provided America with a very strong small business background, but have failed to create national leaders such as the Chinese Governor of Washington, Gary Locke. As minorities grow in size the time is ripe for an emergence of a Korea-American intelligentsia. In order for Korean-Americans to carve their niche in America, they must end self-segregating doubts and harness their natural talent to access social networks to power. As immigrants, we have made the first step to success, but there is a long road ahead to true power.

Selected Bibliography

Abelmann, Nancy and John Lie. *Blue Dreams: Korean Americans and the Los Angeles Riots.* Cambridge: Harvard University Press, 1995.

Chang, Robert and Wayne Patterson. *The Koreans in Hawaii: A Pictorial History, 1903-2003.* Honolulu: University of Hawaii Press, 2003.

Charr, Easurk Emsen. *The Golden Mountains.* Boston: Forum Publishing Co., 1961.

Chin, Soo-Young. *Doing What had to be done* [electronic resources]: the life narrative of Dora Yum Kim. Philadelphia: Temple University Press, 1999.

Choy, Bong Youn. *Koreans in America.* Chicago: Nelson Hall, 1979.

Ho, Moon H. *Korean Immigrants and the Challenge of Adjustment.* Westport, CT: Greenwood Press, 1999.
Hur, Won Moo. *The Korean Americans.* Westport, CT: Greenwood Press, 1998.

Hur, Won Moo and Kwang Chung Kim, eds. *Korean Immigrants in America: A Structural Analysis of Ethnic Confinement and Adhesive Adaptation.* Rutherford, N. J.: Fairleigh Dickinson University Press, 1984.

Kim, Elaine and Eui-Yong Yu, eds. *East to America: Korean American Life Stories.* New York: New Press, 1996.

Kim, Illsoo. *New Urban Immigrants: the Korean Community in New York.* Princeton, N.J.: Princeton University Press, 1981.

Kim, Kwang Chung. Ed. *Koreans in the Hood: Conflict with African Americans*. Baltimore: Johns Hopkins University Press, 1999.

Kim,Won Yong. *Koreans in America*. Seoul: Po Chin Chae Printing Co., 1971.

Lee, Mary Paik. *Quiet Odyssey: A Pioneer Korean Woman in America*. Seattle: University of Washington Press, 1990.

Light, Ivan and Edna Bonacich. *Immigrant Entrepreneurs: Koreans in Los Angles, 1965-1982*. Berkeley: University of California Press, 1988.

Min, Pyong Gap. *Changes and Conflicts: Korean Immigrant Families in New York*. Boston: Allyn and Bacon, 1998.

Min, Pyong Gap. *Caught in the Middle: Korean merchants in America's multiethnic cities*. Berkeley: University of California Press, 1996.

Park, Kyeyoung. *The Korean American Dream: Immigrants and Small Business in New York City*. Ithaca: Cornell University Press, 1997.

Patterson, Wayne. *The Korean Frontier in America: Immigration to Hawaii, 1896-1910*. Honolulu: University of Hawaii Press, 1988.

Patterson, Wayne. *The Ilse: First-Generation Korean Immigrants in Hawaii, 1903-1973*. Honolulu: University of Hawaii Press, 2000.

Yoon, In-Jin. *On My Own: Korean businesses and race relations in America*. Chicago: University of Chicago Press, 1997.

About the Editor

Ilpyong J. Kim (Ph.D. Columbia University) is Professor Emeritus of Political Science and International Relations at the University of Connecticut, Storrs and also served as founding President of International Council on Korean Studies (ICKS) in 1996-2000. He was Fulbright Professor at Tokyo University of Japan in 1976-1977 and at Seoul National University in 1991-1992. He served as President of the New England Conference of the Association for Asian Studies in 1979-1980 and also Chairman of Columbia University Faculty Seminar on Korea in 1985-1987. He was a Visiting Professor at Columbia University and a Visiting Scholar at Harvard University's Fairbank Center for East Asian Research. He has lectured at Brown, Indiana, Princeton, and Yale Universities and also lectured on "U.S. Foreign Policy" at American Cultural Centers in Japan, Korea, and Southeast Asia under the auspices of the United Information Agency of the State Department. He has also participated in the Scholar-Diplomat Program at the State Department and the research seminars organized by the Bureau of Intelligence and Research (INR) of the State Department in the 1970s. Dr. Kim served as a ROK Army Officer during the Korean War and was awarded the U. S. Bronze Star Medal for his distinguished service and bravery in 1953.

Dr. Kim received his Ph.D. degree in Political Science from Columbia University and also worked at the East-West Center in the early 1960s and has taught at various universities in the United States for the past 35 years. His specialty is Comparative Politics and International Relations of East Asia. Thus he has authored or edited a dozen books and contributed more than thirty-eight articles to academic and professional journals and edited volumes. His chapter on "South Korea's Transition to Democracy" was published in *Encyclopedia of Democracy* by the Congressional Quarterly Press in Washington. Dr. Kim has also served as editor of the five volume series "China in New Era" of which *Chinese Politics from Mao to Deng; Chinese Defense and Foreign Policy; Chinese Economic Reform;* and *Reform and Transformation in Communist System* (with Jane Shapiro Zacek) have been published to wide acclaim. He has edited *Korean Challenges and American Policy* and *The Two Koreas in Transition: Implication for U.S. Policy* (1998). His most recent book, *Historical Dictionary of North Korea* was published in March 2003.